Metaheuristics for Portfolio Optimization

Metaheuristics Set

coordinated by
Nicolas Monmarché and Patrick Siarry

Volume 11

Metaheuristics for Portfolio Optimization

An Introduction using MATLAB®

G.A. Vijayalakshmi Pai

WILEY

First published 2018 in Great Britain and the United States by ISTE Ltd and John Wiley & Sons, Inc.

ISTE Ltd
27-37 St George's Road
London SW19 4EU
UK

www.iste.co.uk

John Wiley & Sons, Inc.
111 River Street
Hoboken, NJ 07030
USA

www.wiley.com

Library of Congress Control Number: 2017955798

British Library Cataloguing-in-Publication Data
A CIP record for this book is available from the British Library
ISBN 978-1-78630-281-6

MATLAB® is a registered trademark of The MathWorks, Inc. MATLAB Financial Toolbox™, MATLAB Statistics Toolbox™ and MATLAB Optimization Toolbox™ are products of MATLAB®.

For MATLAB and SIMULINK product information, please contact:
The MathWorks, Inc.
3, Apple Hill Drive
Natick, MA, 01760-2098 USA
Tel: 508-647-7000, Fax: 508-647-7001
Email: info@mathworks.com
Web: http://www.mathworks.com
How to buy: http://www.mathworks.com/store

Contents

Preface

Portfolio Optimization, that deals with the choice and appropriate allocation of capital over assets comprising a portfolio so that it is better off than any other, given the investment objectives and preferences of the investor, has been a traditional and hardcore discipline of Finance in general or *Financial Engineering*, in particular.

Modern Portfolio Theory (MPT) – a theory pioneered by Harry Markowitz in his paper "*Portfolio Selection*" published in the *Journal of Finance* in 1952 and expounded in his book *Portfolio Selection: Efficient Diversification*, in 1959, which eventually won him the Nobel Prize in Economics in 1990, did make a huge impact on the discipline, despite its shortcomings pointed out by its critics. MPT harped on the expected risk and return of an asset, the benefits of diversification where one avoids putting all eggs in one basket, the categorization of risks as systematic and unsystematic, the role played by efficient frontier and risk-free assets in determining the expected portfolio returns and so on, which "*...for over six decades... provided money managers and sophisticated investors with a tried-and-true way to select portfolios.*" ("Harry Markowitz Father of Modern Portfolio Theory Still Diversified", *The Finance Professionals' Post*, December 28, 2011). This book subscribes to MPT and all the portfolio optimization models discussed in it are built over the MPT framework.

Nevertheless, Markowitz's framework assumed a market devoid of transaction costs or taxes or short selling, to list a few, that resulted in simple portfolio optimization models that could be easily solved using a traditional method such as Quadratic Programming, to yield the optimal portfolios desired. However, markets in reality are not as naïve as they were assumed to be. In practice, market frictions, investor preferences, investment strategies, company policies of investment firms etc., have resulted in complex objectives and constraints that have made the problem of portfolio optimization *difficult*, if not *intractable*. The complex mathematical models defining the portfolio have found little help from traditional or analytical methods in their efforts to arrive at optimal portfolios, forcing the need to look for non-traditional algorithms and non-orthodox approaches from the broad discipline of *Computational Intelligence*. Fortunately, the emerging and fast-growing discipline of *Metaheuristics*, a sub discipline of Computational Intelligence, has refreshingly turned out to be a panacea for all the ills of such of these notorious problem models. Metaheuristics has not just turned out to be a viable alternative for solving *difficult optimization* problems, but in several cases has turned out to be the *only alternative* to solve the complex problem models concerned.

Metaheuristic approaches represent efficient ways to deal with complex optimization problems and are applicable to both continuous and combinatorial optimization problems. *Nature-inspired Metaheuristics* is a popular and active research area which relies on natural systems for the solution of optimization problem models and one of its genres, *Evolutionary Algorithms,* which is inspired by biological evolution, is what has been applied to solve the portfolio optimization problem models discussed in the book.

Objectives of the book

Metaheuristics for Portfolio Optimization elucidates Portfolio Optimization problems/models that employ metaheuristics for their effective solutions/decisions and demonstrates their application and results using MATLAB®. The book views a traditional hardcore finance discipline from an interdisciplinary perspective, with the cornerstones of:

– finance (Portfolio Optimization, in particular);

– metaheuristics (Evolutionary Algorithms, in particular), and

– computing (MATLAB®, in particular).

The book, therefore, presents a compilation of ideas, models, algorithms and experiments that were explored, investigated and worked upon by the author independently and in collaboration with the investment and finance industry, during a decade-old highly productive collaborative stint, beginning in 2006.

Notwithstanding the complex constraints that can make most Portfolio Optimization models difficult to solve using traditional methods, the presence of multiple objectives (two or more) in the model can render the problems even more difficult. Fortunately, metaheuristics endowed with their innate capabilities and strengths have exhibited strong potential to solve even such problems, finding what are called Pareto optimal solutions that are acceptable solutions. However, in this book the discussion is restricted only to *single objective optimization models* with complex constraints though.

The objective of the book, therefore, is not to get the readers lost in the labyrinth of encyclopedic work in the niche area of metaheuristic portfolio optimization. It is to lead them through a charted path on tested waters, just as a boatman does while taking the tourists on a pleasure trip across a lake! The book therefore, is target-specific and intensive in content, presenting a modest set of metaheuristic portfolio optimization models worked upon by a specific set of metaheuristic algorithms implemented in MATLAB®, to lead the reader slowly but surely through a selective set of systems. The aim is to demonstrate the tricks of the trade to the reader, so as to equip him/her to explore and innovate further, for solving their own complex problems in hand.

The motivation behind the choice of MATLAB® for the implementation and experimentation of the metaheuristic portfolio optimization models discussed in the book is the availability of an interactive programming environment and accessibility to a repertoire of toolboxes and libraries that render the tasks of coding, testing, execution and simulation easier. Also, the accessibility to a toolbox such as MATLAB's Financial Toolbox™ together with MATLAB's Statistics Toolbox™ and MATLAB's Optimization Toolbox™, coupled with the exclusive Command Line Mode execution of MATLAB®, for example, can help users execute most of their fundamental Portfolio Optimization tasks with minimal or nil program scripts. Some examples to this effect have been illustrated in the book at appropriate places of discussion. While a working knowledge of MATLAB® can help understand the implementations presented in the book better, the algorithms and concepts pertaining to the metaheuristic portfolio optimization models have been kept software independent, so that a reader who comprehends the ideas discussed can implement the same in a software of his/her choice.

The coding style adopted by the MATLAB® code fragments and functions presented in the book has been kept simple and direct to favor readers who are novices in MATLAB®. Nevertheless, such readers are advised to refer to the extensive and elaborate help manuals provided by MATLAB®.

Target audience of the book

Being an interdisciplinary work, the book targets:

– finance practitioners, theorists and "quants", who are interested to know how Metaheuristics, an ally of Computational Intelligence, can serve to solve their complex portfolio optimization models;

– computer scientists and information technologists with little or no knowledge of Metaheuristics as a specialization, who wish to foray into the exciting world of Portfolio Management as practitioners;

– metaheuristic researchers wanting to make inroads into the fertile ground of Portfolio Optimization in particular or Computational Finance in general, to explore applications of their innovative algorithms;

– academic researchers from both Finance and Computer Science / Information Technology communities, and

– graduate/senior undergraduate students from the disciplines of STEM (Science, Technology, Engineering and Management) aspiring to get into the interdisciplinary field, either out of curricular or career interests.

Organization of the book

The book comprises seven chapters grouped under two parts, Part 1 and Part 2. Part 1 of the book comprising chapters 1 and 2, serves as a compact introduction to the disciplines of Portfolio Optimization and Metaheuristics respectively, to readers unfamiliar with the same.

Part 2 of the book comprising chapters 3–7, elaborately discusses five different metaheuristic portfolio selection/optimization models that are built over the fundamentals discussed in Part 1 of the book.

All the Portfolio Optimization concepts and models have been experimented or demonstrated over realistic portfolios, selected from global stock universes, S&P BSE200 Index (Bombay Stock Exchange, India) and Nikkei 225 Index (Tokyo Stock Exchange, Japan), to name a few. The MATLAB® demonstrations of the functions and algorithms governing the portfolio models or discussions in the chapters concerned have been included at the end of each chapter of the book. Projects to be undertaken to reinforce learning and application of concepts discussed in the chapters concerned and suggested material for further reading are included at the end of each chapter.

A brief outline of the chapter contents are as follows:

Chapter 1– Introduction to Portfolio Optimization, introduces the fundamentals of Portfolio Optimization based on Modern Portfolio Theory, targeting readers who are unfamiliar with concepts and theories surrounding financial portfolios. However, the discussion on the fundamentals has been kept very specific and comprehensive enough only to follow the portfolio optimization models discussed in the subsequent chapters.

Chapter 2 – A Brief Primer on Metaheuristics, introduces the broad metaheuristics framework and elaborates on two popular genres of metaheuristic methods, namely *Evolution Strategy* and *Differential Evolution Strategy*, their approach, algorithms and performance characteristics. This chapter targets readers who are unfamiliar with metaheuristics and therefore the discussion has been deliberately restricted to the aforementioned two genres on which the Portfolio Optimization models discussed in the rest of the book are dependent upon.

Chapter 3 – Heuristic Portfolio Selection, elaborates on how a heuristic algorithm such as k-means clustering can be effectively used to select securities in a portfolio. The heuristic selection has been demonstrated over two benchmark portfolios, which are equal weighted portfolios and inverse volatility weighted portfolios.

Chapter 4 – Metaheuristic Risk Budgeted Portfolio Optimization, details the application of metaheuristics for a popular investment strategy such as Risk Budgeting. Differential Evolution strategy is employed for the optimization of risk budgeted long-short portfolios with the objective of maximizing its Sharpe Ratio.

Chapter 5 – Heuristic Optimization of Equity Market Neutral Portfolios, discusses how metaheuristics can help ensure market-neutral investing, a popular form of investing. A refined version of Differential Evolution strategy is used to optimize equity market neutral portfolios that incorporate risk budgets.

Chapter 6 – Metaheuristic 130-30 Portfolio Construction, elaborates on the application of Differential Evolution Strategy and MATLAB's Financial Toolbox^{TM}, for the construction of 130-30 portfolios and a comparison of the same with long-only portfolios.

Chapter 7 – Metaheuristic Portfolio Rebalancing with Transaction Costs, discusses the application of Evolution Strategy for rebalancing a portfolio with the additional constraint of curtailing transaction costs and with the objective of maximizing its Diversification Ratio.

Software Download

The MATLAB® demonstrations discussed in this book were implemented using MATLAB® R2011b and MATLAB® R2012 versions. The programs and functions

Acknowledgements

The author would like to express her profound gratitude to Thierry Michel, presently Systematic Portfolio Manager, TOBAM, Paris, France, for introducing her to the challenging discipline of Portfolio Optimization, way back in 2006, during the course of his lectures at the *CIMPA-UNESCO-IMAMIS School on Financial Information Systems*, organized by *Centre international de mathématiques pures et appliquées*, Nice, France, at Kuala Lumpur, Malaysia. This exciting field in hardcore finance, which eventually turned out to be a fertile ground for applications of algorithms and approaches from the broad field of Computational Intelligence, led to a long, highly productive collaborative stint with Thierry Michel, spanning over a decade and resulting in a spate of research publications in journals and conferences, about 14 in all, besides sanctioning of a funded Major Research Project by University Grants Commission, New Delhi, India, 2011–14, in recognition of the work undertaken in the cross-discipline. The ideas gathered, the rich intellectual experience gained and the lessons learned, the hard way though, metamorphosed into writing a monograph, for the sheer joy of disseminating the knowledge discovered to the research fraternity at large. In all these regards, the unstinted support and help provided by Thierry Michel, during every stage of the saga of learning and research, including finding time to read all the chapters of this monograph and offering valuable suggestions, is gratefully acknowledged.

The author expresses her sincere thanks to Vitaliy Feoktistov, author of *Differential Evolution, In search of solutions* (Springer, 2006), an inspiring book that influenced several aspects of her work discussed in this book, besides the useful correspondence that emboldened her to observe more freedom with regard to interpretation and application of concepts to the problems in hand, which served to tide over stumbling blocks during her explorations.

The author expresses her grateful thanks to Patrick Siarry, Université de Paris 12, France and Nicolas Monmarché, University of Tours, France, coordinators of the Metaheuristics Set of ISTE Ltd for accepting this book and sharing their reviews and suggestions.

The support extended by the production team of ISTE Ltd is gratefully acknowledged.

The assistance and support provided by The MathWorks, Inc., USA to upload the MATLAB® Demonstrations illustrated in the book in the MATLAB® Central File Exchange and promote its narratives, is sincerely acknowledged.

The explorations that contributed to writing this monograph were undertaken in the *Soft Computing Research Laboratory*, during the tenure of Major Research Projects sanctioned by the University Grants Commission (UGC), New Delhi, India and All India Council of Technical Education (AICTE), New Delhi, India and thereafter. The state-of-the-art equipment, software and infrastructure support for the laboratory, funded by UGC and AICTE, besides PSG College of Technology, Coimbatore, India, is gratefully acknowledged.

The author places on record her deep admiration for her father, Late Prof G A Krishna Pai, for teaching her things without saying words, her mother Rohini Krishna Pai, for her boundless encouragement and prayers and her sisters, Dr Rekha Pai and Udaya Pai, for their unstinted support and help whenever and wherever she wanted them, without all of which this work would never have fructified.

G.A. Vijayalakshmi PAI
October 2017

PART 1

Introduction to Portfolio Optimization

This chapter delineates the fundamental concepts of portfolio optimization that are essentially required to comprehend the heuristic finance models discussed in the book, explains these concepts through an example case study and demonstrates the implementation of the concepts discussed using MATLAB® code fragments and Toolbox functions.

1.1. Fundamentals of portfolio optimization

Portfolio

A *portfolio* is a basket of tradable assets such as bonds, stocks and securities held by one or several investors.

Portfolio optimization

Portfolio optimization or *Portfolio selection* primarily concerns itself with finding the best combination of assets that conforms to the investor needs. Each individual asset has its own characteristics and history, and the goal of portfolio optimization is to allocate capital between these assets, in the most efficient way.

Rate of return

Consider purchasing an asset such as stocks, bonds, options etc. at time t_0 for a price P_{t_0} and selling it at time t_1 for a price P_{t_1}. The time period T between t_0 and t_1 is called the *holding period*. In the absence of any intermediate cash flows, for example dividends, the rate of return in percentage, known as the *holding period return* indicated by R_T, is given by:

$$R_T = \frac{(P_{t_1} - P_{t_0})}{P_{t_0}} \times 100 \qquad [1.1]$$

The holding period could be any calendar time such as days, months or years or any amount of time for that matter.

In the case of stocks, if P_{t_1} denoted today's closing price, P_{t_0} denoted yesterday's closing price and the holding period T was considered to be one trading day, then R_T shown in [1.1] represents the *daily stock return*.

Portfolio risks

The fluctuations of the prices of the various assets are not independent, as they are exposed to common sources of *risk*, and thus become correlated. In the universe of stocks, the most common source of fluctuations is the price of the global equity factor, also called the *market*. *Assets relatively insulated from the market are less risky*, all things being equal, and thus *yield less profit. Assets most exposed to the market deliver high profits for a higher level of risk.*

A portfolio is therefore typically exposed to two types of risks, namely *systematic risk* and *idiosyncratic risk*. Systematic risk, also known as *undiversifiable risk, volatility* or *market risk* is a risk inherent to the market and can affect the market as a whole, not just a stock or a segment. Events such as earthquakes or other natural disasters, war and epidemics trigger systematic risks. Undiversifiable risk that is a common risk is present in every asset and hence cannot be averaged away.

Idiosyncratic risk, unsystematic risk or *diversifiable risk,* has little or no correlation with market risk but is associated with an asset or an asset class and hence can be mitigated using appropriate *diversification* or *hedging*. Poor production, fall in earnings, and strikes are examples of events that can trigger the risk of the asset concerned. Investing in assets belonging to different asset classes or assets can mitigate such a risk. Since idiosyncratic risk is different for each asset and since it can be reduced by aggregating many assets, it is not valued for there is no reason to incur it per se.

Beta

The fact that assets most exposed to the market deliver high profits for a higher level of risk triggers interest in what is termed stock Beta. *Beta* (β) or *beta coefficient,* also referred to as *financial elasticity,* is a measure of volatility or systematic risk of an asset in a portfolio, in comparison to that of the market as a whole. Thus β measures the risk of an investment that cannot be dispensed with by means of diversification. β = 0 implies that the asset return is uncorrelated with the market moves, β < 0 implies that the asset return inversely follows the market and β > 0 indicates that the asset return follows the market. Beta of an asset *i* within a portfolio P is given by:

$$\beta_i = \frac{\text{cov}\left(r_i, r_P\right)}{\text{var}\left(r_P\right)} \qquad\qquad [1.2]$$

where $\text{cov}\left(r_i, r_P\right)$ is the covariance of the rate of return r_i of the asset *i* and the rate of return r_P of the portfolio P, $\text{var}\left(r_P\right)$ is the variance of the rate of return r_P of portfolio P. In practice, r_P is replaced by the return of the markets.

A stock with a beta lower than one will move less than the average (the stock is notionally less volatile than the market); a stock with a beta greater than one moves more than the average (the stock is notionally more volatile than the market), and lastly, a stock with beta equal to one, will move with the average (the stock price moves with the market).

Beta is also represented by the *slope* of the regression line obtained by regressing stock returns r_i (dependent variable *y*) over market returns r_P (independent variable *x*).

Portfolio weights

The proportions of investments made over assets in a portfolio are termed *weights.* In other words, weights indicate the amount of capital invested over individual assets comprising a portfolio.

Portfolio beta

A *portfolio beta* in the context of general equities, is the weighted sum of the individual betas (β_i) where *weights* W_i are the proportions of investments in the respective assets of the portfolio, that is:

$$\beta_{Portfolio} = \sum_{i=1}^{N} \beta_i.W_i \qquad\qquad [1.3]$$

Harry Markowitz [MAR 52] proposed a mathematical framework known as *Modern Portfolio Theory (MPT)* or *Mean-Variance Analysis* that won him the 1990 Nobel Prize in Economics. The prime assumption of the framework is that the investors search for higher return (yield) under a constraint of risk, or alternatively, search for the lowest level of risk that will allow them to get a certain level of return. The return is the capital gain that can be expected from holding the portfolio and the risk is defined here as the extent of the capital losses that the portfolio can potentially suffer. In the original formulation, and in most cases after that, return and risk are identified by the *mean* and *variance of the portfolio's fluctuations* respectively.

Following Markowitz's pioneering work, Modern Portfolio Theory has operated under a set of assumptions and stylized facts that are now common knowledge, and fully internalized by practitioners. We proceed to define portfolio return and risk, and the objectives of portfolio optimization in light of Markowitz's model from this point forward.

Portfolio return

A portfolio comprising N assets $A_1, A_2,...A_N$ with $W_1, W_2,...W_N$ as their individual *weights* and $r_1, r_2,...r_N$ as their individual returns, respectively, has its *return* given by:

$$r = W_1.r_1 + W_2.r_2 +...W_N.r_N$$
$$= \sum_{i=1}^{N} W_i.r_i \qquad\qquad [1.4]$$

If the number of trading days in a year were T_y (e.g. 261 out of 365 days in a year) and $r_1, r_2,...r_N$ represented daily returns (%) of the assets, then the *annualized portfolio return* in percentage r_{Ann}, would be given by:

$$r_{Ann} = \sum_{i=1}^{N} W_i.r_i \times T_y \qquad\qquad [1.5]$$

Portfolio risk

The *risk* of a portfolio P is given by the standard deviation of its returns, which is:

$$\sigma = \sqrt{\sum_i \sum_j W_i.W_j.\sigma_{ij}}$$

[1.6]

where σ_{ij} is the covariance between returns of assets i and j. σ_{ij} is also referred to as the *variance-covariance matrix of returns*. The *annualized portfolio risk* in percentage σ_{Ann}, if σ_{ij} is the *covariance between daily returns(%) of assets i* and j, and T_y represents the number of trading days in a year, is given by:

$$\sigma_{Ann} = \sqrt{\sum_i \sum_j W_i.W_j.\sigma_{ij} \times T_y}$$

[1.7]

Portfolio optimization objectives

In reality, the *expected rate of return*, which is obtained by attaching a probability to each possible rate of return, is used to compute the return of the portfolio. If μ_i is the expected return of an asset i, then the portfolio return is given by the weighted sum of expected returns, that is:

$$r = \sum_{i=1}^{N} W_i.\mu_i$$

[1.8]

The twin objectives of portfolio optimization primarily turn out to be:

– maximizing portfolio return; and

– minimizing portfolio risk, that is:

$$Max\left(\sum_{i=1}^{N} W_i.\mu_i\right)$$

$$Min\left(\sqrt{\sum_i \sum_j W_i.W_j.\sigma_{ij}}\right)$$

[1.9]

Thus, portfolio optimization is a methodology that serves to control portfolio risk and return. However, complex portfolio optimization models may involve multiple objective functions. Thus, a portfolio optimization problem by and large turns out to be a *bi-objective* or *multi-objective optimization* problem.

Portfolio constraints

In reality, portfolio optimization problems are governed by *constraints* imposed due to investor preferences, investment strategies or market norms.

The following are constraints commonly imposed on the problem model by an investor–

Basic constraint: each weight W_i lies between 0 and 1 and the sum total of the weights equals 1, that is:

$$\sum_{i=1}^{N} W_i = 1 \quad and \quad 0 \le W_i \le 1 \qquad [1.10]$$

A portfolio which exhibits such a constraint is referred to as a *fully invested portfolio*.

Bound constraints: weights of assets lie between upper and lower bounds, as selected by the investor, that is:

$$\varepsilon_i \le W_i \le \delta_i \qquad [1.11]$$

where ε_i, δ_i are the lower and upper bounds for the weights W_i.

Class constraints or group constraints: assets belonging to a specific sector or asset class A have bounds imposed on their respective sum of weights, that is:

$$\varepsilon_i \le \sum_{i \in AssetClass\ A} W_i \le \delta_i \qquad [1.12]$$

Cardinality constraint: the investor chooses to invest in only K out of a stock universe of size N. In practice, a portfolio of size K, where $1 \le K \le 30$ is referred to as a *small portfolio* or a *large portfolio*, otherwise.

Budget constraints: constraints that restrict the sum of portfolio weights to fall between specified bounds, that is:

$$\varepsilon \leq \sum_k W_k \leq \delta \qquad [1.13]$$

For $\varepsilon = 0$, $\delta = 1$ and $k = N$, the constraint represents a fully invested portfolio.

Turnover constraint: the constraint ensures that the estimated optimal portfolio differs from an initial portfolio by no more than a specified amount. It controls the *buys* and *sells* (purchases and sales) and is computed as:

$$0 \leq \sum_i |W_i - W_i^O| \leq \tau \qquad [1.14]$$

where W_i^O are the weights of the optimal portfolio, W_i the weights of the original portfolio and τ is the upper bound for turnover. There are several ways to compute turnover.

Markowitz's Mean-Variance optimization model

The portfolio optimization problem, therefore, given a universe of assets and their characteristics, deals with a method to spread the capital between them in a way that maximizes the return of the portfolio per unit of risk taken. There is *no unique solution* for this problem, but *a set of solutions*, which together define what is called an *efficient frontier* – the portfolios whose returns cannot be improved without increasing risk, or the portfolios where risk cannot be reduced without reducing returns as well.

The *Markowitz model* [MAR 52] for the solution of the portfolio optimization problem with its twin objectives of maximizing return and minimizing risk, built on the *Mean-Variance* framework of asset returns and holding the basic constraint, reduces to the following:

$$Max\left(\sum_{i=1}^{N} W_i . \mu_i\right)$$

$$Min\left(\sqrt{\sum_i \sum_j W_i . W_j . \sigma_{ij}}\right)$$

subject to

$$\sum_{i=1}^{N} W_i = 1$$

$$0 \le W_i \le 1$$

[1.15]

Devoid of other constraints, the above model is loosely referred to as the "unconstrained" portfolio optimization model. Solving the mathematical model yields a set of *optimal weights* representing a set of *optimal portfolios*.

Efficient frontier

An *efficient frontier* is the set of optimal portfolios that yield the *highest expected portfolio return* for a *defined level of risk* or the *lowest possible risk* for a *defined level of expected portfolio return*. In other words, an efficient frontier is a set of portfolios whose expected portfolio returns for a defined level of risk cannot be surpassed by any other portfolio. It is a *risk-return tradeoff graph* that obtains the optimal structure of the portfolio which yields the maximum expected return for a given level of risk or vice-versa. Thus it is not possible to have points above the efficient frontier. Also, points below the efficient frontier are only sub-optimal. Portfolio optimization, therefore, strives to build portfolios, which are on the efficient frontier and not below it. The set of all optimal portfolios that lie on the efficient frontier, in other words, those portfolios that generate the largest return for a given level of risk or vice-versa, are known as the *Markowitz efficient set*.

The efficient frontiers traced by the Markowitz model are termed as "*exact*" or "*ideal*" in the literature. The Markowitz model, as stated earlier, represents an "Unconstrained Optimization" problem that can be easily solved using *quadratic programming*. However, when constraints reflective of investor preferences, investment strategies and market norms are included, the problem model becomes complex, warranting the need to look for *heuristic methods* for its solution. This would be the subject matter of the rest of the book.

Sharpe Ratio

Sharpe Ratio, which is a measure of calculating risk adjusted return, defines the average return earned in excess of the *risk free rate* per unit of volatility or total risk in an investment asset or a trade strategy.

Sharpe Ratio is defined as:

$$\frac{\left(r_x - R_f\right)}{\sigma} \qquad [1.16]$$

where r_x is the average rate of return on an investment x, R_f the best available rate of return of a risk free security and σ the standard deviation of r_x. The higher the Sharpe Ratio value, the more excess returns can be expected for the extra volatility that they are exposed to by holding a risk free asset. Again a Sharpe Ratio of 0 obviously indicates a risk free asset or a portfolio with no excess return. However, Sharpe Ratio, despite being widely used to compute risk adjusted returns, has its disadvantages if the expected returns do not follow a normal distribution, or portfolios possess non-linear risks, to list a few. Hence alternative methodologies such as *Sortino Ratio* and *Treynor Ratio* have emerged. A portfolio optimization problem that serves to include Sharpe Ratio, has its objective of maximizing Sharpe Ratio as follows:

$$\max\left(\frac{\left(r_x - R_f\right)}{\sigma}\right) \qquad [1.17]$$

To compute Sharpe Ratio of a portfolio, the *ex-ante* Sharpe Ratio uses expected returns while the *ex-post* Sharpe Ratio uses realized returns.

The risk free rate R_f should be considered for the same period (daily or yearly as the case may be) as was considered for the return r_x and risk σ. The following formulae can be useful in transforming the daily risk free rate to yearly and vice-versa, in practical situations, given R_f^{daily} or R_f^{yearly} as the daily or yearly risk free rates expressed as decimals, respectively. $R_f^{daily}.100$ or $R_f^{yearly}.100$ would yield the percentage rates respectively.

$$R_f^{daily} = \left(1 + R_f^{yearly}\right)^{\left(\frac{1}{360}\right)} - 1$$

$$R_f^{yearly} = \left(1 + R_f^{daily}\right)^{(360)} - 1 \qquad [1.18]$$

1.2. An example case study

The fundamental concepts of portfolio optimization discussed in section 1.1 have been illustrated over a case study portfolio:

Portfolio P: Asset returns and market returns

Consider a portfolio P of 10 assets (equities) selected from S&P BSE200 index (Bombay Stock Exchange, India). Table 1.1 shows the asset characteristics and stock prices (closing prices) for the period illustrated (February 16, 2009–March 06, 2009). The daily returns (%) of the stocks, following [1.1] are shown in Table 1.2.

	RIL IB Equity	INFO IB Equity	ITC IB Equity	LT IB Equity	ICICIBC IB Equity	HDFCB IB Equity	ONGC IB Equity	SBIN IB Equity	HUVR IB Equity	TCS IB Equity
NAME	RELIANCE INDUSTRIES LIMITED	INFOSYS TECHNOLOGIES LTD	ITC LTD	LARSEN & TOUBRO LIMITED	ICICI BANK LTD	HDFC BANK LIMITED	OIL & NATURAL GAS CORP LTD	STATE BANK OF INDIA	HINDUSTAN UNILEVER LIMITED	TATA CONSULTANCY SVS LTD
Industry_sector	Energy	Technology	Consumer, Non-cyclical	Industrial	Financial	Financial	Energy	Financial	Consumer, Non-cyclical	Technology
SECTOR_CODE	2	1	8	9	6	6	2	6	8	1
16/02/09	1319.05	1221.55	180.4	666.3	409.2	914.75	687.65	1136	255.85	500.85
17/02/09	1267.6	1177.65	180.55	659.05	385.9	880.25	677.45	1100.35	251.75	485.9
18/02/09	1294.75	1178.75	179.7	654.05	369.35	876.6	674.9	1070.8	253.75	480.55
19/02/09	1293.65	1208.2	180.9	640.65	361.5	884.8	680.25	1059.55	249.55	489.75
20/02/09	1253.55	1178.45	180.25	622.5	335.95	866.95	672.75	1046.6	249.2	473.95
24/02/09	1253.3	1184.1	180.75	625.45	335.5	856.9	680.6	1028.25	252.85	466.5
25/02/09	1266	1216.25	181.8	612.45	340.5	864.15	696.75	1037.75	251.45	479.8
26/02/09	1290.45	1236.35	183.8	610.8	324.75	873.05	715.25	1024.15	253.05	481.8
27/02/09	1265.05	1231.3	182.95	611.45	328.1	884.85	691.15	1027.1	253.8	480.6
02/03/09	1225.15	1218.75	178.7	584.55	304.2	845.65	664.05	995.25	244.6	459.5
03/03/09	1199.05	1197.6	172	574.8	296.4	831	648.35	975.85	241.5	445.15
04/03/09	1209.6	1197.9	173.7	580.35	284.3	838.8	664.45	957.55	240.9	461.05
05/03/09	1149.1	1182.8	167.5	568.55	269.6	800.7	651.85	934.55	230.05	463
06/03/09	1170.55	1219.2	164.8	580.15	269.3	801.1	673.45	940.85	223.95	480.8

Table 1.1. *Asset characteristics and prices of 10 equity assets from S&P BSE200 index (Bombay Stock Exchange, India) comprising a sample portfolio P*

Thus the daily return (%) of the stock INFOSYS TECHNOLOGIES LTD (INFO) on 20/02/2009 would be:

$$\frac{(\text{closing price of INFO on } 20/02/2009 - \text{closing price of INFO on } 19/02/2009)}{\text{closing price of INFO on } 19/02/2009} \times 100$$

$$= \frac{(1178.5 - 1208.2)}{1208.2} \times 100 \quad = \quad -2.46\%$$

The daily returns (%) for rest of the assets may be similarly computed.

The historical closing prices of the S&P BSE 200 market index for the period concerned and their corresponding daily returns (%), following similar computations as undertaken for assessing asset returns using [1.1], have been shown in Table 1.3.

Thus the daily market return (%) of S&P BSE200 index on 06/03/2009 would be:

$$\frac{(981.69 - 972.15)}{972.15} \times 100 \quad = \quad 0.981\%$$

NAME	RIL IB Equity RELIANCE INDUSTRIES LIMITED Energy	INFO IB Equity INFOSYS TECHNOLOGIES LTD Technology	ITC IB Equity ITC LTD Consumer, Noncyclical	LT IB Equity LARSEN & TOUBRO LIMITED Industrial	ICICIBC IB Equity ICICI BANK LTD Financial	HDFCB IB Equity HDFC BANK LIMITED Financial	ONGC IB Equity OIL & NATURAL GAS CORP LTD Energy	SBIN IB Equity STATE BANK OF INDIA Financial	HUVR IB Equity HINDUSTAN UNILEVER LIMITED Consumer, Non-cyclical	TCS IB Equity TATA CONSULTANCY SVS LTD Technology
Industry_sector SECTOR_CODE	2	1	8	9	6	6	2	6	8	1
17/02/09	-3.90	-3.50	0.08	-1.09	-5.69	-3.77	-1.48	-3.14	-1.60	-2.98
18/02/09	2.14	0.09	-0.47	-0.76	-4.29	-0.41	-0.38	-2.69	0.79	-1.10
19/02/09	-0.08	2.50	0.67	-2.05	-2.13	0.04	0.70	-1.05	-1.66	1.91
20/02/09	3.10	-2.46	0.36	-2.83	-7.07	-2.02	-1.10	-1.22	-0.14	-3.23
24/02/09	-0.02	0.48	0.28	0.47	-0.13	-1.16	1.17	-1.75	1.46	-1.57
25/02/09	1.01	2.72	0.58	-2.08	1.49	0.85	2.37	0.92	-0.55	2.85
26/02/09	1.93	1.65	1.10	-0.27	-4.63	1.03	2.66	-1.31	0.64	0.42
27/02/09	-1.97	-0.41	-0.46	0.11	1.03	1.35	-3.37	0.29	0.30	-0.25
02/03/09	-3.15	-1.02	-2.32	-4.40	-7.28	-4.43	-3.92	-3.10	-3.62	-4.39
03/03/09	-2.13	-1.74	-3.75	-1.67	-2.56	-1.73	-2.36	-1.95	-1.27	-3.12
04/03/09	0.88	0.03	0.99	0.97	-4.08	0.94	2.48	-1.88	-0.25	3.57
05/03/09	-5.00	-1.26	-3.57	-2.03	-5.17	-4.54	-1.90	-2.40	-4.50	0.42
06/03/09	1.87	3.08	-1.61	2.04	-0.11	0.05	3.31	0.67	-2.65	3.84

Table 1.2. *Daily returns (%) of the equities shown in Table 1.1*

Portfolio P: Computation of betas

The computation of beta for the asset STATE BANK OF INDIA using [1.2] substituting market returns for r_P , yields the results shown in Table 1.4. Table 1.5 shows the betas computed for all the assets in the portfolio P. As can be observed, all the assets in the portfolio follow the market with assets RIL, INFO, ICICIBC, HDFCB, ONGC and TCS reporting greater volatility ($\beta >1$) and the rest, like ITC, LT, SBI and HUVR reporting lesser volatility ($0 <\beta < 1$).

As mentioned earlier, Beta can also be computed as the slope of the regression line obtained by regressing stock returns r_i over market returns r_P. For the historical period considered from January 02, 2012 to January 02, 2014, regressing SBIN daily stock returns (%) with the S&P BSE 200 market index daily returns (%) yields the line $Y = (1.4187)X + (-0.0579)$ over the scatter plot of the returns in Figure 1.1. The slope of the line, 1.4187 is the beta of the stock SBIN, for the historical period concerned.

Date	Closing Price	Daily Returns (%)
16/02/09	1095.87	
17/02/09	1065.78	-2.746
18/02/09	1063.92	-0.175
19/02/09	1066.1	0.205
20/02/09	1044.06	-2.067
24/02/09	1037.66	-0.613
25/02/09	1045.55	0.760
26/02/09	1049.35	0.363
27/02/09	1044.94	-0.420
02/03/09	1013.88	-2.972
03/03/09	994.84	-1.878
04/03/09	998.03	0.321
05/03/09	972.15	-2.593
06/03/09	981.69	0.981

Table 1.3. *S&P BSE 200 market index closing prices and daily returns (%) for the period February 16, 2009 to March 06, 2009*

Portfolio P: Computation of risk/return characteristics

Assuming that the investor opting for a fully invested portfolio had apportioned his/her capital following the weights listed in Table 1.6 and the asset returns were represented using their respective historical mean returns (average of their returns during the period considered, viz. August 25, 2004 to February 13, 2009), the mean returns, covariance of returns, the expected portfolio daily return (%), annualized return (%) (assuming 261 trading days) and portfolio risk (%) (daily and annualized) following [1.4]–[1.7] respectively, are as shown in Table 1.6.

To explain further, the weight vector W_i [0.06, 0.07, 0.16, 0.10, 0.07, 0.07, 0.07, 0.16, 0.18, 0.06] chosen by the investor sums up to 1 (100%) and hence denotes a fully invested portfolio. For the historical data set considered, the daily return matrix

$[R]_{1116X10}$ where 1,116 is the number of trading days during the period concerned and 10 is the number of assets in the portfolio P, yields the mean daily returns of the assets (%) as $[r_1, r_2, ... r_{10}] = [0.14 \quad 0.06 \quad 0.10 \quad 0.12 \quad 0.05 \quad 0.10 \quad 0.06 \quad 0.10 \quad 0.08 \quad 0.02]$ and the covariance matrix of daily returns (%) $(\sigma_{ij})_{10X10}$ obtained by computing the covariance of the return matrix $[R]_{1116X10}$, as shown in the appropriate row of Table 1.6.

Date	17/02/09	18/02/09	19/02/09	20/02/09	24/02/09	25/02/09	26/02/09	27/02/09	02/03/09	03/03/09	04/03/09	05/03/09	06/03/09
Stock daily return (%) r_i	-3.14	-2.69	-1.05	-1.22	-1.75	0.92	-1.31	0.29	-3.10	-1.95	-1.88	-2.40	0.67
Market daily return (%) r_P	-2.75	-0.17	0.20	-2.07	-0.61	0.76	0.36	-0.42	-2.97	-1.88	0.32	-2.59	0.93
Covariance (r_i, r_P)	1.353												
Variance (r_P)	2.023												
Beta	0.67												

Table 1.4. *Computation of beta for the stock STATE BANK OF INDIA using daily returns (%) of the stock and market, shown in Tables 1.2 and 1.3, respectively*

NAME	RIL IB Equity / RELIANCE INDUSTRIES LIMITED	INFO IB Equity / INFOSYS TECHNOLOGIES LTD	ITC IB Equity / ITC LTD	LT IB Equity / LARSEN & TOUBRO LIMITED	ICICIBC IB Equity / ICICI BANK LTD	HDFCB IB Equity / HDFC BANK LIMITED	ONGC IB Equity / OIL & NATURAL GAS CORP LTD	SBIN IB Equity / STATE BANK OF INDIA	HUVR IB Equity / HINDUSTAN UNILEVER LIMITED	TCS IB Equity / TATA CONSULTANCY SVS LTD
Industry_sector	Energy	Technology	Consumer, Non-cyclical	Industrial	Financial	Financial	Energy	Financial	Consumer, Non-cyclical	Technology
SECTOR_CODE	2	1	8	9	6	6	2	6	8	1
beta	1.44	1.17	0.61	0.72	1.30	1.28	1.28	0.67	0.54	1.47

Table 1.5. *Betas of the assets comprising the portfolio (period: February 16, 2009 to March 06, 2009)*

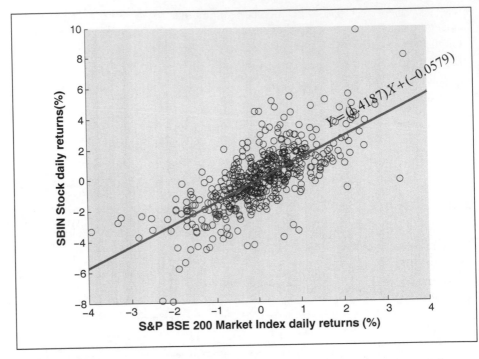

Figure 1.1. *Beta of the stock SBIN computed as slope of the least squares line*
Y = (1.4187)X + (–0.0579), obtained by regressing SBIN stock daily returns (%)
with S&P BSE 200 market index daily returns (%) for the historical period
(January 02, 2012 to January 02, 2014) graphed as a scatter plot

Following [1.4] and [1.5], and using the weight vector W_i and mean return vector r_i, the expected portfolio daily return r and annualized return r_{Ann} are obtained as 0.09% and 22.70% respectively. Similarly, the daily portfolio risk σ and annualized portfolio risk σ_{Ann} of the portfolio P, following [1.6] and [1.7] and making use of the weight vector W_i and covariance matrix of returns σ_{ij}, are computed as 1.71% and 21.14%, respectively.

NAME / Industry_sector	RIL IB Equity RELIANCE INDUSTRIES LIMITED Energy	INFO IB Equity INFOSYS TECHNOLOGIES LTD Technology	ITC IB Equity ITC LTD Consumer, Non-cyclical	LT IB Equity LARSEN & TOUBRO LIMITED Industrial	ICICB IB Equity ICICI BANK LTD Financial	HDFCB IB Equity HDFC BANK LIMITED Financial	ONGC IB Equity OIL & NATURAL GAS CORP LTD Energy	SBIN IB Equity STATE BANK OF INDIA Financial	HUVR IB Equity HINDUSTAN UNILEVER LIMITED Consumer, Non-cyclical	TCS IB Equity TATA CONSULTANCY SVS LTD Technology
SECTOR_CODE	2	1	8	9	6	6	2	6	8	1
Weights	6%	7%	16%	10%	7%	7%	7%	16%	18%	6%
Mean daily returns (%)	0.14	0.06	0.10	0.12	0.05	0.10	0.06	0.10	0.08	0.02
Covariance of daily returns (%) — RIL	6.38	2.55	2.28	3.89	4.65	3.29	3.29	3.65	2.00	3.04
INFO	2.55	4.75	1.49	2.53	3.13	2.29	2.07	2.18	1.29	3.57
ITC	2.28	1.49	4.42	2.25	2.46	1.95	1.95	2.30	1.91	1.83
LT	3.89	2.53	2.25	7.29	4.73	3.36	3.26	3.76	2.07	2.92
ICICIBC	4.65	3.13	2.46	4.73	9.54	5.01	3.75	5.08	2.49	3.40
HDFC	3.29	2.29	1.95	3.36	5.01	6.27	2.89	3.64	1.70	2.52
ONGC	3.29	2.07	1.95	3.26	3.75	2.89	5.37	2.94	1.07	2.37
SBIN	3.65	2.18	2.30	3.70	5.08	3.64	2.94	6.59	1.98	2.65
HUVR	2.00	1.29	1.91	2.07	2.49	1.70	1.97	1.98	4.52	1.67
TCS	3.04	3.57	1.83	2.92	3.40	2.52	2.37	2.65	1.67	5.59
Expected portfolio daily return(%)	0.09									
Portfolio daily risk (%)	1.71									
Expected portfolio annualized return (%)	22.70									
Annualized portfolio risk (%)	21.14									

Table 1.6. *Risk/Return characteristics of the portfolio P of assets listed in Table 1.1, using historical returns for the period August 25, 2004 to February 13, 2009*

1.2.1. *Portfolio P: Unconstrained portfolio optimization*

The risk/return characteristics of portfolio P were discussed for a specific set of weights shown in Table 1.6. However, in practice, the problem paves way for a portfolio optimization model when the investor desires to know those *optimal weights* that will maximize the expected portfolio return and minimize portfolio risk.

Let us suppose that the investor chose to work on optimizing the portfolio adopting the following problem model, the unconstrained optimization model defined by [1.15], while employing the historical dataset S&P BSE 200 index: August 25, 2004 to February 13, 2009, with regard to the 10 assets comprising the portfolio P:

$$Max\left(\sum_{i=1}^{10} W_i.\mu_i\right)$$

$$Min\left(\sqrt{\sum_i \sum_j W_i.W_j.\sigma_{ij}}\right)$$

subject to

$$\sum_{i=1}^{10} W_i = 1$$

$$0 \le W_i \le 1$$

[1.19]

The basic constraint simply underlines a fully invested portfolio.

The mean returns μ_i and covariance of returns σ_{ij} for assets comprising the portfolio P, which are inputs to the problem model, are obtained as explained earlier for the period concerned. To solve the multi-objective problem, we obtain the optimal weights that minimize risk for given values of the expected return, with the expected returns kept varying from that which yields maximum return to that which yields minimum risk. To accomplish this, the problem is decomposed into three sub-problem models, which are (1) obtaining the maximal expected return R^{Max_Ret} of the portfolio, (2) obtaining the optimal expected return R^{Min_Risk} of the portfolio that yields minimum risk, and (3) for the given values of the expected portfolio return, R kept varying between R^{Min_Risk} and R^{Max_Ret}, that is $R^{Min\_Risk} \le R \le R^{Max\_Ret}$, obtain the optimal weights of the portfolio sets that minimize risk. The optimal portfolio sets arrived at, are those that form the efficient set.

To obtain the optimal weights that yield the maximum expected return R^{Max_Ret}, the following linear programming problem [1.20] extracted from [1.19] is employed.

$$Max \left(\sum_{i=1}^{10} W_i . \mu_i \right)$$

subject to

$$\sum_{i=1}^{10} W_i = 1$$

$$0 \le W_i \le 1$$

[1.20]

The optimal weights $W_i^{Optimal}$ arrived at determines the maximum expected return given by $R^{Max\_Ret} = \sum_{i=1}^{10} W_i^{Optimal} . \mu_i$.

To obtain the optimal weights that minimize risk, [1.21] extracted from [1.19] is employed.

$$Min\left(\sqrt{\sum_i\sum_j W_i.W_j.\sigma_{ij}}\right)$$

subject to

$$\sum_{i=1}^{10} W_i = 1$$

$$0 \le W_i \le 1$$

[1.21]

The optimal weights $W_i^{Optimal}$ arrived at determines the optimal return that minimizes risk as $R^{Min\_Risk} = \sum_{i=1}^{10} W_i^{Optimal}.\mu_i$.

For each R, $R^{Min\_Risk} \le R \le R^{Max\ Ret}$, the following problem model is repeatedly solved to ultimately arrive at the optimal weights $W_i^{Optimal}$ that represent the optimal weight sets corresponding to the portfolio sets that minimize risk and maximize return:

$$Min\left(\sqrt{\sum_i\sum_j W_i.W_j.\sigma_{ij}}\right)$$

subject to

$$\sum_{i=1}^{10} W_i.\mu_i \le R$$

[1.22]

$$\sum_{i=1}^{10} W_i = 1$$

$$0 \le W_i \le 1$$

Portfolio P: Efficient frontier for unconstrained portfolio optimization model

For each of the optimal weight sets $W_i^{Optimal}$, arrived at by solving [1.22], that define portfolios belonging to the efficient set, the risk/ return couples computed using [1.4] and [1.6] trace an efficient frontier. Figure 1.2 shows an efficient frontier traced using 60 optimal portfolios belonging to the efficient set. Table 1.7 shows the risk/return characteristics of some of the optimal portfolios belonging to the efficient set.

1.2.2. *Portfolio P: Constrained portfolio optimization*

Let us consider the case where a moderately risk aggressive investor is interested in enforcing constraints on the capital to be invested on various assets and asset classes comprising portfolio P. The investor trying to exercise caution over the volatility of the stocks in the portfolio decides to invest 60% of the capital on low volatility stocks and 40% on high volatility stocks. Making use of betas from Table 1.5, the stocks are categorized into two asset classes which are High volatile and Low volatile. Thus, of the stocks labeled 1 to 10 (in the order of their appearance in the table), assets with labels (1, 2, 5, 6, 7, 10) with betas greater than one are categorized as *High_Volatility* assets and those with labels (3, 4, 8, 9) as *Low_Volatility* assets. The class constraint imposed to this effect by the investor has been shown in the problem model defined by [1.23]. The non-zero lower bounds of the class constraints are indicative of the fact that the investor expects some investment to be definitely made on both High volatile and Low volatile stocks, as a class.

Also, let us suppose that each of the assets belonging to the *High_Volatility* and *Low_Volatility* sets had bounds imposed on their individual weights or proportion of investments. Thus while there were no specific upper or lower limits imposed on low volatile assets, the high volatile assets had a specific upper limit of only 1% of the capital to be invested on any of the assets. The appropriate bound constraints for the corresponding assets in the portfolio have also been shown in the problem model defined by [1.23].

The constrained portfolio optimization problem model that now includes bound, class and basic constraints is as given below:

$$Max\left(\sum_{i=1}^{10} W_i.\mu_i\right)$$

$$Min\left(\sqrt{\sum_i\sum_j W_i.W_j.\sigma_{ij}}\right)$$

subject to

$$\sum_{i=1}^{10} W_i = 1$$

$$0 \le W_1, W_2, W_5, W_6, W_7, W_{10} \le 0.01$$

$$0 \le W_3, W_4, W_8, W_9 \le 1$$

$$0.01 \le \sum_{i \in Low\_Volatility} W_i \le 0.6 \qquad\qquad [1.23]$$

$$0.01 \le \sum_{i \in High\_Volatility} W_i \le 0.4$$

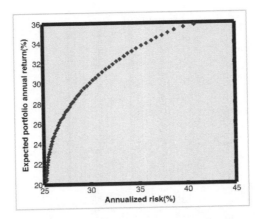

Figure 1.2. *Unconstrained Portfolio Optimization: Efficient frontier for the portfolio P of S &P BSE 200 Index (listed in Table 1.1) with only basic constraints, defined by the problem model described in [1.22] and traced over historical returns for the period August 25, 2004 to February 13, 2009*

Solving the optimization problem yields an efficient frontier as shown in Figure 1.3. The efficient frontier has been compared with the exact or ideal frontier to graphically illustrate the differences in the risk/return characteristics of a constrained portfolio with its unconstrained counterpart. The efficient frontier for the constrained portfolio justifies the investor's moderately risk aggressive nature in that the risks vary between 25%–35% corresponding to the returns varying between 20%–30%.

The characteristics of some of the optimal constrained portfolios belonging to the efficient set have been shown in Table 1.8. The shaded rows indicate the weights of the high volatility assets and the non-shaded rows those of the low volatility assets. The characteristics of the optimal constrained portfolios could be compared with those of the optimal unconstrained portfolios shown in Table 1.7 to study the characteristics of the respective portfolios.

Portfolio P: Sharpe ratios of the unconstrained and constrained portfolios

The Sharpe Ratio, described in [1.16], for the optimal constrained portfolio P whose expected annualized return (%) $r_x = 20.28$ and annualized risk (%) $\sigma = 25.58$, for a risk free rate $R_f = 5\%$ annually, is given by

$$\frac{(r_x - R_f)}{\sigma} = \frac{(20.28 - 5)}{25.58} = 0.597$$

The Sharpe ratios for the sample optimal portfolios P (constrained and unconstrained), shown in Table 1.7 and Table 1.8 respectively, for a risk free rate of 5% are shown in Table 1.9.

1.2.3. *Portfolio P: Sharpe Ratio-based portfolio optimization*

The Sharpe Ratio-based portfolio optimization problem model where the objective is to maximize Sharpe ratio subject to constraints imposed is defined as shown below. Here r_x and σ in the Sharpe Ratio definition shown in [1.16] are represented by the expected portfolio return and risk of the portfolio and R_f as explained before indicates the risk free rate of return.

		Optimal portfolio 1 (minimum return portfolio)	Optimal portfolio 2	Optimal portfolio 3	Optimal portfolio 4 (maximum return portfolio)
Optimal weights (W_i)	W_1	0	0.0666	0.2815	1
	W_2	0.2514	0.2220	0.0302	0
	W_3	0.2508	0.2666	0.2818	0
	W_4	0	0.0259	0.1193	0
	W_5	0	0	0	0
	W_6	0.0771	0.0887	0.0806	0
	W_7	0.1049	0.0385	0	0
	W_8	0.0194	0.0259	0.0045	0
	W_9	0.2703	0.2658	0.2021	0
	W_{10}	0.0261	0	0	0
Basic Constraint $\sum_{i=1}^{10} W_i = 1$		Satisfied	Satisfied	Satisfied	Satisfied
Annualized Risk (%)		25.2713	25.5025	28.0176	40.8013
Expected portfolio annualized return (%)		20.3692	22.7182	27.9382	35.7682

Table 1.7. *Risk/Return characteristics of some of the optimal portfolios P of assets listed in Table 1.1 belonging to the efficient set following the unconstrained portfolio optimization problem model described in [1.19], using historical returns for the period August 25, 2004 to February 13, 2009*

$$Max \left(\frac{\sum W_i \mu_i - R_f}{\left(\sqrt{\sum_i \sum_j W_i W_j \sigma_{ij}} \right)} \right)$$

subject to

$$\sum_{i=1}^{N} W_i = 1$$
$$0 \le W_i \le 1$$

[1.24]

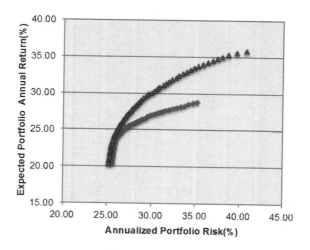

♦ Constrained Portfolio Optimization: Efficient frontier

▲ Unconstrained Portfolio Optimization: Efficient frontier

Figure 1.3. *Constrained Portfolio Optimization: efficient frontier for the portfolio P of S&P BSE 200 Index (listed in Table 1.1) with bound, class and basic constraints imposed over it, defined by the problem model described in [1.23] and traced over historical returns for the period August 25, 2004 to February 13, 2009 and compared with the exact frontier (for a color version of this figure, see www.iste.co.uk/pai/metaheuristics.zip)*

		Optimal Constrained portfolio 1 (minimum return portfolio)	Optimal Constrained portfolio 2	Optimal Constrained portfolio 3	Optimal Constrained portfolio 4 (maximum return portfolio)
Optimal weights (W_i)	W_1	0	0.041	0.1	0.1
	W_2	0.1	0.1	0.1	0.1
	W_3	0.274	0.276	0.278	0
	W_4	0.004	0.016	0.036	0.6
	W_5	0	0	0	0
	W_6	0.1	0.1	0.1	0.1
	W_7	0.1	0.092	0.082	0.1
	W_8	0.032	0.027	0.021	0
	W_9	0.29	0.281	0.265	0
	W_{10}	0.1	0.067	0.018	0

Basic Constraint $\sum_{i=1}^{10} W_i = 1$	Satisfied	Satisfied	Satisfied	Satisfied
Bound Constraints $0 \le W_1,W_2,W_5,W_6,W_7,W_{10} \le 0.1$ $0 \le W_3,W_4,W_8,W_9 \le 1$	Satisfied	Satisfied	Satisfied	Satisfied
Class Constraints $0.01 \le \sum_{i \in Low\_Volatility} W_i \le 0.6$ $0.01 \le \sum_{i \in High\_Volatility} W_i \le 0.4$	Satisfied	Satisfied	Satisfied	Satisfied
Annualized Risk (%)	25.58	25.66	25.94	35.19
Expected portfolio annualized return (%)	20.28	21.58	23.44	28.74

Table 1.8. *Risk/Return characteristics of some optimal constrained portfolios P of assets listed in Table 1.1 belonging to the efficient set, using historical returns for the period August 25, 2004 to February 13, 2009*

The solution to the problem yields a portfolio that has the maximal Sharpe Ratio, which incidentally turns out to be a maximum return portfolio, for the portfolio P illustrated in Table 1.1 over the historical data set August 25, 2004 to February 13, 2009. Table 1.10 shows the characteristics of the maximal Sharpe Ratio-based portfolio.

		Expected portfolio annualized return (%) r_x	Annualized risk (%) σ	Sharpe Ratio
Unconstrained portfolios	Optimal portfolio 1	20.3692	25.2713	0.608
	Optimal portfolio 2	22.7182	25.5025	0.694
	Optimal portfolio 3	27.9382	28.0176	0.818
	Optimal portfolio 4	35.7682	40.8013	0.754
Constrained portfolios	Optimal constrained portfolio 1	20.28	25.58	0.597
	Optimal constrained portfolio 1	21.58	25.66	0.646
	Optimal constrained portfolio 1	23.44	25.94	0.711
	Optimal constrained portfolio 1	28.74	35.19	0.674

Table 1.9. *Sharpe ratios of the optimal unconstrained/constrained portfolios P listed in Tables 1.7 and 1.8, for an annualized risk free rate of 5%*

		Optimal portfolio (maximum Sharpe Ratio)
Optimal weights (W_i)	W_1	0.3992
	W_2	0
	W_3	0.2644
	W_4	0.1625
	W_5	0
	W_6	0.0432
	W_7	0
	W_8	0
	W_9	0.1307
	W_{10}	0
Maximal Sharpe Ratio		0.8347
Basic Constraint $$\sum_{i=1}^{10} W_i = 1$$		Satisfied
Annualized Risk (%)		29.9661
Expected portfolio annualized return (%)		30.0141

Table 1.10. *Risk/Return characteristics of the optimal portfolio P of assets listed in Table 1.1 based on Sharpe Ratio-based maximization described in [1.24], using historical returns for the period August 25, 2004 to February 13, 2009*

1.3. MATLAB® demonstrations

In this section, the following concepts are demonstrated through MATLAB® Toolbox functions executed in the command line mode or MATLAB® code fragments, so as to illustrate the computation or implementation of the concepts in a naïve way. The coding style has been deliberately kept simple and direct to favor novice MATLAB readers.

A. Computing the mean and covariance of asset returns for portfolio optimization.

B. Graphing the efficient frontier for the unconstrained portfolio optimization model.

C. Graphing the efficient frontier for the constrained portfolio optimization model.

D. Sharpe Ratio based portfolio optimization.

A. *Computing the mean and covariance of asset returns for portfolio optimization*

Given the prices time series for the assets comprising the portfolio over a historical period (downloadable from authentic or reliable websites), the first step to portfolio optimization involves computing the return series and thereafter obtaining the mean and covariance of returns. MATLAB Financial Toolbox™ provides the following functions to quickly arrive at this result.

1) `tick2ret` : this function converts prices time series to its return series;

2) `ewstats` : this function obtains the mean and covariance of asset returns, given their return series

Figure 1.4 demonstrates the application of these functions in MATLAB® command line mode (>>), to arrive at the mean and covariance of returns denoted as mean_data and cov_data, of portfolio P (listed in Table 1.1), from its historical prices time series considered over the period August 25, 2004 to February 13, 2009.

```
convert daily price time series of  assets to
return series
>>daily_return_dat = tick2ret(daily_prices_dat);

compute daily return series in  percentage
>>return_percentage_dat = daily_return_dat*100;

obtain mean and covariance of daily returns (%)
of the assets
>>[mean_data, cov_data] =
               ewstats(return_percentage_dat);
```

Figure 1.4. *Demonstration of computation of mean and covariance of daily returns (%) of portfolio P (listed in Table 1.1) in MATLAB® command line mode (for a color version of this figure, see www.iste.co.uk/ pai/metaheuristics.zip)*

Table 1.1 shows a sample set of daily prices for the assets comprising portfolio P and Table 1.2 the daily return prices (%) for the same.

The function `tick2ret` converts the prices series `daily_prices_dat` to its equivalent return series `daily_return_dat`. `daily_prices_dat` is a matrix of prices of equity assets with the rows indicative of the trading days and the columns the prices of the assets on the respective trading days. The matrix should represent the asset prices in the chronological order of the trading days, with the first row indicating the oldest of the observations. `return_percentage_dat` computes the daily returns (%) of the assets. The function `ewstats` works over `return_percentage_dat` to obtain the mean and covariance of daily returns (%) as `mean_data` and `cov_data`. The `mean_data` and `cov_data` of Portfolio P for the historical price time series concerned have been shown in Table 1.6.

B. *Graphing the efficient frontier for the unconstrained portfolio optimization model*

For `portfolio_size` = 10 and `mean_data` and `cov_data` representing the daily mean returns (%) vector and variance-covariance matrix of daily returns (%) of portfolio P listed in Table 1.1, Figures 1.4–1.7 illustrate MATLAB® code fragments that serve to trace the efficient frontier for the unconstrained portfolio optimization problem model defined over portfolio P. Equations [1.19]–[1.22] describe the computations undertaken by the MATLAB® code fragments to arrive at the efficient frontier.

Figure 1.5 illustrates the MATLAB® code fragments that work over [1.20] to arrive at the maximal expected portfolio return R^{Max_Ret} using linear programming. Function `max_ret_objfun` computes R^{Max_Ret} (represented by variable `exp_pf_ret_max`) using the optimal weights available in `var_x`. Observe the use of the function `linprog` available in the Optimization Toolbox of MATLAB® to undertake linear programming.

The MATLAB® code fragment for obtaining minimum variance expected portfolio return, using [1.21] is shown in Figure 1.6. Function `min_var_objfun` computes the optimal weights `var_x` corresponding to the minimal variance and the expected portfolio return (R^{Min_Risk}) (represented by variable `exp_pf_ret_min`). Observe the use of the function `quadprg`, available in MATLAB® Optimization Toolbox, to undertake quadratic programming.

```
%max portfolio return computation using linear
%programming
[x, fval] = max_ret_objfun(portfolio_size,
mean_data);
exp_pf_ret_max = (mean_data  * x);
disp('the maximum expected portfolio return');
exp_pf_ret_max
```

```
function [var_x,  max_ret_fun_val]=
           max_ret_objfun(portfolio_size, mean_data)

% vector f represents the mean returns
f=-1*mean_data;

% matrix Aeq and vector beq represent equality
% constraints
Aeq=ones(1, portfolio_size);
beq=1;

% vectors lb and ub are lower and upper bounds for
% variables xi
lb = zeros(1, portfolio_size);
ub = ones(1, portfolio_size);

% invoke linprog function to compute the optimal
% weights for the maximal portfolio return as var_x

[var_x, max_ret_fun_val] = linprog(f,[],[],Aeq,
                                    beq, lb,ub )

end
```

Figure 1.5. *MATLAB® code fragments for graphing efficient frontier for Portfolio P (Table 1.1) using [1.19]–[1.22]: obtaining maximal expected portfolio return using [1.20] (for a color version of this figure, see www.iste.co.uk/ pai/metaheuristics.zip)*

Using [1.22] and by varying R, $R^{Min\_Risk} \leq R \leq R^{Max\_Ret}$, the MATLAB® code fragment shown in Figure 1.7 obtains the optimal weights for the portfolios that lie on the efficient set. Here exp_pf_ret_min represents R^{Min_Risk} and exp_pf_ ret_max represents R^{Max_Ret}. The function min_var_cnstrobjfun uses mean_data, cov_data and R as its main inputs to obtain the optimal weights through function quadprog.

```
% min variance return computation using quadratic
% programming
[y,  min_obj_fun_val]=
min_var_objfun(portfolio_size, cov_data);
exp_pf_ret_min= mean_data*y;
disp(' expected portfolio return corresponding to
      min variance');
exp_pf_ret_min
```

```
function [var_x,  min_obj_fun_val]=
min_var_objfun(portfolio_size, cov_data)


H=2*cov_data;                        % matrix H
f=zeros(portfolio_size, 1);          % vector f

% Aeq and beq represent equality constraints
Aeq=ones(1, portfolio_size);
beq=1;

% lower and upper bounds for variables xi
lb=zeros(1, portfolio_size);
ub=ones(1, portfolio_size);


% obtain optimal weights  using quadratic
% programming
[var_x,min_obj_fun_val] = quadprog(H,f,[],[],Aeq,
                                   beq, lb,ub );
end
```

Figure 1.6. *MATLAB® code fragments for graphing the efficient frontier for Portfolio P (Table 1.1) using [1.19]–[1.22]: obtaining minimal variance expected portfolio return using [1.21] (for a color version of this figure, see www.iste.co.uk/ pai/metaheuristics.zip)*

The annualized risk / return couples for each of the optimal portfolios lying on the efficient frontier are computed as minimum_var_point and expected_pf_ret_point, respectively.

```
% generate portfolio returns R between the minimum
% and   maximum  points and compute minimum variance
% for each of the portfolio returns using
% quadratic programming

i1=1;
for R = exp_pf_ret_min :0.001:   exp_pf_ret_max
    [var_x,  min_obj_fun_val]=

    min_var_cnstrobjfun(portfolio_size,
                        mean_data, cov_data, R);
    x_optimal(i1,:) = var_x;
    exp_pf_ret_point(i1) =  R;
    min_var_point(i1)= min_obj_fun_val;
    i1=i1+1;
    clear var_x  min_obj_fun_val;
end

% compute annualized return and annualized risk of
% the portfolio sets

minimum_var_point = sqrt(min_var_point *261)
expected_pf_ret_point= exp_pf_ret_point * 261
```

Figure 1.7. *MATLAB® code fragments for graphing efficient frontier for Portfolio P (Table 1.1) using [1.19]–[1.22]: obtaining optimal weights using [1.22] and computing the corresponding annualized risk / return couples (for a color version of this figure, see www.iste.co.uk/pai/metaheuristics.zip)*

Figure 1.8 demonstrates the MATLAB® code fragment that traces the corresponding efficient frontier (already shown in Figure 1.2). Here, minimum_var_point and expected_pf_ret_point, represent the risk / return points of the optimal portfolios belonging to the efficient set that are provided as inputs to the plot function of MATLAB®.

C. *Graphing the efficient frontier for the constrained portfolio optimization model*

Equation [1.23] defines a constrained portfolio optimization problem model defined over portfolio P (listed in Table 1.1), with basic, bound and class constraints. Employing function frontcon (available in MATLAB Financial Toolbox™) could easily serve to obtain the expected return, risk and optimal weights besides tracing the efficient frontier for the constrained portfolio. Figure 1.9

illustrates a demonstration of `frontcon` in the MATLAB® command line mode that solves the said problem model for portfolio P.

```
%graph efficient frontier
plot(minimum_var_point, expected_pf_ret_point,'bd');

title('Efficient frontier for the portfolio P over
S&P BSE 200 index');
xlabel('Annualized risk(%)');
ylabel('Expected portfolio annual return(%)');
```

Figure 1.8. *MATLAB® code fragment for graphing efficient frontier for Portfolio P (Table 1.1) using equations [1.19] – [1.22]: Tracing the efficient frontier (for a color version of this figure, see www.iste.co.uk/ pai/metaheuristics.zip)*

The inputs provided to `frontcon` function are:

`mean_data` : the mean daily return (%) vector of the assets in portfolio P, of size 1 X 10.

`cov_data` : the variance-covariance matrix of daily returns (%) of portfolio P, of size 10 X 10.

`NumPorts = 60` : number of portfolios generated along the efficient frontier.

`PortReturn = []` : `PortReturn` a vector of dimension 1 X `NumPorts`, is the target return values on the efficient frontier. In case of [], equally spaced returns between the maximum and minimum values are used.

`Asset Bounds` : a matrix of dimension 2 X 10 representing the lower bounds and upper bounds on the weights of each of the assets, in the first and last rows respectively. The matrix entries can be easily related to the bound constraints shown in [1.23].

`Group` : the number of groups or asset classes G forming the portfolio and the assets that belong to each of these G asset classes. Groups is a Boolean matrix of dimension G X 10, where `Groups(i,j) = 1`, if asset j belongs to asset class i and Groups(i,j) = 0, otherwise.

As can be observed, the High Volatility and Low Volatility asset classes of portfolio P and the respective assets comprising them have been represented under the parameter Groups as a 2 X 10 matrix.

Group Bounds   : this is a G X 2 matrix which specifies the lower and upper bounds for the total weights of all assets in the group.

For portfolio P, the bounds specified on the total weights of the assets comprising the High Volatility and Low Volatility asset classes as shown in [1.23] are specified here.

The outputs of function frontcon, [PortRisk, PortReturn, PortWts] represent the optimal portfolio risk, return and weights of the portfolio concerned. Invocation of function frontcon, without its output arguments, automatically traces the efficient frontier of the portfolio.

Thus for portfolio P, employing frontcon to solve its constrained portfolio optimization problem model represented by [1.23] to obtain their expected daily returns and risks, arriving at the annualized risk (%) and expected portfolio return (%) by computing PortRisk *sqrt(261) and PortReturn *261 and plotting the efficient frontier using the function plot, as demonstrated in Figure 1.8, yields the efficient frontier already shown in Figure 1.3.

```
Obtain optimal portfolio return, risk and weights for
the constrained portfolio P

>>[PortRisk, PortReturn, PortWts] =
frontcon(mean_data,cov_data, 60, [], [[0 0 0 0 0 0 0
0 0 0]; [0.1 0.1 1 1 0.1 0.1 0.1 1 1 0.1]], [[0 0 1 1
0 0 0 1 1 0]; [1 1 0 0 1 1 1 0 0 1]], [[0.01 0.6];[0
0.4]])


graph efficient frontier for constrained portfolio P
>> plot(PortRisk*sqrt(261), PortReturn*261, 'rd')
```

Figure 1.9. *Graphing efficient frontier for Portfolio P (listed in Table 1.1) for the constrained portfolio optimization problem model defined over it (shown in [1.23]) using MATLAB® functions frontcon and plot (for a color version of this figure, see www.iste.co.uk/ pai/metaheuristics.zip)*

D. *Sharpe Ratio-based portfolio optimization*

The portfolio optimization model, based on obtaining the maximal Sharpe Ratio as shown in [1.24], can be solved using `Portfolio` object available for mean-variance portfolio optimization and analysis, and its associated methods which are `estimateMaxSharpeRatio`, `estimatePortRisk` and `estimatePort Return`, available in MATLAB Financial Toolbox[TM].

Figure 1.10 demonstrates the declaration of the `Portfolio` object for portfolio P to satisfy the requirements of [1.24] and the invocation of `estimate MaxSharpeRatio`, `estimatePortRisk` and `estimatePortReturn` as methods over the object instance, to arrive at the optimal weights that yield the Maximal Sharpe Ratio and the corresponding risk and return of the portfolio.

```
% declare Portfolio object p
p = Portfolio('RiskFreeRate', r0, 'AssetMean',
mean_data, 'AssetCovar', cov_data, 'LowerBound',
LB, 'UpperBound', UB, 'AEquality', AE,
'bEquality', BE );


% invoke method estimateMaxSharpeRatio to obtain
% the optimal weights of the portfolio p with
% maximal Sharpe Ratio
pwgt = p.estimateMaxSharpeRatio;
display(pwgt)


% invoke methods estimatePortRisk and
% estimatePortReturn to obtain the risk and return
% of the portfolio p and compute the annualized
% risk and return
risk_p = p.estimatePortRisk(pwgt) *sqrt(261);
return_p = p.estimatePortReturn(pwgt)*261;
disp(risk_p)
disp(return_p)
```

Figure 1.10. *Sharpe Ratio-based optimization of portfolio P (listed in Table 1.1) modeled on [1.24] using MATLAB® Portfolio object and its associated methods (for a color version of this figure, see www.iste.co.uk/pai/metaheuristics.zip)*

For the portfolio P, the inputs provided to the `Portfolio` object are:

`"RiskFreeRate"` : risk free rate of return (daily), r0 = 0.01365%, obtained from an annualized risk free rate of 5% using [1.18]

`"AssetMean"` :   mean daily return (%) of assets in portfolio P, that is `mean_data`

`"AssetCovar"` : variance-covariance matrix of daily returns (%) `cov_data`

`"LowerBound"` : lower bounds of asset weights LB = [0 0 0 0 0 0 0 0 0 0]

`"UpperBound"` : upper bounds of asset weights UB = [1 1 1 1 1 1 1 1 1 1]

`"AEquality"` : linear equality constraint matrix AE = [1 1 1 1 1 1 1 1 1 1]

`"bEquality"` : linear equality constraint vector BE = [1]

The "`AEquality`" and "`bEquality`" parameters serve to model the equality constraint $\sum_{i=1}^{N} W_i = 1$.

`p.estimateMaxSharpeRatio` invokes the method `estimateMaxSharpe Ratio` over the portfolio object p to arrive at the optimal weights. `p.estimatePortRisk(pwgt)` and `p.estimatePortReturn(pwgt)` in a similar fashion obtain the risk and return of the optimal portfolio respectively. `risk_p` and `return_p` indicate the computation of annualized risk and return of the portfolio P.

Project

An investor wishes to invest in 12 equity stocks from Nikkei225 (Tokyo Stock Exchange, Japan). She downloads the historical data set for the stock index from January 01, 2013 to January 01, 2015, from a reliable finance site. The investor decides on the following:

(i)   to invest her capital only in the asset classes of "Automotive", "Electric Machinery" and "Steel Products". List the stocks available at her disposal.

(ii)   being highly risk aggressive, she decides to pick stocks with high volatility in all the three asset classes. If she decided to make the pick based on the individual betas of the assets, what are the possible assets that she might have chosen? Assume that she chose four stocks A1, A2, A3, A4 from

Automotive, six stocks E1, E2, E3, E4, E5, E6 from Electric Machinery and two stocks S1, S2 from Steel Products.

(iii) having decided on her portfolio of 12 assets, with a capital investment of ¥ 200,000, she decides to work on different portfolio optimization models by imposing a variety of constraints to explore various possibilities. The following are some choices that she has made:

(a) portfolio A: a fully invested portfolio with the basic constraints $0 \leq W_i \leq 1$, where W_i indicates the optimal weights.

(b) portfolio B: a fully invested portfolio with the bound constraints of

$$0 \leq W_{A_1}, W_{A_2}, W_{A_3}, W_{A_4} \leq 0.7$$

$$0 \leq W_{E_1}, W_{E_2}, W_{E_3}, W_{E_4}, W_{E_5}, W_{E_6} \leq 0.8$$

$$0 \leq W_{S_1}, W_{S_2} \leq 0.6$$

(c) portfolio C: a fully invested portfolio with 50% of her capital to be invested on the asset class Electric Machinery, 35% of her capital to be invested on the asset class Automotive and the hssssalance 15% to be invested on Steel Products. The basic, bound and class constraints are as follows:

$$0 \leq W_{A_1}, W_{A_2}, W_{A_3}, W_{A_4}, W_{S_1}, W_{S_2} \leq 1$$

$$0.01 \leq W_{E_1}, W_{E_2}, W_{E_3}, W_{E_4}, W_{E_5}, W_{E_6} \leq 1$$

$$0.01 \leq \sum_{i \in \{A_1, A_2, A_3, A_4\}} W_i \leq 0.35,$$

$$0.01 \leq \sum_{i \in \{E_1, E_2, E_3, E_4, E_5, E_6\}} W_i \leq 0.50$$

$$0.01 \leq \sum_{i \in \{S_1, S_2\}} W_i \leq 0.15$$

She decides to compute the efficient frontiers for each of these three models and explore those portfolios from those models that yield her an expected portfolio annualized return of at least 30%. Was she successful in finding out one such optimal portfolio? Help her to find one, if available, making use of MATLAB Finance Toolbox™.

Suggested Further Reading

The book *Modern Portfolio Theory and Investment Analysis* [ELT 14] is a widely followed textbook on Modern Portfolio Theory. *Streetsmart Guide to Managing your Portfolio* [YAO 02] is a lucid book that offers interesting insights into investment strategies and methods for novices too.

MATLAB Finance Toolbox™ offers a wealth of tools that can be directly used in the command line mode to solve practical problems with regard to portfolio analysis and optimization. With some knowledge of MATLAB® coding and a judicious combination of the Toolbox functions, complex Portfolio optimization models demanding innovative heuristic algorithms can be more than acceptably solved.

Mathworks offers a lot of online tutorials and courses to learn MATLAB® programming (https://in.mathworks.com/support/learn-with-matlab-tutorials.html).

Michael Best's [BES 10] book on *Portfolio Optimization* elaborately discusses how the traditional approaches of linear algebra and quadratic programming can be employed for optimization of portfolios and provides quite a few practical examples in MATLAB® to illustrate this. Bernhard Pfaff's [PFA 16] book on *Financial Risk Modelling and Portfolio Optimization with R* introduces techniques for measuring financial market risk and portfolio optimization. Bernd Scherer and Douglas Martin's [SCH 05] book *Introduction to Modern Portfolio Optimization with NUOPT and S-PLUS,* Gilli *et al.*'s [GIL 11] book on *Numerical Methods and Optimization in Finance,* and Dietmar Maringer's [MAR 05] book on *Portfolio Management with Heuristic Optimization* are good reads on the theories and problem models in portfolio management.

A Brief Primer on Metaheuristics

In this chapter, the framework of Metaheuristics and the advantages and pitfalls involved in its application to real world combinatorial optimization problems are first discussed. Next, two metaheuristic algorithms, namely Evolution Strategy and Differential Evolution, belonging to two different genres of Population-based Metaheuristics and which would form the basis of heuristic finance models discussed in this book, are introduced. The application of the algorithms is demonstrated over a test-suite problem and the MATLAB® code fragments/ toolbox functions that serve to implement the same are also detailed.

2.1. Metaheuristics framework

Real-world combinatorial optimization problems in general have always taken recourse to two categories of algorithms for their solution:

– *exact methods*, and

– *approximate* methods.

Exact methods or analytical methods are constructed in such a way that they are guaranteed to obtain the *global optimum*, by enumerating all sets of solutions, evolving methods to determine which of these could be eliminated from examining and working on the *candidate solution sets* before finally establishing which of these is the *best* or *optimal*. As can be expected, exact methods are time consuming and hence are deemed fit only for small-scale problems. Besides, some of these methods, for example *gradient-based optimizers*, despite their sophisticated versions, depend on a suitable *starting point* or *initial point* x_0 in the search space, to begin their exploration for the optimal solution point. Finding the appropriate x_0 can be a major hurdle when unmanned or automatic optimization is called for in a problem. Also, when the number of variables in a problem increases, the number of evaluations increases resulting in impractical scenarios that may deter the application of the method to the problem concerned.

Approximate algorithms, on the other hand, do not guarantee the best solution for the problem. Instead, they are content to obtain a *"close-to-optimal"* solution, a solution that lies within a certain admissible percentage of proximity to the optimal solution. The algorithm settles down possibly to a solution point, to account for a time/quality compromise. *NP-Hard optimization* (*N*on-deterministic *P*olynomial time *H*ard optimization) problems are classic examples where approximation algorithms have found application. NP-Hard optimization problems are *intractable problems*, which despite exponential growth in computing power have been evading algorithms that solve them in polynomial time. Hence, approximation algorithms yield a compromise solution by allowing themselves to run over these problems for a time that is at most polynomial time or possibly until a solution satisfies a quality criterion that is laid down as a compromise.

Heuristic algorithms are a kind of approximation algorithms, in that they too may not serve to find optimal solutions but only *"near-optimal"* or *"worse-than-optimal"* or *"acceptable"* solutions. They strive to obtain a good-enough solution quickly by applying simple or complex rules of thumb. Thus when exact methods, due to their impracticality arising due to exhaustive search, report unrealistic time estimates with regard to arriving at solutions for large-scale problems, heuristic algorithms have turned out to be a safe bet in arriving at acceptable solutions to the problem concerned within reasonable time. In these aspects, heuristic algorithms have been highly sought after when compared to exact methods. Quite often heuristic algorithms are designed specific to a problem or its instance and by and large are inapplicable for other problems. In fact, early heuristic algorithms, which emphasized the inclusion of aspects such as *learning, intuition* and *insight,* which are characteristics exclusive to *human intelligence* ("natural" intelligence), have made commendable inroads in solving complex problems in the discipline of *Artificial Intelligence.*

Over the last few years, the discipline of Optimization methods has begun to see a steady rise of what are called *Metaheuristic* methods or *Metaheuristics.*

Sorensen and Glover [SOR 13] defined Metaheuristics as:

> "...A *metaheuristic* is a high-level problem-independent algorithmic *framework* that provides a set of guidelines or strategies to develop heuristic optimization algorithms. The term is also used to a problem-specific implementation of a heuristic optimization *algorithm* according to guidelines expressed in such a framework..."

Unlike heuristics, which are severely problem dependent, Metaheuristics serves to offer a collection of tools or mechanisms that are problem independent and could serve as a framework to solve a problem or a broad class of problems. In recent times, Metaheuristics refers not just to a framework but also to specific algorithms that are built subject to its specifications. In other words, Metaheuristics refers to a set of mechanisms, operators or processes that help construct heuristic optimization algorithms.

From the standpoint of approach to problem solving, metaheuristic methods:

1) represent efficient ways to deal with complex optimization problems,

2) are more universal,

3) are applicable for both continuous and combinatorial optimization problems,

4) are amenable for application on multi-modal or multi-objective optimization problems,

5) are expected to avoid problems concerning local optima, something that their exact algorithm counterparts are vulnerable to, and

6) nurture fewer qualms about the objective functions or constraints that define the optimization problem.

Hence metaheuristic approaches have turned out to be viable alternatives to exact methods, especially to solve *"difficult optimization"* problems and in many of the cases *the only alternative* to solve the problems concerned.

However, metaheuristic methods are not without their fair share of criticisms such as:

1) mostly based on metaphors derived from nature and hence lack scientific rigor or are not backed by strong convergence proofs,

2) fairly high computational times,

3) testing of algorithms are mostly done in an *ad hoc* or empirical fashion,

4) influenced by the choice of control parameters, and

5) non-guarantee of obtaining *the* optimal solution.

Population-based metaheuristics is a successful and highly sought after category of metaheuristic algorithms. In these methods, a set of candidate solutions in the search space of the problem domain progress towards the optimal solution point(s). *Genetic Algorithms, Evolutionary Algorithms, Particle Swarm Optimization* and *Differential Evolution* are examples of population-based metaheuristics. These algorithms exhibit an innate ability to find multiple optimal solutions, unlike exact methods.

In this chapter we shall detail two population-based metaheuristic algorithms, namely Evolution Strategy and Differential Evolution, which will form the basis of the heuristic portfolio optimization models discussed in the ensuing chapters of this book.

2.2. Exact methods versus metaheuristics

In this section we demonstrate the differences in the characteristics of metaheuristic and exact algorithms while solving a non-linear optimization problem.

Let us consider the non-linear Beale function:

$$f(x_1, x_2) = (1.5 - x_1 + x_1.x_2)^2 + (2.25 - x_1 + x_1.x_2^2)^2 + (2.625 - x_1 + x_1.x_2^3)^2$$
$$-4.5 \leq x_1, x_2 \leq 4.5 \qquad\qquad [2.1]$$

The Beale function is usually evaluated on a square [-4.5, 4.5] for x_1 and x_2. Figure 2.1 illustrates a plot of the Beale function. The global minimum is attained at $f(x_1, x_2) = 0$, for $(x_1, x_2) = (3, 0.5)$.

Exact method: MATLAB® `fmincon` solver for Beale function optimization

We first proceed to optimize Beale function by adopting MATLAB® solver, `fmincon`, which is a gradient-based solver that finds the minimum of constrained non-linear multi-variable functions with inequality, equality and bound constraints. Such an optimization is generally referred to as *constrained non-linear optimization* or *non-linear programming*.

A typical definition of the `fmincon` function is as follows, where `fun` is the optimization function, `x0` is the initial point or estimate, `A,b` define inequality constraints, `Aeq,beq` define equality constraints, `lb,ub` define the lower and upper bounds of the variables and `[x, fval]` define the optimal variables `[x]` and the function value `fval`.

```
[x, fval] = fmincon(fun,x0,A,b,Aeq,beq,lb,ub)
```

The gradient-based solver obtains the solution of the following non-linear programming problem, where the non-linear function *f(x)* is to be minimized, subject to the generic constraints given. Here *c(x)* and *ceq(x)* can be non-linear functions that return vectors, matrix A and   vector b represent linear inequality constraints, Aeq and beq represent linear equality constraints and *lb, ub* the bounds of the design variable vector x.

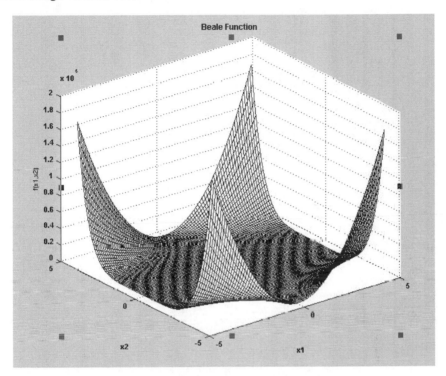

Figure 2.1. *A grid plot of the non-linear Beale function*

$$\min(f(x))$$
subject to
$$c(x) \le 0$$
$$ceq(x) = 0$$
$$A.x \le b$$
$$Aeq.x = beq$$
$$lb \le x \le ub$$

[2.2]

A naïve invocation of $\texttt{fmincon}$ to optimize the Beale function defined in [2.1] would be as follows:

```
[x, fval] = fmincon(@beale,x0,[],[],[],[],[-4.5, -4.5],
                                               [4.5, 4.5])
```

Here, @beale is a function handle to a MATLAB® function beale (shown in Figure 2.2) that computes the function value, [] represents null linear inequality and equality constraints and vectors [-4.5, -4.5] and [4.5, 4.5] represent the lower and upper bounds of Beale function respectively.

As can be observed, the fmincon function typical of exact methods, expects an initial estimate x_0 as input which is often times a guess. Table 2.1 displays the behavior of fmincon when different guesses were made for the initial point x0.

```
% Beale function
function [z] = beale(x)
x1 = x(1);
x2 = x(2);
z =    (1.5 - x1 + x1*x2)^2 +    (2.25 - x1 + x1*x2^2)^2
                        +    (2.625 - x1 + x1*x2^3)^2;
end
```

Figure 2.2. MATLAB® function beale (x) (for a color version of this figure, see www.iste.co.uk/pai/metaheuristics.zip)

Initial point x0	Function count	Iterations	Optimal variables [x]	Optimal function value fval
[1, 1]	46	14	[2.999, 0.4998]	3.3969e-07
[-2, 2]	54	15	[2.9997, 0.4999]	1.0939e-08
[-1, 1]	71	21	[-4.5, 1.1864]	0.7621
[2, 2]	79	23	[3, 0.5]	3.6066e-11
[3, 1]	47	14	[3.0001, 0.5]	9.7386e-09
[-3, 2]	51	16	[2.9997, 0.4999]	4.2002e-08
[-2, 1]	60	17	[-4.5, 1.1864]	0.7621

Table 2.1. Behavioral characteristics of Exact methods: Demonstration of fmincon solver over Beale function optimization for various initial points x0

Function count indicates the number of function evaluations during the iterations of the solver for the given initial point x0. To recall, the global minimum for Beale function is attained at $f(x_1, x_2) = 0$, for $(x_1, x_2) = (3, 0.5)$. It can be seen how for different initial points, the solver built on an exact method displays different behavior, some close to the optimal zone and some away from it, justifying the fact that initial point selection is a major hurdle in exact methods.

Metaheuristic method: Differential Evolution for Beale function optimization

Differential Evolution, a metaheuristic method was adopted to undertake Beale function optimization. Differential Evolution is a population-based metaheuristic method that is built on the principles of natural evolution. The strategy explores the search space for the optimal solution sets, through a population of candidate solutions that evolve generation after generation, until the optimal solution sets arc searched out. We defer elaboration of the method in this section and only present its behavioral characteristics, which is of relevance to the subject under discussion. Section 2.5 elaborates the design and working of Differential Evolution algorithm.

Table 2.2 shows the behavioral characteristics of Differential Evolution for a standard set of control parameters that were set to solve the Beale function optimization problem. It can be observed that for just around 25 generations, the metaheuristic strategy has entered the optimal zone and continues to linger around with stability in the optimal zone, for the ensuing number of generations too.

Generations	Optimal variable x	Optimal function value $f(x)$
25	[3.0386, 0.5065]	4.3545e-04
30	[3.0028, 0.5027]	9.5672e-05
35	[3.0123, 0.5023]	3.7798e-05
40	[2.9975, 0.4996]	2.4124e-06
45	[3.0012, 0.5003]	2.3950e-07

Table 2.2. *Behavioral characteristics of metaheuristic methods: demonstration of Differential Evolution over Beale function optimization*

The performance of metaheuristic methods are distinctly visible when applied over problems that deal with large-scale optimization or complex/ multiple objective functions and constraints.

2.3. Population-based metaheuristics – Evolutionary Algorithms

Population-based metaheuristic algorithms, ideally work iteratively over a population of candidate solution sets, combining and reworking on them until the near-optimal solution sets are discovered. *Evolutionary Algorithms* are an important class of population-based metaheuristics and are mostly built on the principles of natural *evolution.*

Evolutionary Algorithms typically involve an *initial population* of *chromosomes* or *individuals* that are randomly generated and represent candidate solution sets to the optimization problem concerned. The objective is to explore the search space of the problem and finally arrive at the optimum solution set. The initial population of individuals, termed *parent population,* evaluate their individual *"fitness"* by way of assessing how promising a solution each one is. The parent population following principles of natural evolution, undergo *reproduction* amongst themselves to yield a new population of individuals termed *offspring.* The offspring population is yet another candidate solution set existing in the problem's search space. The offspring population too evaluate their respective fitness values and the *best fit* amongst the offspring, which are the most promising amongst the candidate solution sets they represent, are chosen as the next set of parent population for the *next generation.*

The cycle repeats with the new parents reproducing to generate new offspring and the best fit individuals amongst the offspring passing on to the subsequent generation and so on. Thus during each generation cycle, the search strategy shepherds the population of individuals through the search space enabling them to explore diverse or better candidate solution sets.

A variety of *genetic inheritance operators* such as *selection, crossover* and *mutation,* to quote a prominent few, are employed to bring about what are called *exploration* and *exploitation* in the Evolutionary Computation literature. In line with principles of natural evolution, exploration is when the strategy is endowed with the capability to explore the search space in all its vastness picking on diverse individuals who are plausible solution sets, and exploitation is when the most promising candidate solution sets are preserved or retained through various mechanisms, to be passed on to the ensuing generation. The generation cycles are repeated until specific *termination criterion* or *stopping criterion* specified for the problem concerned are met with, at which point of time, the new population generated represents an "acceptable" or "near-optimal" solution set.

Figure 2.3 illustrates a generic Evolutionary Algorithm at work to obtain the optimal solution set. The parent population represents the candidate solution set garnered from the problem search space and currently under exploration, with the size of the diamond shapes in the diagram symbolically indicative of the fitness values of the individuals. Employing genetic inheritance operators such as selection, crossover and mutation – one or more or all of these – the offspring population also representative of candidate solution points in the problem search space is generated. With the help of appropriate genetic inheritance operators, the best fit individuals from the offspring are selected and these move on to become the parent population for the next generation. At the end of the generation cycle, an appropriate termination or stopping criterion that is framed to aid efficient problem solving is checked for its satisfiability. The generation cycles continue until the criterion is met with at which stage the best fit individuals in the population generated deliver the optimal solution sets.

2.3.1. *Evolutionary Algorithm basics*

In this section we define the basic building blocks of Evolutionary Algorithms which when mapped to the problem structure and objectives, serves to obtain the optimal solution set for the problem concerned.

Gene

A *gene* is the most fundamental building block and is representative of the design variable of the optimization problem. Thus if the problem dealt with n variables, then the number of genes would be n. Encoding of genes could be done in *binary* form (as is done in conventional Genetic Algorithms) or in *real coded* form, where each gene naturally represents the numerical value of the design variable concerned, or other forms such as *octal* or *hexadecimal* coding etc.

In this book we shall adopt real coded genes to represent the numerical values of the financial variables constituting the finance models.

Chromosome

Also referred to as *individual* in certain metaheuristic algorithms, a chromosome is a collection of genes representative of all the design variables that need to be optimized in the problem. Thus, if a problem had n design variables $x_1, x_2, x_3, \ldots x_n$, a chromosome structure with n genes, with each gene i representing a design variable x_i, could be represented as follows:

X_1	X_2	X_3	$\ldots$	X_n

Each chromosome or individual represents a point in n-dimensional search space for the problem. The Evolutionary algorithm strives to either transform candidate solution points into feasible solution points or directly identify feasible solution points, while navigating through the search space, in search of optimal or near-optimal solution points.

Population

A collection of chromosomes or individuals with different admissible values for their respective genes is called as a *population*. The number of chromosomes or individuals in the population is termed *population size*.

While the *length* of the chromosome or individual is fixed (*n* for example), the population size N could be fixed by the designer after observing the performance characteristics of the algorithm.

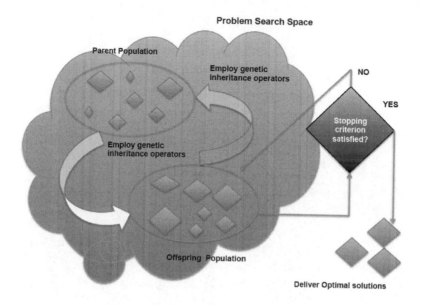

Figure 2.3. *A Generic Evolutionary algorithm at work*

Thus a population of chromosomes or individuals could be represented as follows where each vector x_{ij}, $i=1,2,3...n$ represents a point in n dimensional search space for the problem and each x_{ij}, $j=1,2,3...N$ for a specific gene index i, represents a set of admissible values for the design variable x_i, in case of the chromosome representing a feasible solution point.

Population of chromosomes / individuals:

x_{11}	x_{21}	x_{31}	...	x_{n1}

x_{12}	x_{22}	x_{32}	...	x_{n2}

x_{13}	x_{23}	x_{33}	...	x_{n3}

x_{1N}	x_{2N}	x_{3N}	...	x_{nN}

Fitness value

The fitness value or *fitness function value* is that which determines how promising a candidate solution represented by the chromosome is. While there are several methods to determine fitness functions suitable to the problems concerned, a simple and ideal method in the case of optimization problems is to choose the objective function as the fitness function itself. For reasons of simplicity we confine our discussion to optimization problems with a single objective function.

To obtain the fitness values of each of the chromosome, the design variables in the problem objective function, like $x_1, x_2, x_3, \ldots x_N$ are substituted by the values represented by the respective genes of the chromosomes concerned, to arrive at the objective function value for the corresponding point in the search space.

The population of chromosomes is sorted according to their fitness values. In case of minimization problems, those chromosomes with smallest objective function value are deemed "best fit" and those with large values are deemed "worst fit". In the case of maximization problems the roles are reversed. The metaheuristic strategy inherently tries to preserve or explore "high-fit" individuals during its navigation through the search space thereby aiding a natural evolution towards solution points that have optimal or near optimal objective function values, in course of a definite number of generation cycles.

The metaheuristic methods discussed in this book will only resort to modeling fitness functions using the appropriate objective functions of the optimization problems concerned.

Selection

This is a genetic inheritance operator that serves to select parents from a population or select individuals (parent or offspring) for the new population in the ensuing generation. However, for the selection of parents, most Evolutionary Algorithms adopt random selection. For the selection of individuals for the next generation, various strategies have been devised and it is left to the designer to adopt any one of these methods suitable to the problem in hand.

The metaheuristic methods adopted in this book make use of *random selection* to select their parents and a variant of *(μ +λ) strategy* for the selection of individuals in the new population for the next generation, which will be explained subsequently.

Crossover

Crossover is an important genetic inheritance operator that selects two or more parent individuals to yield offspring individuals, by exchanging their respective genes.

A variety of crossover operators are available in the Evolutionary Computation literature. In this book we restrict the application to *Two-point crossover*, where two parent individuals are randomly selected and the string of genes between two randomly selected sites in the parent chromosomes, termed *cross sites,* are exchanged.

A schematic diagram of Two-point crossover is shown in Figure 2.4. Here the cross sites are randomly chosen to be *(p, q)* and therefore it can be seen how the string of genes between genes p and q (both inclusive) are exchanged to yield the respective offspring chromosomes. As said earlier, the offspring individuals, different from their parents are potential candidate solution sets for they represent two different points in the n dimensional problem search space.

Mutation

Mutation operator is a genetic inheritance operator analogous with biological mutation. The operator serves to maintain the diversity of the population from one generation to another by changing one or more randomly selected genes in a set of randomly selected chromosomes in a population. However, mutation is always accompanied by a probability factor termed *mutation rate*, which is deliberately kept small, for overdoing it could result in the evolutionary search deteriorating to random search.

The metaheuristic methods adopted in this book will resort to mutation in a special form.

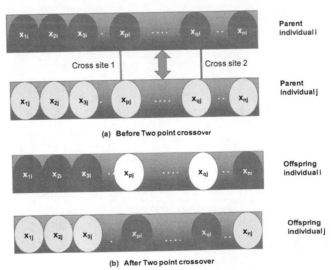

Figure 2.4. *A schematic diagram for Two-point crossover*

2.4. Evolution Strategy

In this section, we detail the method and application of Evolution Strategy, a population-based metaheuristic strategy that has had a respectable track record of solving complex portfolio optimization problems in particular.

Approach

Evolution Strategy (ES) [PAI 09] is a population-based metaheuristic strategy that follows the typical framework of such a metaheuristic category. Thus, an initial randomly generated population of parent chromosomes evolving into offspring population, the application of genetic inheritance operators such as selection, crossover and mutation in generating offspring and preparing new populations for the next generation, the role played by fitness functions in determining the high-fit individuals in each parent/offspring population during each generation to aid navigation through search space, the presence of a termination or stopping criteria to exit from the generation cycles and deliver the optimal solution sets, are all left undisturbed in the strategy.

However, ES distinguishes itself from its counterparts with regard to the following:

1) resorts to specific choices of genetic inheritance operators with regard to Selection, Crossover and Mutation;

2) instead of exterminating the entire parent population as is commonly done, preserves the best amongst the parent individuals to co-exist along with the best offspring in the next generation, and participate in the evolutionary process;

3) employs what is termed *elitism* in Evolutionary Computation literature when the best-of-the-best solutions are preserved in a repository termed *Hall of Fame*, with the chromosome last inducted into it yielding the optimal solution.

2.4.1. *Evolution Strategy: genetic inheritance operators*

Chromosome representation

Evolution Strategy adopts real coded genes representing the problem design variables, for its chromosome structure. Thus an optimization problem with n decision or design variables would be represented by a chromosome of length n, that is n real coded genes.

Selection

Evolution Strategy uses random selection for choosing the parent individuals to produce offspring. Thus, the strategy generates a pair of offspring from only a pair of randomly selected parent individuals. Evolution Strategy does not take recourse to multi-parent selection, which has also been discussed in the literature.

With regard to selection of individuals for the next generation, ES adopts a variant of $(\mu + \lambda)$ strategy recorded in the Evolutionary Computation literature, where μ best fit parent individuals and λ best fit offspring individuals, in the ratio of $(s{:}t)$, where $(s + t = N)$, $s, t \neq 0$ and N is the population size, are selected. The fact that $s \neq 0$ ensures exploitation, in that the best fit parents are preserved for the next generation, and $t \neq 0$ ensures exploration where the newly generated individuals are retained in the next generation.

The ES strategy discussed in this book resorts to a uniform choice of $(s{:}t) = 1{:}2$.

Crossover

Evolution Strategy employs a special form of two point crossover called *arithmetic variable point crossover* [OSY 02] that works over a pair of real coded parent chromosomes to yield a pair of offspring chromosomes.

If P_1 and P_2 are two parent chromosomes belonging to a population in generation t, $x1$ (t) and $x2(t)$ are two genes in P_1 and P_2 respectively, then the corresponding updated genes in the offspring chromosomes O_1 and O_2 in generation $(t+1)$ are given by $x1(t+1), x2(t+1)$, where

$$x1(t+1) \quad = \quad (a).\, x2(t) + (1\text{-}a).\, x1(t)$$
$$x2(t+1) \quad = (1\text{-}a).\, x2(t) + (a).x1(t) \qquad\qquad [2.3]$$

for a random number a. The cross over operation is associated with a *crossover rate ρ*.

Figure 2.5 illustrates the arithmetic variable point crossover operation undertaken on two specific genes of the parent chromosome pairs.

Mutation

Evolution Strategy adopts *Real Number Uniform Mutation* [OSY 02], a mutation operator that contributes to preserving the diversity of population and is undertaken for a specified mutation rate τ, which is usually kept very small. Real number uniform mutation serves to "tweak" a randomly chosen gene as

$$gene\_lb + b * (gene\_ub - gene\_lb) \qquad\qquad [2.4]$$

for a random number *b* and with *gene_lb* and *gene_ub* representing the lower bounds and upper bounds respectively of the design variables representing the genes concerned.

Fitness function

Evolution Strategy employs the objective function as its fitness function. Thus in the case of minimization problems those chromosomes yielding minimal fitness values are deemed "best-fit" and in the case of maximization problems those chromosomes yielding maximal fitness values are deemed "best-fit".

Elitism using Hall of Fame

The Hall of Fame, which finally yields the optimal solution is initialized to null and the best fit chromosome amongst the root parent population is inducted into it to initialize the same. Subsequently, during the generation cycles, every time the offspring population is generated the best fit chromosome from the offspring competes with the one in the Hall of Fame. If the new entrant is better fit than the incumbent then the former is inducted into the Hall of Fame and the latter is deleted. This competition continues until the stopping criterion is met with at which stage the chromosome in the Hall of Fame is declared to represent the optimal solution. The genes extracted from the chromosome represent the optimal values of the decision variables and the fitness function value, which is its objective function value represents the optimal function value for the problem.

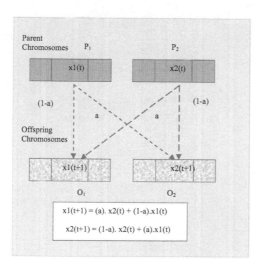

Figure 2.5. *Arithmetic variable point crossover demonstrated over two specific genes in the parent chromosome pair*

In this book, ES deals with Hall of Fame accommodating only one best fit member. However, there are no limits enforced and therefore it is not unusual to find applications (for example Pareto Optimal solution sets) where the Hall of Fame may have to accommodate multiple best-fit solutions.

Stopping or termination criterion

The stopping criterion is fixed to be a definite number of generations, often decided upon after a few trial runs.

2.4.2. *Evolution Strategy process flow chart*

Figure 2.6 illustrates the Process flow chart for Evolution Strategy.

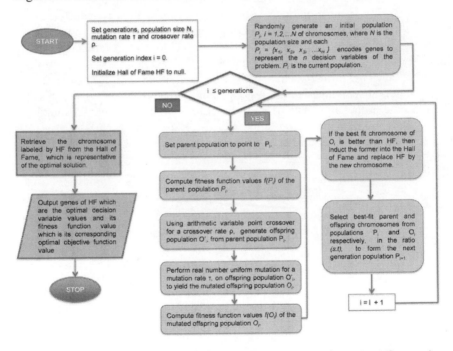

Figure 2.6. *Evolution Strategy with Hall of Fame: process flow chart (for a color version of this figure, see www.iste.co.uk/pai/metaheuristics.zip)*

2.4.3. *Demonstration of Evolution Strategy*

In this section we demonstrate the working of Evolution Strategy in optimizing the Beale function described in [2.1], for a simplified selection of Evolution Strategy parameters for purposes of illustration, for a single generation. To recall, Beale

function is usually evaluated on a square [-4.5, 4.5] for x_1 and x_2 and the global minimum is attained at $f(x_1, x_2) = 0$, for $(x_1, x_2) = (3, 0.5)$.

Step 1: set Evolution Strategy parameters. Chromosome length $n = 2$ (two design variables x_1, x_2), population size $N = 10$, mutation rate $\tau = 0.01$, crossover rate $\rho = 0.61$, generations = 500, parent/offspring ratio $(s{:}t)$ in the next generation − (1:2), bounds $[lb, ub]$ − [-4.5, 4.5].

Initialize Hall of Fame to null and set fitness value HF of the chromosome in Hall of Fame to be a large number (9999999, for example).

Set generation index $i = 0$.

Step 2: randomly generate the initial population of chromosomes so that they satisfy their bounds [-4.5, 4.5]. Let $(P_j)_{10X2}$ be the parent population as shown below:

P_j:

P_1	3.815	1.255
P_2	-1.051	-0.880
P_3	-1.867	-0.110
P_4	-4.135	-0.369
P_5	4.275	-3.689
P_6	-1.286	2.501
P_7	-3.686	3.365
P_8	-2.529	-2.122
P_9	-3.738	-2.218
P_{10}	4.310	-1.876

Step 3: compute fitness function values of P_j, $f(P_j)$ by substituting each gene value of the chromosome, representing the values of the variables x_1, x_2, into the Beale function to yield the respective objective function values. The sorted list of fitness values and the corresponding chromosome labels are as listed below:

$f(P_j)$:

37.6	49.7	66.0	133.7	283.5	991.6	1198.9	2559.0	19339.7	50298.4
P_2	P_3	P_1	P_4	P_6	P_8	P_{10}	P_9	P_7	P_5

Step 4: undertaking arithmetic crossover operator over P_j, for a crossover rate $\rho = 0.61$, yields the offspring population O_j:

O_j:

O_1	-0.021	-0.428
O_2	2.784	0.802
O_3	-1.867	-0.110
O_4	-4.135	-0.369
O_5	4.275	-3.689
O_6	-1.286	2.501
O_7	-3.377	1.899
O_8	-2.838	-0.655
O_9	-3.594	-2.218
O_{10}	4.166	-1.876

Step 5: executing Real number uniform mutation over O_j, for a mutation rate $\tau = 0.01$ yields the mutated offspring population $O_j^{mutated}$ shown below. As can be observed, considering the mutation rate that is kept very small, no changes whatsoever have taken place over the original offspring population, in this specific generation.

$O_j^{mutated}$:

$O_1^{mutated}$	-0.021	-0.428
$O_2^{mutated}$	2.784	0.802
$O_3^{mutated}$	-1.867	-0.110
$O_4^{mutated}$	-4.135	-0.369
$O_5^{mutated}$	4.275	-3.689
$O_6^{mutated}$	-1.286	2.501
$O_7^{mutated}$	-3.377	1.899
$O_8^{mutated}$	-2.838	-0.655
$O_9^{mutated}$	-3.594	-2.218
$O_{10}^{mutated}$	4.166	-1.876

Step 6: compute fitness function values of $O_j^{mutated}$ viz., $f(O_j^{mutated})$ by substituting each gene value of the chromosome, representing the values of the variables x_1, x_2, into the Beale function to yield the respective objective function

values. The sorted list of fitness values and the corresponding chromosome labels are as listed below:

$f(O_j^{mutated})$:

4.12	14.48	49.74	92.60	133.74	283.50
$O_2^{mutated}$	$O_1^{mutated}$	$O_3^{mutated}$	$O_8^{mutated}$	$O_4^{mutated}$	$O_6^{mutated}$

337.87	1115.66	2373.80	50298.44
$O_7^{mutated}$	$O_{10}^{mutated}$	$O_9^{mutated}$	$O_5^{mutated}$

Step 7: check if the best fit chromosome from the mutated population $O_j^{mutated}$, viz., $O_2^{mutated}$ is better than the one in the Hall of Fame (lesser in value than HF). Since it is less than HF, induct $O_2^{mutated}$ into the Hall of Fame and set HF value to 4.12.

Step 8: select the best fit chromosomes (least fitness values) from the parent population P_j and the mutated offspring population $O_j^{mutated}$, in the ratio of 1:2 to move to the next generation.

Next Generation:

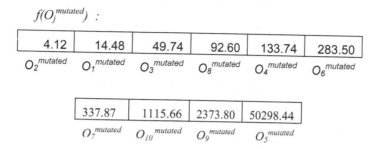

P_2	-1.051	-0.880
P_3	-1.867	-0.110
P_1	3.815	1.255
$O_2^{mutated}$	2.784	0.802
$O_1^{mutated}$	-0.021	-0.428
$O_3^{mutated}$	-1.867	-0.110
$O_8^{mutated}$	-2.838	-0.655
$O_4^{mutated}$	-4.135	-0.369
$O_6^{mutated}$	-1.286	2.501
$O_7^{mutated}$	-3.377	1.899

Step 9: $i = i+1$. Check if the generation index i has reached the number of generations. If not, set parent population P_j to the population in Next Generation and go to Step 3 to repeat a similar set of operations on P_j.

Thus, at the end of a generation cycle, a new population of chromosomes, a mix of best fit parent and offspring chromosomes are generated, ready to get into the next cycle of operations and so on, until the stopping criterion is met with. At this stage the best-of-the-best fit chromosomes inducted into the Hall of Fame represents the optimal solution set (decision variables) and HF represents the optimal objective function value.

For the Beale function optimization problem, Evolution Strategy was able to fetch the following optimal solution set from the Hall of Fame, for a population size of 100 and number of generations set as 500, with all other parameters set in Step 1 above remaining intact.

Optimal solution set: $(x_1, x_2) = (3.0018, 0.5005)$

Optimal function value: $f(x_1, x_2) = 5.7248e\text{-}07$

2.4.4. Experimental results and analysis

Consistency of performance

Since population based metaheuristic methods are stochastic search processes with the randomly generated initial population determining the starting points of search in the search space for the problem concerned, it is essential to ensure the consistency of performance by these methods by repeatedly running the algorithm for a definite number of times. Table 2.3 illustrates the optimal results obtained by Evolution Strategy during 15 sample runs for the Beale function optimization problem for population size of $N = 100$ and number of generations GEN set as 500. It can be seen that Evolution Strategy is by and large consistent in delivering optimal results.

Convergence characteristics

The convergence characteristic of population-based metaheuristic methods can be studied by observing the behavior of the objective function value during the generation cycles.

Figure 2.7 illustrates a trace of the objective function values of the best of the best fit chromosomes inducted into the Hall of Fame during the generation cycles, during a specific run. It can be seen how the objective function value, hovering around 0.8 initially, very quickly slumps to its global minimum of 0 in less than 20 generations. Thus Evolution Strategy records a respectable convergence characteristic for the appropriate choice of its control parameters.

Runs	Optimal function value $f(x_1, x_2)$	Optimal solution set (x_1, x_2)
R1	8.0075e-25	[3, 0.5]
R2	5.6532e-21	[3, 0.5]
R3	0	[3, 0.5]
R4	0	[3, 0.5]
R5	0	[3, 0.5]
R6	0.0014	[2.9171, 0.4759]
R7	8.2176e-06	[2.9936, 0.4981]
R8	1.9025e-07	[3.0011, 0.5003]
R9	9.6757e-13	[3, 0.5]
R10	0	[3, 0.5]
R11	1.5335e-12	[3, 0.5]
R12	1.1387e-14	[3, 0.5]
R13	1.1371e-30	[3, 0.5]
R14	1.1259e-19	[3, 0.5]
R15	6.6985e-20	[3, 0.5]

Table 2.3. *Beale function optimization: performance of Evolution Strategy for N = 100 and GEN =500, over 15 sample runs*

Sensitivity to control parameters

Population-based metaheuristic methods by and large record some amount of sensitivity to the control parameters that define the algorithms. A lot of empirical testing and analysis have been undertaken and recorded in the Evolutionary Computation literature, suggesting bench marks for certain classes of problems.

In the case of Evolution Strategy, with regard to Beale function optimization as an example case study, the strategy is sensitive to the parameters of population size and the number of generations, which acts as its stopping criterion.

Table 2.4 illustrates the optimal solution sets arrived at for different values of population size and generations.

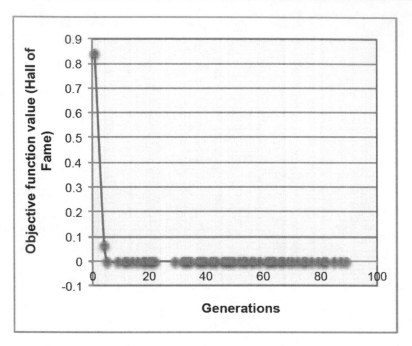

Figure 2.7. *Convergence characteristics of Evolution Strategy during Beale function optimization: Trace of the objective function values of the best-of-the-best fit chromosomes, inducted into the Hall of Fame, during the generation cycles*

[Population Size, Generations]	Optimal function value $f(x_1, x_2)$	Optimal solution set (x_1, x_2)
[150, 1000]	5.5295e-12	[3, 0.5]
[150, 500]	2.7621e-22	[3, 0.5]
[150, 200]	8.1653e-16	[3, 0.5]
[150, 100]	3.9226e-13	[3, 0.5]
[100, 1000]	1.1421e-17	[3, 0.5]
[100, 500]	5.7248e-07	[3.0018, 0.5005]
[100, 200]	4.6727e-04	[2.9475, 0.4867]
[100, 100]	7.5175e-04	[2.9378, 0.4821]
[50, 100]	0.2599	[2.245, 0.1950]
[50, 200]	1.5519e-04	[2.9707, 0.4919]
[50, 500]	4.7699e-06	[2.9946, 0.4986]
[50, 1000]	0.0173	[2.7214, 0.42]

Table 2.4. *Beale function optimization: sensitivity of Evolution Strategy to the control parameters of population size and number of generations*

2.5. Differential Evolution strategy

In this section, we detail the method and implementation of Differential Evolution, a population based metaheuristic strategy that has been successfully applied for the solution of complex portfolio optimization problems, besides multifarious problems from various disciplines.

Approach

The Differential Evolution (DE) algorithm proposed by Kenneth Price and Rainer Storn [STO 95] is a simple yet powerful global optimizer. A year after its discovery, the method was successfully demonstrated at the First International Contest on Evolutionary Optimization, which was held in conjunction with the 1996 IEEE International Conference on Evolutionary Computation, by winning third place for the proposed benchmarks. In due course Storn and Price's papers on DE [PRI 97, STO 97] coupled with its good track record over solution of benchmark problems, served to popularize DE to a large extent amongst the scientific community.

Unlike ES, which takes recourse to organic evolution operators, DE relies on *distance* and *direction* information to guide its search process through the search space. Differential Evolution has therefore turned out to be a promising global optimizer that ensures fast convergence, high precision, capability to work over continuous landscapes and flat surfaces of the search space, commendable success rate in attaining global optimum, besides universal applicability to a wide variety of optimization problems, namely linear, nonlinear, continuous, combinatorial or mixed integer ones.

2.5.1. *Differential Evolution operators*

Mutation, Crossover and Selection are the three major operators of DE. While most evolutionary algorithms rely on some probability distribution to determine the mutation step size, DE relies on the *vector differences between individuals* constituting the population. The initial population of individuals that are generated in any evolutionary algorithm serve to provide useful information about the search space or fitness landscape. Thus if the individuals in the population are strewn across the search space with large distances separating the individuals, then that ensures a better search space representation by the population concerned. With the onset of generation cycles, when the search progresses, the distances between individuals in the respective populations are expected to get smaller and smaller until at one point of time the entire set of individuals in the population could be expected to converge to the same point in the search space that represents the solution. Also, when the search is in progress during the generation cycles, prudence lies in keeping the mutation step sizes large if the differences between the individuals in the population are large, to cover as much ground as possible and keeping the mutation step sizes small to favor local search, if the differences between individuals in the population are small. Differential Evolution successfully adopts this expected behavior by calculating mutation step sizes as *weighted differences between randomly selected individuals in the population*. Thus DE computes one or more difference vectors between the individuals constituting the population concerned and uses these to determine the magnitude and direction of the step size.

Mutation

Differential Evolution produces what are called *trial vectors* for each individual in the population to define its mutation operator. Trial vectors are obtained by mutating a *target vector* with a *weighted differential*.

Thus, for generation t, if $x_i(t)$ is an individual in a parent population $P(t)$ then its corresponding trial vector $t_i(t)$ is produced by randomly choosing a target vector $x_{i_1}(t)$, $i \neq i_1$ and two other individuals $x_{i_2}(t)$, $x_{i_3}(t)$, $i \neq i_1 \neq i_2 \neq i_3$ from the population of individuals and computing

$$t_i(t) = x_{i_1}(t) + \beta.(x_{i_2}(t) - x_{i_3}(t)),$$ [2.5]

where $\beta \in (0, \infty)$ is the *scale factor* controlling the amplification of the differential variation. β helps to ensure a trade-off between exploration and exploitation of the search space and the term $\beta.(x_{i_2}(t) - x_{i_3}(t))$ defines the direction and length of each search step.

The trial vectors are produced for each individual in the population, thus forming a population of trial vectors.

Crossover

The DE *crossover* operator produces *offspring vectors* by recombining the parent vectors and the trial vectors concerned. Thus for a parent vector $x_i(t)$ and trial vector $t_i(t)$, an offspring $O_i(t)$ which is a discrete recombination of the parent and the corresponding trial vector is computed as

$$O_{ij}(t) = \begin{cases} t_{ij}(t) & if \ j \in \tau \\ x_{ij}(t) & otherwise \end{cases}$$ [2.6]

where $x_{ij}(t)$ refers to the jth element of the vector $x_i(t)$ and τ is the set of *crossover points*. The crossover points can be obtained through various approaches, the following two of which are most popular:

— *binomial crossover*

— *exponential crossover*.

Binomial Crossover

If n_d is the number of genes (components) in an individual in the population, Binomial Crossover randomly selects the crossover points τ from the set of possible crossover points $\{1, 2, 3, ... n_d\}$, for a selection probability p_s. To ensure that τ stays non-empty, it is mandatorily initialized to any one random element.

Exponential Crossover

For the list of crossover points $\{1, 2, 3, ... n_d\}$, Exponential Crossover views the list as a circular array $\{0, 1, 2, 3, ... n_d - 1\}$ and chooses a sequence of crossover points beginning from a randomly selected index, so long as the choice conforms to the selection probability p_s or $|\tau| - n_d$.

Selection

In a DE, selection operator is used on two occasions, namely (1) to determine the individuals that would take part in the mutation operation to produce a trial vector and (2) to determine those individuals from the parent and offspring population, which will move to the next generation.

In case of (1), random selection is often used. In case of (2), *deterministic selection*, where the better of the parent and offspring individual in a population, based on a one-to-one comparison of the two individuals concerned, is undertaken. Deterministic selection serves to keep a check on the average fitness of the population.

2.5.2. Differential Evolution strategy process flow chart

Figure 2.8 illustrates the Process flow chart for Differential Evolution strategy.

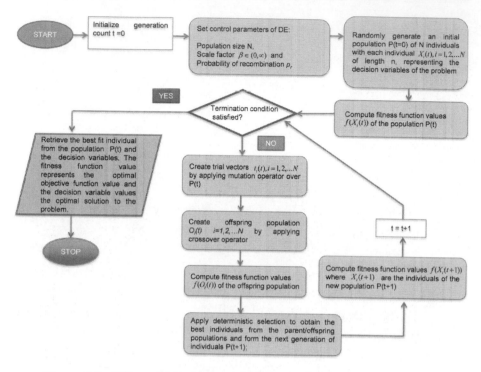

Figure 2.8. *Differential Evolution strategy: process flow chart (for a color version of this figure, see www.iste.co.uk/pai/metaheuristics.zip)*

Remarks on control parameters of Differential Evolution

Just as in other evolutionary algorithms, the performance of DE is influenced by the choice of its control parameters, namely population size N, scale factor β and probability of recombination or crossover p_r.

The population size N has a direct bearing on DE's search abilities since the larger the population the larger the search prospects and more directions in the search space can be explored. Empirical studies over DE, however, have revealed that a choice of $N \approx 10. n$, where n is the dimension of the problem variable, can be a good guideline value.

The choice of scaling factor β affects convergence in that smaller values of β implies smaller mutation step sizes and hence longer times for convergence, and larger values of β may result in the algorithm overstepping or overlooking good optima. Therefore, while large β may ensure diversity, small β can help ensure exploring tight valleys facilitating local area search. Hence as the population size increases, scaling factor β should decrease. Empirical studies have shown that large values of N and β result in premature convergence. $\beta = 0.5$ has generally been observed to provide good performance [STO 97].

The probability of recombination p_r has an influence over the diversity of DE since it controls the number of elements that will change in an individual. The higher the probability p_r, the higher is DE's diversity and exploration and the faster its convergence, since more variation is introduced in the population.

While it is essential to explore the ideal choice of control parameters for a problem, most empirical results have shown that convergence of DE is relatively insensitive to the choice of the control parameters. Several problems have stuck to bench mark values for DE's control parameters and have reaped success in their performances by way of accuracy, robustness and speed.

2.5.3. *Differential Evolution strategies*

A number of variations to the basic Differential Evolution algorithm have been proposed in the literature. The variations revolve around the way in which the target vector is chosen, the number of difference vectors that are selected, and which crossover operator is employed [FEO 06]. In order to describe these variations the notation *DE/x/y/z* has been employed in the literature. Here *x* refers to the method of choosing the target vector, *y* the number of difference vectors and *z* the crossover operator. For example, *DE/rand/1/bin* refers to a variation of DE where the target vector is randomly ("*rand*") selected, the number of difference vectors chosen is *1* and the crossover operator used is binomial ("*bin*"). Again, *DE/rand/1/exp* refers to the variation as explained before with the crossover operator chosen being Exponential ("*exp*").

Some of the popular DE variations have been listed below.

DE/best/1/z

In this strategy the target vector is selected as the best individual $x^{best}(t)$ of the population. $x^{best}(t)$ is chosen as the best by way of its fitness value. The strategy employs one difference vector $(x_i(t) - x_j(t))$ and uses the crossover operator indicated by z. The trial vector is computed as

$$t_i(t) = x^{best}(t) + \beta(x_{i_1}(t) - x_{i_2}(t))$$

[2.7]

DE/x/v/z

In this strategy the choice of target vector is indicated by x and that of crossover operator is indicated by z. However, for the difference vector indicated by v, v difference vectors (v more than 1) are employed. The choice of v difference vectors facilitates exploration in several different directions at a point of time. For a target vector $x_i(t)$ the trial vector is computed as

$$t_i(t) = x_i(t) + \beta \sum_{k=1}^{v} (x_{i_{1,k}}(t) - x_{i_{2,k}}(t))$$

[2.8]

where $\left(x_{i_{1,k}}(t) - x_{i_{2,k}}(t)\right)$ indicates the kth difference vector.

DE/current-to-best/1+v/z

In this strategy the target vector $x_i(t)$ is mutated using at least two difference vectors. While one difference vector is computed with the target vector and the best vector, the rest of the v difference vectors are computed as usual from the randomly selected vectors. Hence the notation (1+v) where "1" indicates the difference vector between the target and the best vector and "v" the rest of the difference vectors. Thus the trial vector is given by

$$t_i(t) = x_i(t) + \beta(x^{best}(t) - x_i(t)) + \beta \sum_{k=1}^{v} (x_{i_{1,k}}(t) - x_{i_{2,k}}(t))$$

[2.9]

DE/rand-to-best/v/z

This strategy as the notations suggest, is a combination of *rand* and *best* strategies explained above. The trial vector is given as

$$t_i(t) = \gamma . x^{best}(t) + (1 - \gamma) . x_{i_1}(t) + \beta \sum_{k=1}^{v} (x_{i_{2,k}}(t) - x_{i_{3,k}}(t))$$

[2.10]

where $x^{best}(t)$ is the best individual in the population, $x_i(t)$ is a randomly chosen individual and $(x_{i_{2,k}}(t) - x_{i_{3,k}}(t))$ indicates the kth difference vector. β is the scale factor and $\gamma \in [0,1]$ is the greediness of the mutation operator. Here γ close to *1* favours exploitations and γ close to *0* favours explorations. It is also possible to construct a strategy which employs an adaptive γ, that is $\gamma(0) = 0$, initially and with each new generation $\gamma(t)$ increases tending towards the value *1*.

It can be seen in [2.10] that if $\gamma = 0$ the strategy reduces to *DE/rand/y/z* and if $\gamma = 1$ it reduces to *DE/best/y/z* strategies.

Of the variations in DE discussed above, *DE/rand/1/bin* is noted for its good diversity and *DE/current-to-best/2/bin* has been observed to have good convergence characteristics.

2.5.4. Demonstration of Differential Evolution Strategy

In this section we demonstrate the working of Differential Evolution Strategy (*DE/rand/1/bin*) when it is applied to the Beale function optimization problem described in [2.1]. For purposes of illustration, the demonstration is undertaken for a simple choice of parameters, for a single generation cycle. The demonstration uses random ("*rand*") method to select its target vector, employs one difference vector ($y = 1$) and binomial crossover operator ($z = $ "*bin*").

To recall, Beale function is usually evaluated on a square [-4.5, 4.5] for x_1 and x_2 and the global minimum is attained at $f(x_1, x_2) = 0$, for $(x_1, x_2) = (3, 0.5)$.

Step 1: set Differential Evolution Strategy and problem parameters. Individual length $n = 2$ (two design variables x_1, x_2), population size $N = 10$, scale factor $\beta = 0.5$, probability of recombination $p_r = 0.87$, generations = 45, bounds [*lb, ub*] = [-4.5, 4.5]

Set generation index count $t = 0$.

Step 2: randomly generate initial population of individuals so that they satisfy their bounds [-4.5, 4.5]. Let $(P_i)_{10 \times 2}$ be the parent population as shown below:

P_i:

P_1	1.15	0.24
P_2	2.49	-1.23
P_3	3.31	-3.87
P_4	-4.26	-2.27
P_5	1.04	-3.97
P_6	-2.72	-2.42
P_7	3.28	3.92
P_8	3.85	2.76
P_9	3.13	-4.16
P_{10}	-4.15	4.21

Step 3: compute fitness function values of P_i, $f(P_i)$ by substituting each component value of the individual, representing the values of the variables x_1, x_2, into the Beale function to yield the respective objective function values. The fitness values are as shown below:

$f(P_i)$:

3.98	48.27	39615.07	3661.10	4340.71	2147.09
P_1	P_2	P_3	P_4	P_5	P_6

41344.33	7213.00	53694.41	96887.17
P_7	P_8	P_9	P_{10}

Step 4: Compute trial vectors T for the parent population. The trial vector population T obtained is as shown below:

T:

T_1	4.36	-6.69
T_2	3.23	1.81
T_3	-6.14	-1.49
T_4	3.47	-3.43
T_5	-4.98	1.05
T_6	4.93	0.70
T_7	5.08	-5.32
T_8	5.78	-5.01
T_9	2.25	-5.71
T_{10}	1.90	-7.23

For example, the trial vector T_1 is computed as follows. As described in section 2.5.1 and as illustrated in [2.5], for every parent population individual, DE's mutation operator randomly chooses a target vector and two difference vectors from amongst the parent population. For P_1, the target vector P_5 = [1.04, -3.97] and difference vectors P_2 = [1.04, -3.97] and P_{10} = [-4.15, 4.21] were chosen. Using [2.5] the trial vector T_1 is computed as

$$T_1 = [1.04, -3.97] + \beta. ([1.04, -3.97]- [-4.15, 4.21]) = [4.36, -6.69].$$

Similarly the rest of the trial vector population are determined.

Step 5: undertake crossover operation to generate the offspring population O_i. As discussed in section 2.5.1 and as illustrated in equation [2.6], the offspring population generated by Binomial crossover is

O_i :

O_1	4.36	-6.69
O_2	3.23	1.81
O_3	-6.14	-1.49
O_4	3.47	-3.43
O_5	-4.98	1.05
O_6	4.93	0.70
O_7	5.08	-5.32
O_8	5.78	-5.01
O_9	2.25	-5.71
O_{10}	1.90	-7.23

For example, to generate the offspring O_1, employing [2.6] yields $\tau = \{ 1, 2 \}$ and hence both the components of the corresponding individual P_1 in the parent population are replaced by their respective trial vector components of T_1. However, for the generation cycle concerned, τ turned out to be a uniform $\{1, 2\}$ (need not be since τ is randomly selected) and therefore the offspring population resulted in being the same as the trial vector population for this generation.

Step 6: compute fitness function values of Oi, f(Oi) by substituting each component value of the individual, representing the values of the variables x_1, x_2, into the Beale function to yield the respective objective function values.

$f(P_0)$:

1742848.51	455.73	1155.75	21548.35	7.98	0.41
O_1	O_2	O_3	O_4	O_5	O_6

607920.96	552480.18	179306.09	528854.28
O_7	O_8	O_9	O_{10}

Step 7: undertake deterministic selection as described in section 2.5.1 to yield the following population for the next generation. The selection is made by undertaking a one-on-one comparison of the fitness values of the parent and offspring population individuals and selecting the one with the minimum fitness value (since it is a minimization problem).

Next Generation:

P_1	1.15	0.24
P_2	2.49	-1.23
O_3	-6.14	-1.49
P_4	-4.26	-2.27
O_5	-4.98	1.05
O_6	4.93	0.70
P_7	3.28	3.92
P_8	3.85	2.76
P_9	3.13	-4.16
P_{10}	-4.15	4.21

Step 8: $i = i+1$. Check if the generation count i has reached the number of generations. If not, set parent population P_i to the population in Next Generation and go to Step 3 to repeat a similar set of operations on P_i.

Thus when one generation cycle ends, a new population of chromosomes which is a mix of best fit parent and offspring chromosomes are generated, ready to get into the next cycle of operations and so on, until the stopping criterion is met with. At this stage, the best fit individual which is the one with the minimum fitness function value represents the optimal solution. The fitness function value represents the optimal objective function value and the decision variables extracted from the individual, the optimal solution set.

For the Beale function optimization problem, Differential Evolution Strategy was able to fetch the following optimal solution set for a population size of 20 and number of generations set as 90, with all other parameters set in Step 1 above remaining intact.

Optimal solution set: $(x_1, x_2) = (3, 0.5)$

Optimal function value: $f(x_1, x_2) = 1.25e\text{-}13$

2.5.5. Experimental results and analysis

Consistency of performance

As discussed earlier for Evolution Strategy, since DE is also a population based stochastic search strategy, the consistency of performance for the method can be empirically tested by repeatedly running the algorithm for a definite number of runs. Each run initiates a search from a population of random points across the search space. Table 2.5 illustrates the optimal results obtained by Differential Evolution Strategy during 15 sample runs for the Beale function optimization problem for population size of $N = 20$ and number of generations GEN set as 90. It can be seen that DE is consistent in delivering optimal results.

Convergence characteristics

The convergence characteristics of metaheuristics is an important issue and therefore empirical metrics such as convergence of the objective function (as was discussed for Evolution Strategy earlier) or the number of objective function evaluations or CPU time, in case of comparisons, are always undertaken during an experimental analysis of the metaheuristic methods. Another important criteria known as *Distribution-based criteria*, concerned with the *diversity of the population* during the generational process, is also undertaken. In these criteria, when the individuals in the population get closer and crowd around, during the subsequent generations, then the diversity is said to be low and convergence is said to be obtained.

Runs	Optimal function value $f(x_1 , x_2)$	Optimal solution set (x_1 , x_2)
R1	1.25E-13	[3, 0.5]
R2	9.25E-10	[3, 0.5]
R3	7.06E-09	[3, 0.5]
R4	1.86E-09	[3, 0.5]
R5	9.93E-14	[3, 0.5]
R6	1.25E-11	[3, 0.5]
R7	3.83E-10	[3, 0.5]
R8	3.51E-11	[3, 0.5]
R9	4.84E-05	[2.9832, 0.4961]
R10	1.31E-11	[3, 0.5]
R11	2.80E-13	[3, 0.5]
R12	7.50E-13	[3, 0.5]
R13	7.99E-12	[3, 0.5]
R14	2.04E-11	[3, 0.5]
R15	2.93E-11	[3, 0.5]

Table 2.5. *Beale function optimization: performance of Differential Evolution Strategy for N = 20 and GEN = 90, over 15 sample runs*

Vitaliy Feoktistov [FEO 06] proposed an innovative measure called *Population measure* or P *measure* to study the convergence criterion, which measures diversity using distance measures. P measure is a measure of population dynamics that allows one to measure the convergence rate by closely observing the density of the individuals of a population around the optimum. P measure is thus the radius of the population measured as the Euclidean distance between the center of the population (called the *barycenter*) and the individual farthest from it. The *barycenter* is computed as the average vector of all individuals in the population. The P measure for a population of M individuals (*Ind*$_i$, *i=1, 2, ...M*) with barycenter B is given by,

$$P_M = \max \|Ind_i - B\|_E, i = 1, 2, 3 ... M \qquad\qquad [2.11]$$

where, $B = \sum_{i=1}^{M} \dfrac{Ind_i}{M}$ and $\| \ \|_E$ indicates the Euclidean distance between the vectors.

The P measure trace of DE for 200 generations for a specific run is shown in Figure 2.9. It can be clearly seen that the P measures of the respective populations, in a matter of few generations (close to 50) begin crowding round a small region and within the next few generations converge to 0 and remain stable thereafter. Thus the convergence characteristic of DE with regard to Beale function optimization is surely noteworthy.

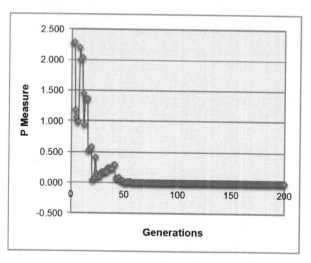

Figure 2.9. *Convergence characteristics of Differential Evolution Strategy during Beale function optimization: trace of the P measure values of the population during the generation cycles, for a specific run of the algorithm*

2.6. MATLAB® demonstrations

In this section, MATLAB® functions for some Evolution Strategy and Differential Evolution operators and the programs concerned for Beale function optimization, as listed below, have been presented. The MATLAB® coding style has been deliberately kept simple and direct to favor novice MATLAB readers.

A. Evolution Strategy: MATLAB® Implementation for Beale function Optimization

- Real number uniform mutation operator;

- Arithmetic variable point crossover operator;

- Computation of fitness function values for the Beale function optimization problem;

- The complete MATLAB® program for Beale function optimization using Evolution Strategy.

B. Differential Evolution: MATLAB® Implementation for Beale function Optimization

- Mutation operator;

- Binomial crossover operator;

- Deterministic selection operator;

- The complete MATLAB® program for Beale function Optimization using Differential Evolution.

A. *Evolution Strategy: MATLAB® Implementation for Beale function Optimization*

Figures 2.10 and 2.11 illustrate the MATLAB® functions for the Evolution Strategy operators of Real number uniform mutation and Arithmetic variable point crossover, respectively.

The function `realnumber_unifrm_mutation` returns the mutated population `mutated_popln` given the population of chromosomes `chromo_popln`, the respective bounds for the individual genes in the population `gene_bounds` and the mutation rate `mut_rate`, as inputs. The condition (`rno < mut_rate`) where `rno` is a random number ensures random mutation subject to the mutation rate and following [2.4].

```
% Evolution Strategy: mutation operator
% mutation ensures that the mutated gene lies within
% their respective bounds

function mutated_popln =
realnumber_unifrm_mutation(chromo_popln,
gene_bounds, mut_rate)
[popln_size,genes] = size(chromo_popln);
 for i = 1 : popln_size
     for j = 1 : genes
         rno = rand;
         if (rno < mut_rate) % mutate the gene
          chromo_popln(i,j) = gene_bounds(1,1) +
          rno *(gene_bounds(1,2)-gene_bounds(1,1));
         end
     end
 end

mutated_popln = chromo_popln;
end
```

Figure 2.10.   *Evolution Strategy: real number uniform mutation operator (for a color version of this figure, see www.iste.co.uk/pai/metaheuristics.zip)*

```
% Evolution Strategy: Arithmetic variable point cross
% over for real coded chromosomes

function [offspring_popln]=
arith_varpoint_crossover(parent_popln,
crossover_rate)

[popln_size,  genes] = size(parent_popln);
for i = 1 : 2: (popln_size-1)
    parent1 = parent_popln(i,:);
    parent2 = parent_popln(i+1,:);
    a = rand;
    for j = 1: genes
       if (rand < crossover_rate)% perform cross over
            temp1 = parent1(j);
            temp2 = parent2(j);
            parent1(j)= a * temp1 + (1-a)* temp2;
            parent2(j)= (1-a)* temp1 + a * temp2;
       end
    end
    offspring_popln(i,:) = parent1;
    offspring_popln(i+1,:)= parent2;
end
end
```

Figure 2.11. *Evolution Strategy: arithmetic variable point crossover operator (for a color version of this figure, see www.iste.co.uk/pai/metaheuristics.zip)*

The function `arith_varpoint_crossover` undertakes arithmetic variable point crossover over the population of chromosomes `parent_popln`, with a crossover rate `crossover_rate`, following [2.3] and returns the offspring population `offspring_popln`.

Figure 2.12 shows the MATLAB® function for computation of fitness function values for the Beale function optimization problem employing function `beale` shown in Figure 2.12.

Figure 2.13 illustrates the complete program for Beale function optimization problem using Evolution Strategy.

```
% Compute fitness function for Beale function
% optimization problem

function popln_fitness= comp_fitness_Beale(popln)
  [popln_size, ~]=size(popln);

  for i =1:popln_size
     individual = popln(i,:);
     function_val(i) = beale(individual);
  end
  popln_fitness = function_val;
end
```

Figure 2.12. *Computation of fitness function values for the Beale function optimization problem using metaheuristic strategies (for a color version of this figure, see www.iste.co.uk/pai/metaheuristics.zip)*

```
% Demonstration of Evolution Strategy with Hall of
% Fame for Optimization of Beale function

clear all
% set Evolution Strategy and Problem parameters
popln_size = 100;           % population size
chromosm_length = 2;        % chromosome length
total_generations = 500;    % total generations

% mu is one third of population size
  mu = round ((1/3)*popln_size);
% lambda is two thirds of population size
  lambda = popln_size - mu;

% crossover rate
  crossover_rate = 0.61;

% mutation rate
  mutation_rate = 0.01;

% bounds
  bounds = [-4.5, 4.5];
```

```
% initialize  Hall of Fame
  HOF_fitness = 9999;
  hof_indx = 0;
  HOF_chromosome = zeros(1, chromosm_length);


% generate random initial population

fix(clock)

initial_popln = bounds(1) + (bounds(2)-bounds(1)) *
                     rand(popln_size, chromosm_length);
next_gen_pool = initial_popln;
gen_indx =1;
t=1;


% while loop for generations begins

while (gen_indx <= total_generations)

% set parent population and compute fitness of parent
% population

parent_popln = next_gen_pool;
parent_popln_fitness = comp_fitness_Beale(parent_popln);


% determine the best fit parents (mu) to be passed on
% to the next generation

[parent_popln_fitness_sort, parent_indx]=
                        sort(parent_popln_fitness);
parent_indx = parent_indx(1:mu);
next_gen_pool(1:mu,:) = parent_popln(parent_indx, :);


% perform cross over and mutation on the parent
% population to obtain offspring population

offsprng_popln= arith_varpoint_crossover(parent_popln,
                                 crossover_rate);
mutat_popln = realnumber_unifrm_mutation(offsprng_popln,
                                 bounds,  mutation_rate);
```

```
% compute fitness of offspring population

 mutat_popln_fitness = comp_fitness_Beale(mutat_popln);


% determine best fit offspring (lambda) to be passed on
% to the next generation

[mutat_popln_fitness_sort, mutat_indx]=
                         sort(mutat_popln_fitness);
offspring_indx = mutat_indx(1:lambda);
next_gen_pool(mu+1:popln_size,:) =
                     mutat_popln(offspring_indx, :);

% induct best of best fit offspring chromosome into
% Hall of Fame

         if (mutat_popln_fitness_sort(1) < HOF_fitness)
         HOF_fitness = mutat_popln_fitness_sort(1)
         HOF_genhistory(t) = gen_indx;
         HOF_funcvalhistory(t) = HOF_fitness,
         t=t+1;
         hof_indx = mutat_indx(1);
         HOF_chromosome = mutat_popln(hof_indx,:)
         end

gen_indx = gen_indx + 1;

end              % while loop for generations ends


% output optimal function values and variables
% represented by the individual in the Hall of Fame

optimal_function_value = HOF_fitness
x_optimal = HOF_chromosome
fix(clock)
disp('Successful execution!')
```

Figure 2.13. *Evolution Strategy for Beale function optimization: complete MATLAB® program (for a color version of this figure, see www.iste.co.uk/pai/metaheuristics.zip)*

B. *Differential Evolution: MATLAB® Implementation for Beale function Optimization*

Figures 2.14, 2.15 and 2.16 illustrate the Differential Evolution operators of Mutation, Crossover (binomial) and Selection respectively.

The function DE_mutation obtains the trial vector population using [2.5] for the population of individuals individual_popln with scale factor β beta_val provided as input.

```
% Differential evolution:    mutation operator

function trialvec_popln =
  DE_mutation(individual_popln, beta_val,
  popln_size)

  for i = 1 : popln_size
      % select target vector  and two difference
      % vectors randomly


      rand_indx = randperm(popln_size);
      for t=1:popln_size
          if (rand_indx(t)==i)
              elimx = t;
          end
      end

      rand_indx(elimx)=[];
      trial_vector_indx = rand_indx(1);
      diff1_vec1_indx = rand_indx(2);
      diff1_vec2_indx= rand_indx(3);

      % obtain trial vectors for each of the parent
      % vectors
      trialvec_popln(i,:) =
      individual_popln(trial_vector_indx,:) +
      beta val*(individual popln(diff1 vec1 indx,:)
      - individual_popln(diff1_vec2_indx,:));
  end
end
```

Figure 2.14. *Differential Evolution : Mutation operator (for a color version of this figure, see www.iste.co.uk/pai/metaheuristics.zip)*

The function DE_bin_Crossover undertakes binomial crossover over population of individuals parent_popln and its trial vectors target_vec_ popln for a probability of recombination prob_recombi, using equation [2.6]. The set of crossover points τ tau is obtained using function DE_compute_tau where component_size is the number of genes or components in the individual.

```
% Differential Evolution: Binomial Cross over

function [offspring_popln]=
DE_bin_Crossover(parent_popln, target_vec_popln,
prob_recombi, components)

tau = DE_compute_tau(components, prob_recombi);
offspring_gen(:,:) = parent_popln(:,:,);
offspring_gen(:, tau)= target_vec_popln(:,tau);
offspring_popln = offspring_gen;
end
```

```
% Computation of Tau for DE Binomial Crossover

function tau = DE_compute_tau(component_size,
                             probab_recombi)
h = randperm(component_size);
% initialize j_star to a random index so that tau
% remains non empty
j_star = h(1);
tau=j_star;
for i=1:component_size-1
    if (rand < probab_recombi)
        tau = union (tau, i)
    end
end
end
```

Figure 2.15. *Differential Evolution : binomial crossover operator (for a color version of this figure, see www.iste.co.uk/pai/metaheuristics.zip)*

```
% Differential Evolution: Selection operator
function next_gen_pool = DE_selection(parent,
      parent_fitness, offsprng, offsprng fitness,
      popln_size)

for i=1:popln_size
    if (parent_fitness(i) <= offsprng_fitness(i))
        next_gen_pool(i,:)= parent(i,:);
    else next_gen_pool(i,:)= offsprng (i,:);

end
end
```

Figure 2.16. *Differential Evolution : deterministic selection operator (for a color version of this figure, see www.iste.co.uk/pai/metaheuristics.zip)*

The function DE_selection undertakes a one-on-one selection of the best fit individuals from the parents parent and offspring offsprng, to determine the individuals for the next generation.

Figure 2.17 illustrates the complete program for Beale function optimization using Differential Evolution.

```
% Demonstration of Differential Evolution over Beale
% function optimization

clear all

% Set Differential Evolution and problem parameters
popln_size = 20;        % set population size
individual_length = 2;  % set individual length
beta = 0.5;

% higher probability of recombination assures greater
% diversity
pr_recombi = 0.87;
total_generations = 100   % total generations
bounds = [[-4.5 -4.5];[4.5 4.5]]; %bounds for Beale function
```

```
% Generate random initial population satisfying bounds of
% Beale function

fix(clock)
initial_popln = bounds (1,1) + (bounds (2,2) - bounds(1,1))
                    .*  rand(popln_size, individual_length);
current_popln = initial_popln;

% begin generation cycles
gen_indx = 1;

% while loop for generation  cycles begins
while (gen_indx < total_generations)

  gen_indx

  % set current population as parent population
  parent_popln = current_popln;

  % compute parent population fitness
  parent_popln_fitness = comp_fitness_Beale(parent_popln);

  % obtain trial vector population through mutation
  trial_vector_popln = DE_mutation(parent_popln, beta,
                                   popln_size);
  % generate offspring population through crossover

   offsprng_popln= DE_bin_Crossover(parent_popln,
   trial_vector_popln, pr_recombi, individual_length);

  % compute offspring population fitness
   offsprng_popln_fitness =
                   comp_fitness_Beale(offsprng_popln);

  % select next generation using deterministic
  % selection
  next_gen_pool = DE_selection(parent_popln,
               parent_popln_fitness, offsprng_popln,
                offsprng_popln_fitness, popln_size);

  % increment generation count
  gen_indx = gen_indx + 1;

  % set the current population

  current_popln = next_gen_pool;

end              % while loop for generation cycles ends
```

```
% Compute fitness of the current population as soon as
% the termination criterion is met with

 popln_fitness = comp_fitness_Beale(current_popln);

% sort fitness values to obtain the individual with the
% maximum fitness
[popln_fitness_sort, final_indx]= sort(popln_fitness);

% obtain maximal objective function value and the
% corresponding optimal values of the variables
j=final_indx(1);
x_optimal = current_popln(j, :);
y_optimal = beale(x_optimal);

% display optimization results
disp('Optimization results:')
x_optimal
y_optimal

fix(clock)
disp('Successful execution!')
```

Figure 2.17. *Differential Evolution for Beale function optimization: Complete MATLAB® program (for a color version of this figure, see www.iste.co.uk/pai/metaheuristics.zip)*

Project

Heuristic optimization literature discusses several test functions that serve as benchmarks for comparing the performances of different heuristic strategies that have been discovered and are actively being discovered. *Rosenbrock's function,* also known as *Rosenbrock's Valley* or *Banana function,* is one such test function. Rosenbrock's function f (x₁, x₂) for the given boundary constraints is defined as below:

Minimize $f(x_1, x_2) = (1 - x_1)^2 + 100.(x_2 - x_1^2)^2$

Subject to, $-5 \le x_1, x_2 \le 5$

The surface plot of the function is shown in Figure 2.18. Rosenbrock's function attains its minima at $f(x_1, x_2) = 0$ with $x_1 = 1, x_2 = 1$.

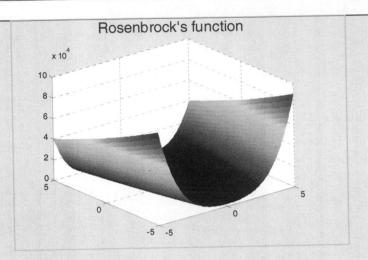

Figure 2.18. *Surface plot of the Rosenbrock's function*

(i) Modify the MATLAB implementations of Evolution Strategy and Differential Evolution algorithms to optimize the Rosenbrock's function.

(ii) Compare the convergence characteristics of the two metaheuristic algorithms using (a) P Measure and (b) Convergence of objective function values. Which of these reports faster convergence?

(iii) How do various Differential Evolution Strategies (see section 2.5.3) behave while solving the Rosenbrock's function optimization problem? Compare their performances.

(iv) Nelder-Mead Simplex method with a "traditionally" chosen initial point of (-1.2, 1) can solve the Rosenbrock's function optimization problem. Function fminsearch available in the Optimization Toolbox™ of MATLAB® is built over Nelder-Mead's Simplex algorithm. Invoke fminsearch with appropriate arguments, in the command line mode of MATLAB®, to solve the Rosenbrock's function optimization problem.

(v) How does fminsearch behave when randomly chosen initial points are fed as inputs to the function?

(vi) What are your observations and conclusions with regard to the performances of the metaheuristic algorithms and the traditional Simplex algorithm, for the Rosenbrock's function optimization problem?

Suggested Further Reading

Rainer Storn's homepage on Differential Evolution:

http://www1.icsi.berkeley. edu/~storn/code.html

presents source codes for DE in a variety of programming languages such as, C, C++, R, Python and MATLAB®, to quote a few. An enriching discussion on history, practical hints, applications of DE to real world problems, books and commercial software tools can be found in the site.

Vitaliy Feoktistov's book, *Differential Evolution in search of solutions*, Springer, 2006, is a lucid treatise on the subject.

Kenneth Sorenson's article on *"Metaheuristics – the metaphor exposed"* [SOR 15] is a must-read paper with its ruthlessly forthright views punched with humor, sounding a warning bell for all those researchers inspired to invent "novel" metaheuristic methods in their enthusiasm to solve their respective problems of interest.

MATLAB® Optimization Toolbox™ offers an array of functions that can be directly used (in the command line mode) to solve optimization problems that adhere to the implementation framework of the functions concerned. The Global Optimization Toolbox™ of MATLAB®, on the other hand, presents solvers that use metaheuristics, namely Genetic Algorithms and Simulated Annealing, to tackle complex optimization problems with multiple maxima or minima.

While a lot of books, monographs and edited volumes have been written in the discipline of Evolutionary Computation, those by Patrick Siarry [SIA 16], Andries Engelbrecht [ENG 07], Michalewicz and Fogel [MIC 04], Eiben and Smith [EIB 08], Dan Simon [SIM 13], Johann Dreo *et al.*, [DRE 06], and Back *et al.*, [BAC 00], to list a few, can serve to offer novices a gamut of information on the theoretical and application perspectives of the discipline.

PART 2

Heuristic Portfolio Selection

This chapter details how a heuristic algorithm such as k-means clustering could be effectively employed to undertake selection of securities in a portfolio. The heuristic security selection method has been demonstrated over specific benchmark portfolios namely equal weighted portfolios and inverse volatility weighted portfolios, to study the characteristics of the portfolios when such a selection is made. The experimental analyses have been undertaken over portfolios selected over S&P BSE200 and Nikkei225 datasets. The MATLAB® demonstrations for the strategies discussed have also been presented.

3.1. Portfolio selection

Given the *vast and variegated universe* of securities, local and global, making a prudent and effective choice of a *finite set of assets* that constitutes an individual portfolio can be a daunting task. The vastness of choices available and the diverse behavioral characteristics of the individual securities in its own regard and most importantly with regard to one another, can turn the interesting process of selection into a mind-boggling exercise.

In this section, we restrict the discussion on security selection to selection of equity stocks alone, to keep it simple and focused. Selection of equity stocks is no less a challenging task for with most asset allocation plans allotting significant portions of their capital to equity investments, the appropriate selection of equity stocks calls for knowledge and evaluation with regard to the companies and the industries of the stocks concerned, the sectors to which they belong and their respective earning potential.

Diversification

All investors are aware of the adage – "Never put all eggs in one basket." Thus selection of securities ought to take care of this significant aspect too and hence the need for *diversification*. Diversification and the process of allocation which involves investments in different assets, asset classes or markets, is a popular strategy to mitigate risk. Diversification need not necessarily mean a large portfolio comprising large number of assets. Researchers are agreed upon that diversification even in a narrow portfolio comprising of assets to the order of 30 or less, is sufficient enough to guarantee the benefits of diversification. With different securities performing differently at any point in time, diversification serves to minimize financial losses by constructing a portfolio of various assets in varying proportions so that under performance of one or more assets does not severely impact the performance of the portfolio as a whole. In fact, one of the objectives of portfolio optimization can also be *maximizing diversification* which can be construed as equivalent to *minimizing risk*.

Again maximizing diversification cannot mean unchecked investment of one's capital in a large number of stocks since the amount of *transaction costs and taxes* accrued on a large portfolio could raise the cost of the portfolio deeming the whole exercise unrealistic. The fact that transaction costs can have severe effects on expected returns from a portfolio rendering the investor's initial capital investment crucial, has already been investigated in the literature.

Diversification index

A measure that serves to quantify diversification is known as *diversification index*. As a consequence, diversification indices serve to quantify portfolio risks and hence minimizing portfolio risk is akin to *maximizing diversification index* of the portfolio. Several diversification indices have been discussed in the literature. Any good measure of diversification takes into account not just the characteristics of assets comprising the portfolio but also their respective allocations in the portfolio (weights).

Three such diversification indices are discussed here:

1) *Weight Entropy*

$$-\sum_{i=1}^{N} w_i . \ln(w_i)$$

[3.1]

2) *Herfindahl Index*

$$1 - \sum_{i=1}^{N} w_i^2 \qquad\qquad\qquad\qquad [3.2]$$

3) *Diversification Ratio (DR)*

$$\left(\frac{\bar{\sigma}.\bar{W}}{\sqrt{\bar{W}'.V.\bar{W}}} \right) \qquad\qquad\qquad\qquad [3.3]$$

Here $\bar{W} = (w_1, w_2, ... w_N)'$ where w_i are the individual asset weights, is the portfolio weight vector or allocations. $\bar{\sigma} = (\sigma_1, \sigma_2, ... \sigma_N)$ are the standard deviations of returns on the assets i, $i = 1, 2, ... N$ and V is the *variance-covariance matrix of returns* on the assets of the universe.

As can be observed, Weight Entropy and Herfindahl Index are weight-based diversification indices where the interdependence between the assets and their diverse risk characteristics are not taken into consideration and the diversification is measured solely using the respective asset allocations (weights). Though Weight Entropy-based diversification is popular, Woerheide and Persson [WOE 93] recommended Herfindahl Index as the best measure of diversification for an unevenly distributed portfolio, beating even entropy-based diversification.

Diversification Ratio, proposed and patented by Yves Choueifaty in 2008 [CHO 08, CHO 13] is another diversification index of recent origin that serves to provide the most diversified portfolio possible in any given stock universe across global and domestic markets. It takes into consideration the interdependence between assets and is the ratio of the weighted sum of individual asset volatilities to the portfolio's volatility. A maximal Sharpe Ratio portfolio or a portfolio that is most diversified would yield maximal DR.

EXAMPLES.– For the portfolio P of assets listed in Table 1.1 and whose risk/return characteristics have been shown in Table 1.6, the portfolio characteristics required for the computation of diversification indices have been extracted and reproduced here.

Weights:

$$\bar{W} = (w_1, w_2, w_3, ... w_{10})' = (0.06,\ 0.07,\ 0.16,\ 0.1,\ 0.07,\ 0.07,\ 0.07,\ 0.16,\ 0.18,\ 0.06)'$$

Variance-covariance matrix of daily returns(%):

$$
V = \begin{bmatrix}
6.38 & 2.55 & 2.28 & 3.89 & 4.65 & 3.29 & 3.29 & 3.65 & 2.00 & 3.04 \\
2.55 & 4.75 & 1.49 & 2.53 & 3.13 & 2.29 & 2.07 & 2.18 & 1.29 & 3.57 \\
2.28 & 1.49 & 4.42 & 2.25 & 2.46 & 1.95 & 1.95 & 2.30 & 1.91 & 1.83 \\
3.89 & 2.53 & 2.25 & 7.29 & 4.7 & 3.36 & 3.26 & 3.76 & 2.07 & 2.92 \\
4.65 & 3.13 & 2.46 & 4.73 & 9.54 & 5.01 & 3.75 & 5.08 & 2.49 & 3.40 \\
3.29 & 2.29 & 1.95 & 3.36 & 5.01 & 6.27 & 2.89 & 3.64 & 1.70 & 2.52 \\
3.29 & 2.07 & 1.95 & 3.26 & 3.75 & 2.89 & 5.37 & 2.94 & 1.97 & 2.37 \\
3.65 & 2.18 & 2.3 & 3.76 & 5.08 & 3.64 & 2.94 & 6.59 & 1.98 & 2.65 \\
2.00 & 1.29 & 1.91 & 2.07 & 2.49 & 1.70 & 1.97 & 1.98 & 4.52 & 1.67 \\
3.04 & 3.57 & 1.83 & 2.92 & 3.40 & 2.52 & 2.37 & 2.65 & 1.670 & 5.59
\end{bmatrix}
$$

Standard deviation of returns (square root of the diagonal of V) :

$$\bar{\sigma} = (2.53,\ 2.18,\ 2.10, 2.70, 3.09, 2.50, 2.32, 2.57, 2.13, 2.36)$$

The diversification indices for the portfolio concerned computed using [3.1]–[3.3] yield the following:

Weight Entropy: $-\sum_{i=1}^{10} w_i . \ln(w_i) = 2.2076$

Herfindahl Index: $1 - \sum_{i=1}^{10} w_i^2 = 1 - 0.1204 = 0.8796$

Diversification Ratio:

$$\left(\frac{\bar{\sigma}.\bar{W}}{\sqrt{\bar{W}'.V.\bar{W}}} \right) = \frac{2.3995}{1.7128} = 1.4009$$

All further discussions in this chapter will only resort to DR as the metric to measure diversification.

3.2. Clustering

G M Loeb [LOE 07] claimed that "…Diversification may be necessary where no intelligent supervision is likely…" With due respects to Loeb's claim but viewing the same from a different perspective and in allegiance to the ideology of this book, if heuristics can serve to undertake such an "intelligent supervision" then diversification practiced in the traditional sense of the term can even turn "unnecessary"!

In this section, we discuss how a clustering algorithm, namely k-means clustering that is a heuristic method, serves to undertake an intelligent portfolio selection without taking recourse to the traditional method of undertaking evaluation of stocks. The heuristic method takes into consideration the individual asset returns and the interdependence of the asset returns, to yield portfolios whose unconstrained efficient frontiers are in close proximity to those of the respective Markowitz's ideal efficient frontier. Testing the asset selection over benchmark portfolios, namely equal weighted portfolios and inverse volatility weighted portfolios, for example, yielded portfolios whose DRs representing their diversification indices and hence the corresponding portfolio volatility, to be commensurate with those displayed by portfolios situated on the ideal efficient frontier (efficient set, to recall).

For ease of reference, portfolios constructed out of k-means clustered assets shall henceforth be referred to as *k-portfolios* in this book.

Definition of clustering

Clustering or *Cluster Analysis* deals with the task of grouping a set of physical or abstract objects into classes so that objects within clusters show more *similarities* between themselves than with those objects belonging to other clusters. A *cluster* is therefore a collection of objects that are similar to one another within a cluster (*intra cluster similarity*) and dissimilar to objects that belong to other clusters (*inter cluster dissimilarity*) testifying the adage, "birds of a feather flock together." Cluster analysis has found wide applications in data analysis, pattern recognition, image and signal processing and market research, to quote a few.

Figure 3.1 shows a group of data objects graphically represented using a scatter plot and the clusters that they have formed by virtue of proximity or closeness to one another chosen as their similarity measure.

Similarity measures

Similarity measures are real valued functions that serve as metrics to measure the similarity or closeness of objects with regard to specific characteristics. Most similarity measures rely on *distance metrics* to measure similarity. Thus the smaller the distance measure between objects, the more similar they are, and the larger the distance, the more dissimilar they are. Alternatively, similarity, measures are also seen described by inverse of distance metrics, in which case the smaller the distance between objects, the larger is the similarity, and the larger the distance between objects, the smaller is its similarity. Clustering algorithms employ similarity measures represented by distance metrics to measure similarity between objects before they are grouped into clusters.

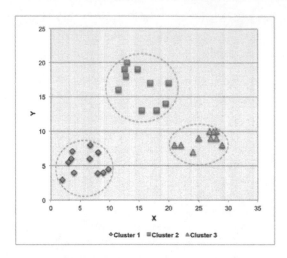

Figure 3.1. *Clustering data objects – an example (for a color version of this figure, see www.iste.co.uk/pai/metaheuristics.zip)*

Given two n-dimensional data objects $X = (x_1, x_2, ... x_n)$ and $Y = (y_1, y_2, ... y_n)$, the following are some popular similarity measures represented by distance metrics to measure the similarity $d(X, Y)$ between the data objects X and Y:

Euclidean distance

$$d(X, Y) = \sqrt{(x_1 - y_1)^2 + (x_2 - y_2)^2 + ... (x_n - y_n)^2} \qquad [3.4]$$

Manhattan or City Block distance

$$d(X, Y) = |(x_1 - y_1)| + |(x_2 - y_2)| + ... |(x_n - y_n)| \qquad [3.5]$$

Minkowski distance

$$d(X, Y) = \left(|(x_1 - y_1)|^q + |(x_2 - y_2)|^q + ... |(x_n - y_n)|^q \right)^{1/q}, \qquad [3.6]$$

where q is a positive integer. For $q = 1$ it represents Manhattan distance and for $q = 2$ it represents Euclidean distance.

Weighted Euclidean distance

$$d(X, Y) = \sqrt{w_1 \cdot |x_1 - y_1|^2 + w_2 \cdot |x_2 - y_2|^2 + ... w_n \cdot |x_n - y_n|^2} \qquad [3.7]$$

where w_i are the weights allotted according to the desired importance.

Given N data objects a *similarity matrix (S)$_{NXN}$* represents the mutual similarities between the data objects and as can be easily seen, S is a symmetric matrix with diagonal elements as zeros when the similarity measure is represented by distance metrics.

EXAMPLE.– Given X_1 = (2, 6, 8), X_2 = (5, 3, 4) and X_3 = (1, 2, 7) to be three data objects, the similarity matrix based on Euclidean distance measure shown in [3.4] is given by

$$
\begin{array}{cccc}
 & X_1 & X_2 & X_3 \\
X_1 & 0 & 5.831 & 4.243 \\
X_2 & 5.831 & 0 & 5.099 \\
X_3 & 4.243 & 5.099 & 0
\end{array}
$$

where $d(X_1, X_2) = d(X_2, X_1) = 5.8341$, for example and the rest of the computations follow similarly. Here X_1 and X_3 are deemed more similar (closer in distance) when compared to the rest of the pairs of objects.

It needs to be emphasized that in a real world application, a collection of data objects can be grouped into different cluster sets based on different choices of characteristics. For example, a   class of students may be grouped into different cluster sets based on the choice of characteristics namely emotional intelligence aspects, socio-economic factors, skill sets, academic achievements and a combination of one or more or all of these, to quote a few. The cluster sets arrived at, needless to say would be different for different choices of characteristics chosen for clustering. Consequently, a prudent choice of characteristics becomes essential to exploit the merits associated with clustering, for the problem in question.

3.3. *k*-means clustering

k-means clustering is a *partitioning based clustering algorithm* where N data objects are partitioned into *k clusters* or groups or partitions of data $(k \le N)$ where each cluster satisfies the following properties:

– each cluster must contain at least one data object, and

– each data object can belong to only one cluster

Algorithm k-means cluster illustrates the clustering procedure. Initially, *k* data objects randomly chosen from X_i, i =1,2,3,...N, are set as the *centroids* or *cluster centers*. In the first iteration, each of the data objects evaluate their respective proximities to the centroids and join that cluster commanded by that centroid with whom it shares closest proximity. At the end of the first iteration, k clusters with their respective data objects sharing close proximity to their respective centroids are formed. In the next and subsequent iterations, the new centroids for each of the clusters are computed using the data objects that form the respective cluster. Once again the data objects X_i, $i = 1,2,3,...N$, work to know which of these k centroids they share close proximity with and join that group around that centroid. The cycle of operations repeats until the centroids computed in two successive iterations do not move at which point k-means clustering algorithm terminates. The k clusters show the data objects that have finally grouped themselves together based on the similarity measure chosen.

```
Algorithm k-means cluster (X, k)

Step 1:    Let X = ( X₁, X₂, X₃,... Xₙ) be the N data objects
           that are to grouped  into k clusters.

Step 2:    Randomly  choose  k  data  objects  to  act  as  the
           initial centroids of the k groups. Let {C₁, C₂, ...
           Cₖ} indicate the k centroids.

Step 3:    Compute the similarity measure (distance measure)
           for  each  of  the  N  data  objects  with  the  k
           centroids.  Assign  each  data  object   Xᵢ  to  that
           cluster  with  whose  centroid  it  has  the  closest
           similarity.  In other words, Xᵢ joins that cluster
           j where d(Xᵢ, Cⱼ) reports the minimal distance.

Step 4:    After all the N data objects have been assigned to
           the    respective    clusters,    compute    the    new
           centroids   { C₁', C₂', ... Cₖ'} where each Cᵢ'   is
           the centroid of the data objects comprising the
           respective  group. As  can  be  expected  the  new
           centroids  may  not  represent  the  actual  data
           objects.

Step 5:    Check if the new   centroids {C₁', C₂', ... Cₖ'} are
           the same as the old centroids      {C₁, C₂, ... Cₖ}.
           If they are different,   the centroids have moved,
           so reset {C₁, C₂, ... Cₖ} to the new centroids and
           go to Step 3.

           If they are same then the centroids have not
           moved, hence terminate the procedure.

Step 6:    Output data objects in each of the k clusters.
```

In reality k-means clustering works to minimize the following objective function which is an error function given by

$$J = \sum_{i=1}^{k} \sum_{j=1}^{N} \left(\left\| X_j - C_i \right\| \right)^2 \qquad [3.8]$$

where $\left\| X_j - C_i \right\|^2$ is the distance measure between the data object X_j and centroid C_i. Although k-means clustering algorithm has been proved to terminate, it does not necessarily find the optimal set of clusters corresponding to the minimal objective function shown in [3.8]. The algorithm is also significantly sensitive to the randomly chosen initial centroids, as a consequence of which k-means clustering may report different cluster configurations for a given set of data objects, for various runs.

However k-means clustering is considered computationally efficient when compared with other clustering algorithms and can produce tighter clusters if the clusters are globular.

EXAMPLE.– Let us consider four data objects { X_1, X_2, X_3, X_4} – { (1,1), (2,1), (4,3), (5,4)} to be grouped into two clusters ($k = 2$). The similarity measure chosen is the Euclidean distance measure.

Let X_1 and X_2 be the randomly chosen initial centroids (i.e.) $C_1 = X_1$ and $C_2 = X_2$. Computing the distance measures of each of the data objects with the centroids yields the following distance matrix:

$$
\begin{array}{c}
 \\
C1 \\
C2
\end{array}
\begin{array}{cccc}
X_1 & X_2 & X_3 & X_4 \\
\left[\begin{array}{cccc}
0 & 1 & 3.61 & 5 \\
1 & 0 & 2.83 & 4.24
\end{array}\right]
\end{array}
$$

For example, $\left\| X_3 - C_1 \right\|^2 = \sqrt{(4-1)^2 + (3-1)^2} = 3.61$ and

$$\left\| X_3 - C_2 \right\|^2 = \sqrt{(4-2)^2 + (3-1)^2} = 2.83$$

At the end of iteration 1, with each data object choosing its minimal distance measure between the two centroids, X_1 joins group C_1 and X_2, X_3, X_4 join group C_2 as illustrated below.

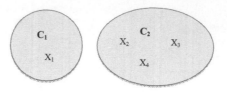

In the second iteration, the new centroids (C_1', C_2') of the clusters using the respective data objects in the clusters yields, $C_1' = X_1 = (1,1)$ and $C_2' = (X_2+X_3+X_4)/3 = (11/3, 8/3)$.

Computing the distance measures of the data objects with the new centroids yields the following distance matrix and the new clusters illustrated thereafter.

$$
\begin{array}{c}
\\
C_1' \\
C_2'
\end{array}
\begin{array}{cccc}
X_1 & X_2 & X_3 & X_4 \\
\left[\begin{array}{cccc}
0 & 1 & 3.61 & 5 \\
3.14 & 2.36 & 0.47 & 1.89
\end{array}\right]
\end{array}
$$

Proceeding in a similar fashion, iteration 3 for the new centroids $C_1' = (3/2, 1)$ and $C_2' = (9/2, 7/2)$ yields the distance matrix,

$$
\begin{array}{c}
\\
C_1' \\
C_2'
\end{array}
\begin{array}{cccc}
X_1 & X_2 & X_3 & X_4 \\
\left[\begin{array}{cccc}
0.5 & 0.5 & 3.2 & 4.61 \\
4.3 & 3.54 & 0.71 & 0.71
\end{array}\right]
\end{array}
$$

and the clusters,

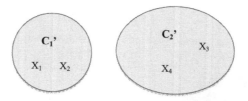

Since the centroids for the current clusters are same as those of the previous iteration's clusters, the centroids have not moved and hence k-means clustering terminates with the grouping of data objects shown above as the final set of clusters.

3.4. Heuristic selection of securities

In this section we detail how heuristic selection of securities could be effected through k-means clustering.

For the application of k-means clustering two important factors need to be determined, (1) k, the number of clusters and (2) the characteristics with which the securities need to be effectively clustered. While the right choice of k can be a lurking problem in some real world applications, fortunately in the case of portfolio selection, k refers to the number of assets in the portfolio or the portfolio size which is quite often or always dictated by the investor and his or her preferences. Thus investors interested in *small portfolios* and going by the thumb rule, may choose $k < 30$ and those interested in *large portfolios* could choose $k > 30$.

In the case of choice of characteristics for clustering, it was decided to employ the following vector of asset characteristics:

Given a stock universe of N assets, for an asset i,

$$[\mu_i, \quad \sigma_{i1}, \sigma_{i2}, \sigma_{i3}, ... \sigma_{ii}, ... \sigma_{iN}]$$

was chosen as the characteristic vector. Here μ_i is the mean return of asset i, $\sigma_{i1}, \sigma_{i2}, \sigma_{i3}, ... \sigma_{ii}, ... \sigma_{iN}$ are the variance and covariance of returns of asset i, with respect to other assets in the stock universe. In other words, $[\sigma_{i1}, \sigma_{i2}, \sigma_{i3}, ... \sigma_{ii}, ... \sigma_{iN}]$ corresponds to row i of the variance-covariance matrix V of N assets in the stock universe. σ_{ii} which is the variance of the asset return is the diagonal element of the matrix V in row i.

EXAMPLE.– For the portfolio P of assets listed in Table 1.1 and whose risk/return characteristics have been shown in Table 1.6, we draw attention to the rows Mean daily returns (%) and Covariance of daily returns(%) of the table. The asset characteristics of some sample assets, to favor clustering of the 10 assets, would be given as follows:

Asset 1 (RIL) : [**0.14**, **6.38**, 2.55, 2.28, 3.89, 4.65, 3.29, 3.29, 3.65, 2.00, 3.04]

Mean return   Variance of return   Covariance of returns

Asset 2 (INFO): [**0.06**, 2.55, **4.75**, 1.49, 2.53, 3.13, 2.29, 2.07, 2.18, 1.29, 3.57]

Asset 10 (TCS): [**0.02**, 3.04, 3.57, 1.83, 2.92, 3.40, 2.52, 2.37, 2.65, 1.67, **5.59**]

Thus in the case of a stock universe comprising N assets, the vector of asset characteristics employed to undertake clustering of assets would be of length $N+1$.

k-means clustering now considers the set of characteristic vectors of the N assets as the data objects X_i each of which is an $(N+1)$ dimensioned vector and making use of a similarity measure represented by an appropriate distance measure, groups the assets into their respective clusters following the procedure discussed in **Algorithm k-means cluster**.

We now illustrate the heuristic selection of assets from two stock universes namely S&P BSE200 (Bombay Stock Exchange, India) and Nikkei 225 (Tokyo Stock Exchange, Japan) making use of their respective historical data sets for the period, March 1999–March 2009.

3.4.1. *Heuristic portfolio selection for S&P BSE200*

A stock universe of 127 assets was selected from S&P BSE200 after eliminating those stocks with short series data during the period March 1999–March 2009 (typically new stocks with partial historical data set were eliminated). The period included both upturns and downturns in the market and hence the specific interest in the historical data set concerned.

As discussed in the earlier section, the mean returns of the assets, viz. $[\mu_i]_{127\times1}$ and the variance-covariance of returns of the assets concerned, viz. $[V]_{127\times127}$ were chosen to act as the asset characteristics matrix for purposes of clustering the 127 assets. The length of the vector of characteristics for each of the assets was 128.

Figure 3.2 illustrates the clusters obtained by k-means clustering for $k = 30$ and when Euclidean distance measure was used as the similarity measure. Each of the boxes in the figure graphically illustrates a group of assets with their serial numbers, asset names and sector codes shown within brackets. The sector codes represent the sectors to which these assets belong and have been described in the legend.

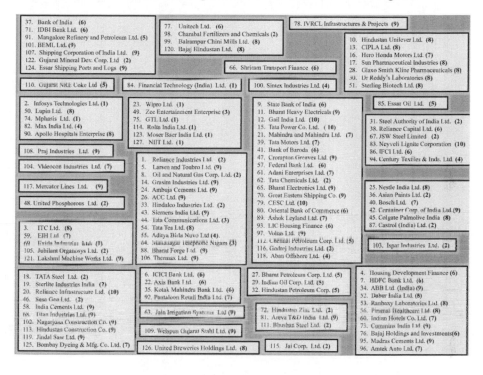

Sector codes: (1) Technology   (2) Basic Materials   (3) Communications
              (4) Diversified   (5) Energy   (6) Financial
              (7) Consumer cyclical   (8) Consumer noncyclical
              (9) Industrial   (10) Utilities

Figure 3.2.   *k-means clustered assets (k = 30) of a universe of 127 assets belonging to S&P BSE 200 data set (March 1999–March 2009) of Bombay Stock Exchange, India, with each cluster shown in a box illustrating the serial numbers, asset names and sector codes of the assets grouped*

We proceed to *randomly* pick 30 stocks, *one from each cluster* to construct a well diversified *k*-portfolio. It needs to be recalled here that *k*-means clustering ensures inter-cluster dissimilarity and intra-cluster similarity and therefore the choice of one asset from each cluster ensures maximal diversification with regard to their characteristics of mean and variance/covariance of asset returns. Three such randomly picked *k*-portfolios showing the serial numbers of the assets listed, have been shown below:

k-portfolio 1:

> {37 109 77 10 50 110 103 63 66 18 115 108 117 78 3 85 126 84
> 44 21 27 40 38 23 104 6 48 53 72 100}

k-portfolio 2:

> {71 109 98 13 82 110 103 63 66 19 115 108 117 78 59 85 126 84
> 54 80 29 45 86 114 104 35 48 76 81 100}

k- portfolio 3:

> {124 109 99 16 90 110 103 63 66 20 115 108 117 78 69 85 126 84
> 1 118 32 87 94 127 104 92 48 96 111 100}

Efficient frontiers of S&P BSE200 k-portfolios

In the first experiment, the efficient frontiers of the three *k*-portfolios were studied in the backdrop of Markowitz's ideal efficient frontier. Markowitz's ideal portfolio involved diversification in all 127 assets in the universe. The unconstrained portfolio optimization problem model discussed in Chapter 1 and defined by [1.19]–[1.22] (with MATLAB® demonstrations for the same shown in section 1.3 B) was employed to compute the efficient frontiers and study their behavior.

Figure 3.3 illustrates the efficient frontiers of the three *k*-portfolios in the backdrop of Markowitz's ideal efficient frontier for a specific run of the *k*-means clustering algorithm.

A visual inspection of the efficient frontiers of the *k*-portfolios, reveals their close proximity to one another and hence similarity of portfolio behavior. Also it can be seen that their behavior is very close to that of the ideal efficient frontier especially for high risk compositions of the *k*-portfolios concerned. In other words, a *k*-portfolio is able to replicate the behavior of an ideal portfolio for high-risk compositions. Since *k*-means clustering yields different clusters during different runs due to their random selection of centroids during each run, repeating the experiment over various runs yielded results that were by and large similar to one another. Figure 3.4 shows the efficient frontiers of the corresponding *k*-portfolios randomly selected from the clusters belonging to two different runs of the *k*-means clustering algorithm. The close proximity of the efficient frontiers of the *k*-portfolios to one another and the ideal efficient frontier is clearly visible.

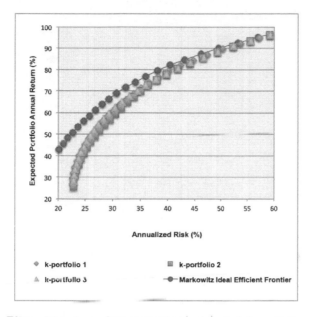

Figure 3.3 *Efficient frontiers of three randomly selected k-portfolios (k = 30) from a specific run of the k-means clustering algorithm for S&P BSE200 data set, against the backdrop of Markowitz's ideal efficient frontier (for a color version of this figure, see www.iste.co.uk/pai/metaheuristics.zip)*

The exercise was repeated for small and large *k*-portfolios, for *k* = 20, *k* = 50 and *k* = 70. Figure 3.5 illustrates the efficient frontiers concerned for a specific run of the *k*-means clustering algorithm.

3.4.2. *Heuristic portfolio selection for Nikkei225*

The aforementioned experiment was tested over Nikkei 225 data set. A universe of 196 stocks was selected after eliminating assets with short series data. The historical period considered was from March 1999 to March 2009, that included both upturns and downturns in the global markets.

The universe of 196 assets was grouped into clusters making use of the mean returns and variance/covariance of asset returns as the clustering characteristics. The length of the characteristic vector was 197. Figure 3.6 illustrates the clusters generated by *k*-means clustering algorithm for *k* = 30 during a specific run. Each box encapsulates a cluster with the serial numbers, asset names and sector codes of the assets shown inside. The legend for the sector codes has been listed below the figure.

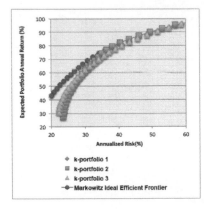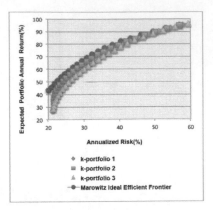

Figure 3.4. *Efficient frontiers of three randomly selected k-portfolios (k = 30) from two different runs of k-means clustering algorithm for S&P BSE200 data set, against the backdrop of Markowitz's ideal efficient frontier (for a color version of this figure, see www.iste.co.uk/pai/metaheuristics.zip)*

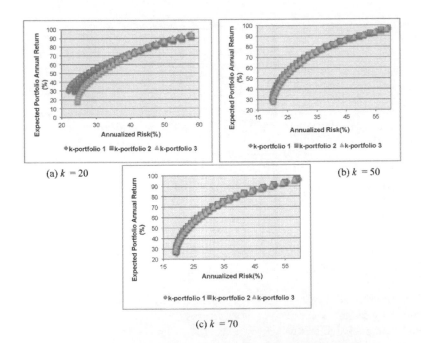

Figure 3.5. *Efficient frontiers of three randomly selected k-portfolios for k = 20, k = 50 and k = 70 from a specific run of k-means clustering algorithm, for S&P BSE200 data set (for a color version of this figure, see www.iste.co.uk/pai/metaheuristics.zip)*

k-portfolios of size $k = 30$ were randomly picked, strictly one from each cluster to ensure diversification. Three such k-portfolios showing the serial numbers of the assets, have been listed below:

k-portfolio 1:

{148 29 130 176 24 80 41 16 63 30 22 106 82 46 179 15 56 8 169 150 12 2 4 117 135 61 36 44 21 6 }

k-portfolio 2:

{148 40 130 163 47 81 118 57 73 192 37 138 84 49 159 15 87 54 171 167 13 10 9 120 141 68 48 51 21 17 }

k-portfolio 3:

{148 50 130 101 64 96 142 129 78 58 71 145 103 59 158 15 93 76 194 182 45 14 32 146 153 122 89 67 21 53}

Efficient frontiers of Nikkei225 k-portfolios

The efficient frontiers of the three k-portfolios in the backdrop of the Markowitz's ideal efficient frontier where the ideal portfolio invests in all 196 assets considered in the stock universe, has been shown in Figure 3.7. A visual inspection of the plots clearly shows the close proximity of the efficient frontiers of the k-portfolios revealing similarity of portfolio behavior. Besides, for low risk and very high risk combinations, the k-portfolios get very close to the ideal efficient frontier.

Figure 3.8 illustrates the results when the experiments were repeated for $k = 80$. The close proximity of the efficient frontiers of the k-portfolios to one another as well as to that of the Markowitz's ideal efficient frontier can be clearly seen. Thus in the case of large portfolios, for the historical period considered, k-portfolios reported similarity of behavior with one another as well as to that of the ideal portfolio.

Summing up, even a random choice of assets for the k-portfolios yielded exemplary results by way of ensuring diversification, similarity of portfolio behaviors as evinced by the respective efficient frontiers and close-to-ideal portfolio by way of proximity to the Markowitz's ideal efficient frontier. On the other hand, a careful choice of assets from each cluster (one each from each cluster of course) as dictated by the investor's preferences and choices, is not going to be anyway different and the same results would be recorded for this case too.

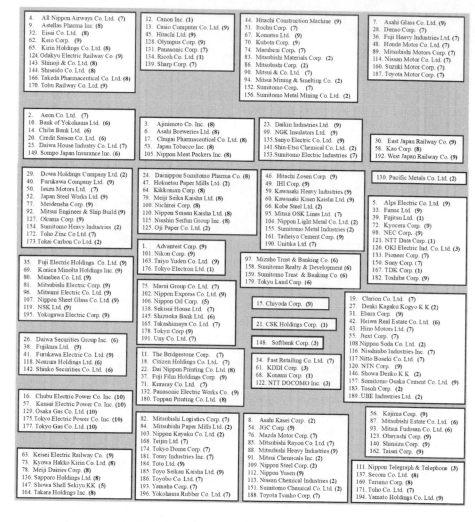

Sector codes:
(1) Technology   (2) Basic Materials   (3) Communications
(5) Energy   (6) Financial   (7) Consumer cyclical
(8) Consumer noncyclical   (9) Industrial   (10) Utilities

Figure 3.6. *k-means clustered assets (k = 30) of a universe of 196 assets belonging to Nikkei225 data set (March 1999–March 2009) of Tokyo Stock Exchange, Japan, with each cluster shown in a box illustrating the serial numbers, asset names and sector codes of the assets grouped*

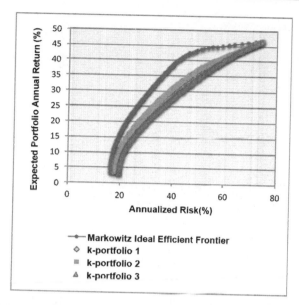

Figure 3.7. *Efficient frontiers of three randomly selected k-portfolios (k = 30) from a specific run of the k-means clustering algorithm for Nikkei225 data set against the backdrop of Markowitz's ideal efficient frontier (for a color version of this figure, see www.iste.co.uk/pai/metaheuristics.zip)*

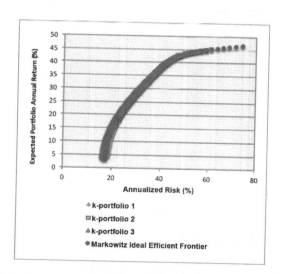

Figure 3.8. *Efficient frontiers of three randomly selected k-portfolios (k = 80) from a specific run of the k-means clustering algorithm for Nikkei225 data set, against the backdrop of Markowitz's ideal efficient frontier (for a color version of this figure, see www.iste.co.uk/pai/metaheuristics.zip)*

3.5. *k*-portfolio performance

In this section, we discuss the application of two benchmark portfolio construction techniques on *k*-portfolios. The objective of this exercise is to mainly study the performance characteristics of *k*-portfolios during their practical application.

We consider two popular portfolio construction techniques, namely Equal Weighted portfolio and Inverse Volatility Weighted portfolio. *Risk parity* is a popular portfolio allocation strategy with the objective of earning better returns for the same level of risk or earning the same returns for a lower level of risk, when compared to traditional portfolio allocation strategies. Thus risk parity approach focuses on low-volatility portfolios, and *equal weighted portfolios and inverse volatility weighted portfolios are just simple approaches to create low-volatility portfolios.*

3.5.1. *Equal Weighted k-portfolio construction*

An *Equal Weighted portfolio* is a portfolio construction technique where all assets comprising the portfolio are assigned equal weights. In other words, all stocks are treated equal and therefore the capital investment is equally apportioned between the assets of the portfolio. Thus the Equal Weighted portfolio has its weights defined by

$$W_i = \frac{1}{N}$$ [3.9]

where N is the portfolio size.

Equal Weighted *k*-portfolios were studied over S&P BSE200 and Nikkei 225 data sets and their risk/return characteristics and respective Diversification Ratios were observed. Their characteristics were compared with those of an "ideal" portfolio – fictitious though – comprising all assets in the stock universe.

S&P BSE200 Equal Weighted k-portfolios

For the *k*-portfolios discussed in section 3.4.1 for *k* = 20, *k* = 30, *k* = 50 and *k* = 70, the risk return characteristics and their respective Diversification Ratios when equal weighted portfolios were constructed out of them, have been listed in Table 3.1. The risk return characteristics and the Diversification Ratio for the "ideal" portfolio that comprises all 127 assets of the stock universe considered has been shown in the same table.

It can be seen that *k*-portfolios display larger Diversification Ratios and higher returns when compared to those of the "ideal" portfolio. Thus *k*-portfolios serve to testify the well-known observation that holding a large number of assets in the portfolio need not increase a portfolio's Diversification Ratio. Also the risk parity quality of the *k*-portfolios can also be observed when *k* is large ($k = 70$ in the sample portfolios considered).

Nikkei225 Equal Weighted k-portfolios

For the *k*-portfolios discussed in section 3.4.2 for $k = 30$ and $k = 80$, the risk return characteristics and their respective Diversification Ratios when Equal Weighted portfolios were constructed out of them have been listed in Table 3.2. The results have been compared against those of the "ideal" portfolio that stays invested in all 196 assets comprising the stock universe considered.

The *k*-portfolios displayed higher returns when compared to those of the "ideal" portfolio and assured risk parity investing by providing higher returns for an equal amount of risk and measure of the diversification ratio.

3.5.2. Inverse Volatility Weighted k-portfolio construction

Inverse Volatility Weighted portfolio is one in which the weights of individual assets in the portfolio are proportional to the reciprocals of their individual volatilities. Thus Inverse Volatility Weighted portfolios result in higher volatility assets being accorded smaller weights and lower volatility assets being accorded larger weights.

The weights are given by,

$$\frac{\dfrac{1}{\sigma_i}}{\sum\limits_{j} \dfrac{1}{\sigma_j}} \qquad\qquad [3.10]$$

where σ_i is the volatility of asset *i*.

The Inverse Volatility Weighted *k*-portfolios were studied over S&P BSE 200 and Nikkei 225 data sets and their risk/return characteristics and Diversification Ratios compared with those of the "ideal" portfolio of the stock universe.

Category	Portfolio	Annualized Risk (%)	Expected portfolio annual return (%)	Diversification Ratio
k = 20	k-portfolio 1	41.21	60.62	2.29
	k-portfolio 2	41.52	56.06	2.26
	k-portfolio 3	41.82	55.40	2.31
k = 30	k-portfolio 1	35.42	55.74	2.38
	k-portfolio 2	35.62	58.46	2.42
	k-portfolio 3	35.91	54.69	2.40
k = 50	k-portfolio 1	31.58	49.92	2.36
	k-portfolio 2	31.46	49.44	2.39
	k-portfolio 3	31.45	48.86	2.40
k = 70	k-portfolio 1	29.80	44.70	2.31
	k-portfolio 2	29.99	44.76	2.32
	k-portfolio 3	29.88	44.69	2.33
"Ideal" Portfolio		27.81	36.53	2.16

Table 3.1. *Risk/Return Characteristics and Diversification Ratios of Equal Weighted k-portfolios compared against those of the "ideal" portfolio for S&P BSE200 data set*

S&P BSE200 Inverse Volatility Weighted k-portfolios

For the k-portfolios discussed in section 3.4.1 for $k = 20$, $k = 30$, $k = 50$ and $k = 70$ and whose Equal Weighted portfolio versions were discussed in section 3.5.1, their risk/return characteristics and their respective Diversification Ratios when Inverse Volatility Weighted portfolios were constructed out of them, have been listed in Table 3.3. The risk return characteristics and the Diversification Ratio for the "ideal" portfolio that comprises all 127 assets of the stock universe considered has been shown in the same table.

In this case also, it can be seen that k-portfolios yield higher returns when compared to those of the "ideal" portfolio, besides vouching for the fact that holding a large number of assets in the portfolio need not increase a portfolio's Diversification Ratio. Also the risk parity characteristics of the Inverse Volatility Weighted k-portfolios can also be observed for all values of k considered.

Category	Portfolio	Annualized Risk (%)	Expected portfolio annual return (%)	Diversification Ratio
k = 30	k-portfolio 1	26.58	7.43	1.77
	k-portfolio 2	26.52	8.62	1.70
	k-portfolio 3	26.25	8.20	1.73
k = 80	k-portfolio 1	26.69	8.07	1.73
	k-portfolio 2	26.33	7.46	1.73
	k-portfolio 3	26.57	8.92	1.74
"Ideal" Portfolio		25.34	6.72	1.70

Table 3.2. *Risk/Return Characteristics and Diversification Ratios of Equal Weighted k-portfolios compared against those of the "ideal" portfolio for Nikkei225 data set*

Nikkei225 Inverse Volatility Weighted k-portfolios

For the k-portfolios discussed in section 3.4.2 for $k = 30$ and $k = 80$ and whose Equal Weighted portfolio versions were discussed in section 3.5.1, the risk return characteristics and their respective Diversification Ratios when Inverse Volatility Weighted portfolios are constructed out of them have been listed in Table 3.4. The results have been compared against those of the "ideal" portfolio of 196 assets comprising the stock universe considered.

The k-portfolios displayed higher returns when compared to those of the "ideal" portfolio and assured risk parity investing by providing higher returns for an equal amount of risk and measure of the diversification ratio.

In summary, k-portfolios constructed as Equal Weighted or Inverse Volatility Weighted portfolios serve to ensure risk parity based investing by yielding higher returns for an equal amount of risk or measure of Diversification Ratio, when compared with those yielded by the respective "ideal" portfolios. They also served to testify the fact that one need not invest in large number of assets to obtain larger Diversification Ratios.

Category	Portfolio	Annualized Risk (%)	Expected portfolio annual return (%)	Diversification Ratio
k = 20	k-portfolio 1	28.37	44.77	2.28
	k-portfolio 2	29.36	40.09	2.20
	k-portfolio 3	29.87	38.34	2.30
k = 30	k-portfolio 1	27.95	43.88	2.25
	k-portfolio 2	28.20	47.73	2.33
	k-portfolio 3	28.72	43.46	2.28
k = 50	k-portfolio 1	27.76	42.19	2.19
	k-portfolio 2	27.53	41.88	2.24
	k-portfolio 3	27.64	41.26	2.26
k = 70	k-portfolio 1	27.11	38.62	2.16
	k-portfolio 2	27.31	38.93	2.17
	k-portfolio 3	27.21	38.93	2.19
"Ideal" Portfolio		26.04	31.98	2.04

Table 3.3. *Risk/Return characteristics and Diversification Ratios of Inverse Volatility Weighted k-portfolios compared against those of the "ideal" portfolio for S&P BSE200 data set*

3.5.3. *Other k-portfolio characteristics*

Pai and Michel's [PAI 09] work on k-means clustered assets demonstrated how the same could be effectively employed to tackle *cardinality constrained portfolio optimization problem*. The cardinality constrained portfolio optimization problem where an investor decides to invest only on K assets (cardinality constraint) with the usual objectives of maximizing return and minimizing risk subject to one or more constraints such as basic, bound, class etc. has attracted a lot of attention amongst researchers. The cardinality constraint turns the problem model into a mixed integer quadratic programming model rendering it difficult for direct solving using

Category	Portfolio	Annualized Risk (%)	Expected portfolio annual return (%)	Diversification Ratio
k = 30	k-portfolio 1	24.76	6.41	1.79
	k-portfolio 2	24.95	7.29	1.71
	k-portfolio 3	24.30	6.49	1.73
k = 80	k-portfolio 1	25.53	7.35	1.74
	k-portfolio 2	24.97	6.61	1.74
	k-portfolio 3	25.34	8.12	1.74
"Ideal" Portfolio		24.17	6.13	1.71

Table 3.4. *Risk/Return characteristics and Diversification Ratios of Inverse Volatility Weighted k-portfolios compared against those of the "ideal" portfolio for Nikkei225 data set*

numerical or analytical methods. Several approaches using Neural Networks, Evolutionary algorithms, local search algorithms such as Simulated Annealing and Threshold Accepting, besides hybrid search algorithms have been explored for the effective solution of the problem model.

Pai and Michel [PAI 09] adopted k-means clustering to tackle the cardinality constraint. The *investable universe* constructed by picking one asset each from the K clusters (as discussed in the earlier sections of this chapter and termed k-portfolio in this book) not only served to eliminate the cardinality constraint and rid the problem model of its notoriety but resulted in the near-optimal behavior of the k-means clustered portfolio sets as evinced by their respective efficient frontiers. They also revealed better portfolio reliability when compared to Markowitz and Random Matrix Theory filtered models.

Thus employing k-means clustering to tackle the cardinality constrained portfolio optimization problem served the four fold objectives of:

1) diversifying the portfolio in K assets;

2) elimination of cardinality constraint from the mathematical model;

3) reduction in the number of design variables for the optimization process leading to faster convergence;

4) improved portfolio reliability with regard to the portfolio's predicted and realized risks.

3.6. MATLAB® demonstrations

In this section we demonstrate MATLAB® functions and programs associated with the construction of k-portfolios, as listed below. The MATLAB® coding style has been kept simple and direct to favor novices in MATLAB®:

A. Computation of Diversification Ratio

B. k-means clustering

C. k-means clustering of assets to obtain k-portfolios

D. Equal weighted k-portfolio construction

E. Inverse volatility weighted k-portfolio construction

A. *Computation of Diversification Ratio*

The function to compute Diversification Ratio illustrated in [3.3] is shown in Figure 3.9. The function assumes that the mean and covariance of returns (daily returns % considered here) viz. `mean_data` and `cov_data` and the portfolio weight set viz. `weight_set` are already computed and available (conformable to the appropriate matrix operations). Chapter 1, section 1.3 A discusses MATLAB® demonstrations for computing the mean and covariance of asset returns.

B. *k-means clustering*

MATLAB® provides *k*-means clustering as a function `kmeans(X, k)` available in its Statistics Toolbox™. Here $[X]_{nxp}$ represents a matrix of observations comprising *n* points (rows) with *p* variables (columns) and `k` the number of clusters to be formed. `kmeans` works to group the n points into k clusters with the function output $[O]_{nx1}$ as a column vector indicating the cluster indices (1, 2, 3, ... k) for the n points in the observation matrix.

```matlab
% Compute Diversification Ratio (DR)  of a
% portfolio given the weights, mean and
% covariance of daily returns

function [DR] =
Compute_DiversificationRatio(mean_data, cov_data,
                                        weight_set)
%Compute portfolio risk
portfolio_risk = sqrt( weight_set * cov_data *
                                weight_set');
% Compute standard deviations of assets(individual
% asset risks)
stdev_assets = sqrt(diag(cov_data));

%Compute DR
DR = ((sum(stdev_assets' .* weight_set)) /
                                portfolio_risk);
end
```

Figure 3.9. *MATLAB® function for computing Diversification Ratio of a portfolio (for a color version of this figure, see www.iste.co.uk/pai/metaheuristics.zip)*

The default distance measure used by `kmeans` is Euclidean distance measure. However, it is possible to specify a distance measure of one's preference (from the available options though) for example, `cityblock`, `hamming` etc. as parameters to the function.

Figure 3.10 illustrates a demonstration of the function in its naïve form, when executed in MATLAB® command line mode. Given the observation matrix $[X]_{7x4}$ `kmeans(X, 3)` groups the seven points in the observation matrix into three clusters with their respective cluster indices in the output indicative of the cluster to which the individual points belong to.

C. *k-means clustering of assets to obtain k-portfolios*

For *k*-portfolio selection, the assets in the stock universe are clustered into *k* groups with the mean returns and their covariance of returns as the clustering characteristics. Figure 3.11 shows the MATLAB® code fragment that illustrates the generation of clusters. ClusterChar_matrx represents the matrix of observations with each row *i* of the matrix representing the mean return and the covariance of return of the asset *i*. company_list refers to the asset names read from a text file and cluster_output the column vector of cluster indices. find (cluster_output == i) returns the linear indices of the assets in cluster *i*.

A random or preferential selection of assets, one from each cluster can be made to construct the desired *k*-portfolio.

```
X =

    1      3      5      6
    2      6      8      9
    1      3      5      2
    7      2      6      9
    4      8      6     10
    1      2      1      4
    6      9      9      7

>> kmeans (X, 3)

ans =

    3
    2
    3
    2
    2
    1
    2

>>
```

Figure 3.10. *Demonstration of* kmeans *function in MATLAB® command line mode*

D. *Equal weighted k-portfolio construction*

For the construction of equal weighted *k*-portfolios, the mean returns and covariance of returns, namely mean_data and cov_data are first obtained. With portfolio_size, set to *k* the size of the *k*-portfolio, and the weights of the

portfolio viz. `eq_weight_mat` set to 1/*k*, Figure 3.12 illustrates the MATLAB®
code fragment for the construction of an equal weighted *k*-portfolio, its annualized
risk and return.

`eq_portfolio_risk` denotes the daily risk (%) and
`eq_ann_portfolio_risk` the annualized portfolio risk (%) of the equal
weighted *k*-portfolio. `eq_ann_portfolio_return` denotes the annualized
return (%) of the equal weighted *k*-portfolio. With `eq_stdev_assets` indicating
the standard deviations of returns (the diagonal of the covariance matrix of returns
denotes the variance) the Diversification Ratio is computed and available in
`eq_DivRatio`.

```
% Set clustering characteristics as mean and
% covariance of returns of an asset

ClusterChar_matrx = [mean_data', cov_data];

% read asset names
company_list =
           textread('BSE127_Companyinfo.txt','%s')

% Invoke kmeans clustering to obtain k groups of
% assets
cluster_output = kmeans(ClusterChar_matrx,k)
for i = 1:k
    w = find (cluster_output == i)
    % display asset names in each cluster
    company_list(w)
end
```

Figure 3.11. *MATLAB® code fragment for k-means clustering of assets*
(for a color version of this figure, see www.iste.co.uk/pai/metaheuristics.zip)

```
% Equal weighted portfolio
eq_weight_mat = ones(1,portfolio_size) *
                              1/portfolio_size;
eq_portfolio_risk = sqrt(eq_weight_mat * cov_data *
                              eq_weight_mat');
eq_ann_portfolio_return = 261*
                    sum(eq_weight_mat.*mean_data);
eq_ann_portfolio_risk = sqrt(261)* eq_portfolio_risk;
eq_stdev_assets = sqrt(diag(cov_data));

eq_DivRatio = ((sum(eq_stdev_assets' .*
           eq_weight_mat)) / eq_portfolio_risk);
```

Figure 3.12. *MATLAB® code fragment for Equal weighted k-portfolio*
construction (for a color version of this figure, see
www.iste.co.uk/pai/metaheuristics.zip)

E. *Inverse Volatility weighted k-portfolio construction*

The Inverse Volatility weighted k-portfolio construction requires mean returns and covariance of returns viz. `mean_data` and `cov_data` as inputs. `iv_weight_mat` denotes the inverse volatility weights computed using equation [3.10]. `iv_ann_portfolio_risk`, `iv_ann_portfolio_return` and `iv_DivRatio` denote the annualized portfolio risk, annualized returns and Diversification Ratio of the Inverse Volatility weighted k-portfolio.

Figure 3.13 illustrates the MATLAB® code fragment for the construction of an Inverse Volatility weighted k-portfolio, its annualized risk and return.

```
% Inverse volatility weighted portfolio
iv_stdev_assets = sqrt(diag(cov_data))';
iv_recipro_stdev_assets = ( 1./iv_stdev_assets );
iv_recipro_stdev_assets_sum =
                    sum(iv_recipro_stdev_assets);
iv_weight_mat =
iv_recipro_stdev_assets/iv_recipro_stdev_assets_sum ;

iv_portfolio_risk = sqrt( iv_weight_mat * cov_data *
                              iv_weight_mat');
iv_ann_portfolio_return = 261*
                    sum(mean_data.*iv_weight_mat);
iv_ann_portfolio_risk = sqrt(261)* iv_portfolio_risk;
iv_DivRatio = ((sum(iv_stdev_assets .* iv_weight_mat))
                              / iv_portfolio_risk);
```

Figure 3.13. *MATLAB® code fragment for Inverse Volatility weighted k-portfolio construction (for a color version of this figure, see www.iste.co.uk/pai/metaheuristics.zip)*

Project

Assume that as an investor, you decide to invest in 30 equity stocks listed in a specific stock exchange of your country or place of residence. Also assume that you have access to the historical data set of the stocks for a modest period of time (minimum of five years).

Explore the outcomes of the following experiments making use of MATLAB® and/or its Toolboxes:

(i) You decide to select a k-portfolio ($k = 30$) by clustering the stock universe into k groups and randomly select k assets one from each cluster to construct your portfolio. Make five such choices of k-portfolios. Assuming that you were interested in an unconstrained portfolio optimization model (discussed in Chapter 1, section 1.2, [1.19]–[1.22]),   how were the efficient frontiers graphed for the five unconstrained k-portfolios chosen?

(ii) You decide to exercise your personal preferences and opt to choose one asset of your choice from each of the k clusters and thus construct your k-portfolios (non-random selection). Make five such choices of k-portfolios. Assuming that you were interested in an unconstrained portfolio optimization model (discussed in Chapter 1, section 1.2, [1.19]–[1.22]), how were the efficient frontiers graphed for the five unconstrained k-portfolios considered?

(iii) For the k-portfolio choices made in (ii), you decide to go for a constrained portfolio optimization model (discussed in Chapter 1, section 1.2, [1.23]), with bound, class and basic constraints imposed on the k-portfolio. Assume that you computed the betas of the assets in the k-portfolio and having classified them as low volatility and high volatility stocks, you imposed class constraints on the two asset classes as illustrated in [1.23]. Also you decide to impose bound constraints of your choice on the individual assets of the k-portfolio. How were the efficient frontiers graphed for the five constrained k-portfolios considered by you?

(iv) You observe that some clusters have some "attractive" stocks and therefore decide to defy the norm of selecting one stock from each cluster. You therefore opt to stick to a specific cluster or clusters holding such stocks and grab as many stocks as you wish from each cluster, choosing to ignore the rest of the clusters, to construct your k-portfolio. In other words, you choose to soft pedal on diversification or chose to put all eggs in one basket, so to say. Assuming that you were interested in an unconstrained portfolio optimization model (discussed in Chapter 1, section 1.2, [1.19]–[1.22]), how were the efficient frontiers graphed for the three k-portfolios considered? What are your observations?

(v) Trace a Markowitz's "ideal" efficient frontier for the stocks in your universe and compare all the k-portfolio efficient frontiers traced, in the background of the "ideal" efficient frontier. What are your observations?

Suggested Further Reading

Pai and Michel's [PAI 09] paper on "*Evolutionary Optimization of constrained k-means clustered assets for diversification in small portfolios*" details the application of k-means clustering for constructing small portfolios and analyses the performances of the portfolios.

Clustering algorithms, however, have found limited applications in the field of portfolio optimization. Vincenzo *et al.*, [VIN 05] applied *Single linkage* and *Average linkage* clustering algorithms to serve as filters for the correlation coefficient matrix, during portfolio optimization. They demonstrated the improved portfolio reliability displayed by the clustering schemes in comparison to that of the Markowitz and Random Matrix Theory (RMT) filtered models.

RMT [MET 90] has emerged as a prominent method in serving as an efficient filtering method in portfolio optimization by de-noising the correlation matrix. Some of the RMT based models have been studied by Laloux *et al.*, [LAL 07], Papp *et al.,* [PAP 05] and Malgorzata and Krzych., [MAL 06].

MATLAB Statistical Toolbox™ provides a brief documentation on the description and application of Cluster Analysis, in its product manual.

Kaufman and Rousseeuw [KAU 05] and Everitt *et al.*, [EVE 11], to quote a few, are comprehensive guides to learn more on clustering techniques.

Metaheuristic Risk-Budgeted
Portfolio Optimization

This chapter discusses metaheuristic optimization of risk budgeted long-short portfolios with the objective of maximizing the portfolio's Sharpe Ratio. The non-linear constraints representing the portfolio's absolute contribution to total risk are tackled using Joines and Houck's dynamic penalty functions. Differential Evolution with Hall of Fame (DE-HOF) is employed to solve the non-linear constrained fractional programming model representing the portfolio optimization problem. MATLAB® demonstrations of the functions used and the programs coded to solve the specific portfolio optimization problem model with DE-HOF have been presented last.

4.1. Risk budgeting

Minimization of risk is a predominant portfolio optimization objective. Nevertheless, the fact that practitioners have to take risks to enable their portfolios to outperform *benchmarks* cannot be ignored. A benchmark is a standard or measure that is used to compare the risk, return and allocation of a portfolio and is generally constructed using broad measures such as indices or specific fund categories or asset classes. Benchmarks serve as guidelines for periodical rebalancing of one's portfolio to manage risk. Mandates often stipulate the allowable risks relative to the benchmarks (known as *Tracking error* or *active risk*) to encourage fund managers mimic or beat the benchmarks to earn more returns.

Risk attribution serves to decompose the total risk of the portfolio into smaller units that correspond to the risks of the individual assets or asset classes comprising the portfolio. *Risk budgeting* also referred to as *Risk decomposition* or *Risk contribution*, is a useful investment strategy, which while ensuring market protection enhances investment exposure. It undertakes this by decomposing the aggregate portfolio risk into its components and imposing limits on the individual risks of the assets / asset classes comprising the portfolio. Thus asset allocation in the case of risk budgeting needs to be made in strict compliance to the risk budgets decided upon. As can be seen, risk budgets are based upon the individual investor's risk appetites.

Risk budgeting could be effected through what is known as *Marginal Contribution to Risk* (MCR). MCR is defined as the partial derivative of the portfolio risk with respect to its weights and is given by

$$\bar{m} = (m_1, m_2, ... m_N)' = \frac{(V.\bar{w})}{\sqrt{\bar{w}'.V.\bar{w}}} \, , \tag{4.1}$$

where $\bar{w}' = (w_1, w_2, ... w_N)$ is the weight set and V is the variance-covariance matrix of asset returns.

The *Absolute Contribution to Total Risk* is given by

$$w_i.m_i, \quad i = 1, 2, ... N \, , \tag{4.2}$$

and the Percentage Contribution to Total Risk is given by

$$\frac{\text{Absolute Contribution to Total Risk}}{\text{Total Risk}} = \frac{w_i.m_i}{\sqrt{\bar{w}'.V.\bar{w}}}, i = 1, 2, ... N \tag{4.3}$$

The sum of Absolute Contributions to Total Risk for a portfolio, always equals its volatility.

EXAMPLE.– For the portfolio P shown in Table 1.6 (Chapter 1) whose characteristics have been reproduced below for convenience, the risk contributions of the individual assets {RIL, INFO, ITC, LT, ICICIBC, HDFC, ONGC, SBIN, HUVR, TCS} comprising P are computed as shown.

Weights:

$$\bar{W} = (w_1, w_2, w_3, ... w_{10})' = (0.06, \; 0.07, 0.16, 0.1, 0.07, 0.07, 0.07, 0.16, 0.18, 0.06)'$$

Variance-covariance matrix of daily returns (%):

$$V = \begin{bmatrix} 6.38 & 2.55 & 2.28 & 3.89 & 4.65 & 3.29 & 3.29 & 3.65 & 2.00 & 3.04 \\ 2.55 & 4.75 & 1.49 & 2.53 & 3.13 & 2.29 & 2.07 & 2.18 & 1.29 & 3.57 \\ 2.28 & 1.49 & 4.42 & 2.25 & 2.46 & 1.95 & 1.95 & 2.30 & 1.91 & 1.83 \\ 3.89 & 2.53 & 2.25 & 7.29 & 4.7 & 3.36 & 3.26 & 3.76 & 2.07 & 2.92 \\ 4.65 & 3.13 & 2.46 & 4.73 & 9.54 & 5.01 & 3.75 & 5.08 & 2.49 & 3.40 \\ 3.29 & 2.29 & 1.95 & 3.36 & 5.01 & 6.27 & 2.89 & 3.64 & 1.70 & 2.52 \\ 3.29 & 2.07 & 1.95 & 3.26 & 3.75 & 2.89 & 5.37 & 2.94 & 1.97 & 2.37 \\ 3.65 & 2.18 & 2.3 & 3.76 & 5.08 & 3.64 & 2.94 & 6.59 & 1.98 & 2.65 \\ 2.00 & 1.29 & 1.91 & 2.07 & 2.49 & 1.70 & 1.97 & 1.98 & 4.52 & 1.67 \\ 3.04 & 3.57 & 1.83 & 2.92 & 3.40 & 2.52 & 2.37 & 2.65] & 1.670 & 5.59 \end{bmatrix}$$

Portfolio daily risk (%) = 1.71

The Marginal Contribution to Risk measure of portfolio P is computed as

$$\bar{m} = (m_1, m_2, m_3, m_4, m_5, m_6, m_7, m_8, m_9, m_{10})' = \frac{(V.\bar{w})}{\sqrt{\bar{w}'. V. \bar{w}}}$$

$$= (3.23 \quad 2.30 \quad 2.44 \quad 3.44 \quad 4.11 \quad 3.04 \quad 2.79 \quad 3.50 \quad 2.38 \quad 2.66) / 1.71$$

$$= (1.88, \ 1.34, \ 1.42, \ 2.01, \ 2.40, \ 1.77, \ 1.63, \ 2.04, \ 1.39, \ 1.55)$$

The Absolute Contribution to Total Risk of portfolio P is computed as

$$(w_i.m_i) \quad i = 1, 2, ... N$$

$$= (0.11, 0.09, 0.23, 0.20, 0.17, 0.12, 0.11, 0.33, 0.25, 0.09)$$

It can be observed that the sum of the Absolute Contributions to Total Risk of the portfolio P equals its volatility, which is 1.71.

The Percentage Contribution to Total Risk (%) of portfolio P is computed as

$$\frac{w_i.m_i}{\sqrt{\bar{w}'.V.\bar{w}}} = (0.07, 0.05, 0.13, 0.12, 0.10, 0.07, 0.07, 0.19, 0.15, 0.05)*100$$

$$= (7, 5, 13, 12, 10, 7, 7, 19, 15, 5)$$

As can be observed, the asset SBIN (State Bank of India) has the highest percentage of contribution to total risk (19%) of the portfolio P.

4.2. Long-Short portfolio

The weights of a portfolio are indicative of the proportions of capital invested over each asset comprising the portfolio. The weights could be *positive* or *negative*. *Positive weights* are indicative of what is termed *long selling* and the assets concerned are known as *long positions*. *Negative weights* are indicative of what is termed *short selling* and the assets concerned are referred to as *short positions*. Long positions yield returns during their rise in prices and short positions yield returns anticipating a fall in their prices. A portfolio comprising only long positions is called a *long-only portfolio* and the same comprising an assortment of long and short positions is called a *long-short portfolio*.

Short selling is when assets are *borrowed* from a third party with the understanding of returning the same to the lender at a later date. The borrower (short seller) anticipates a decline in the prices of assets and "sells" the borrowed assets at the prevailing price. Since the sale involves borrowed assets for which the seller is not the owner, the sale is termed "short" sale. Now assuming that as anticipated by the short seller, the asset prices declined, the short seller repurchases the assets at the declined price and during the process of buy back makes a profit. Thus the short seller hopes to make profit by cashing in on the decline in the prices of assets between the sale and repurchase.

EXAMPLE.– Assuming that the prevailing price of an asset is €50 and a short seller anticipates that the asset price would decline in the future to €35. The short seller now borrows the asset from a lender and sells it for €50. When the prices decline, possibly to €35, as anticipated by the short seller, the short seller buys back the asset and in the process makes a profit of €15.

Needless to say, short selling is risky and a short sale kept open for long can cost more. Nevertheless, short selling is a viable and a profitable investment strategy provided it is handled with discretion and with enough experience of handling risks involved with the strategy.

In respect of long-short portfolios that are fully invested for example, short positions give room to *leveraged* profits considering the fact that poor performing stocks could be shorted to purchase better performing long positions with leveraged weights and thereby gain higher returns. Long-short portfolios when compared with their long-only counterparts are notionally expected to enhance investment exposure and market protection.

4.3. Risk-Budgeted Portfolio Optimization model

In the Risk-Budgeted Portfolio Optimization model, the investor decides to invest on a leveraged long-short portfolio and maximize the Sharpe Ratio of his/her portfolio subject to the following constraints:

– a risk budget of $r\%$ is imposed over the absolute contribution to total risk for each asset i in the portfolio, that is

$$w_i . m_i \leq r\% \text{ of } \sigma_p, i = 1, 2, ...N \qquad [4.4]$$

where m_i is the marginal contribution to risk of asset i, w_i the weight of asset i and σ_p the portfolio risk.

– the portfolio is fully invested, that is

$$\sum_{i=1}^{N} w_i = 1 \qquad [4.5]$$

– unbounded inequality constraints are imposed on specific assets (assets with positive premia, for instance) reflecting the leveraging that is permitted on the portfolio, that is

$$w_i > 0 \quad \text{or} \quad w_j \geq 0 , i \neq j \qquad [4.6]$$

– a constraint imposed on selective assets to define a leveraged long-short portfolio mix, that is

$$-a_i \leq w_i \leq b_i \qquad [4.7]$$

where $(-a_i, b_i)$ are free lower and upper bounds, for any a_i, b_i acceptable to the investor and promoting a leveraged portfolio.

Thus the risk-budgeted portfolio which is a leveraged long-short portfolio comprises three asset classes with specific constraints imposed on each of these asset classes. Some positive premia assets with mandatory and leveraged investment ($w_i > 0$), other positive premia assets with optional and leveraged investment ($w_j \geq 0$) and other assets with free bounds but leveraged and long-short ($-a_i \leq w_i \leq b_i$). Let W^+ , W^{Spl} and W^{Free} indicate the three asset classes respectively.

The mathematical formulation of the problem model is described as

$$\max\left(\frac{\bar{p}.\bar{w}}{\sqrt{\bar{w}'.V.\bar{w}}}\right) \qquad \text{(maximize Sharpe Ratio)} \qquad [4.8]$$

where $\bar{p}$ represents the *premia* (returns) of the assets in the portfolio, $\bar{w}$ the weights and V the variance-covariance matrix of asset returns, $\bar{p}.\bar{w}$ is the expected portfolio return, $\sigma_P = \sqrt{\bar{w}'.V.\bar{w}}$ is the portfolio risk and $\left(\dfrac{\bar{p}.\bar{w}}{\sqrt{\bar{w}'.V.\bar{w}}}\right)$ is the Sharpe Ratio of the portfolio,   subject to the constraints,

$$w_i.m_i \le r\% \text{ of } \sigma_P, \, i = 1, \, 2, \, ...N \qquad \text{(risk budgeting)} \qquad [4.9]$$

where $\bar{m} = (m_1, m_2, ...m_N)' = \dfrac{(V.\bar{w})}{\sqrt{\bar{w}'. V. \bar{w}}}$ are the marginal contributions to risk and $r\%$ is the risk limit,

$$\sum_{i=1}^{N} w_i = 1 \qquad \text{(fully invested)} \qquad [4.10]$$

$$w_j^+ > 0 \qquad \text{(financial leverage)} \qquad [4.11]$$

where w_j^+ are the weights of selective positive premia assets W^+,

$$w_k^{spl} \ge 0, \quad j \ne k \qquad \text{(optional inclusion of special leveraged assets)} \qquad [4.12]$$

where w_k^{spl} are the weights of some special assets W^{Spl} whose inclusion is not mandatory if the optimality so demands, but if included can be leveraged to any extent.

$$-a_i \le w_i^{Free} \le b_i \qquad \text{(long-short mix, promoting leveraging)} \qquad [4.13]$$

where $(-a_i, b_i)$ are free bounds for any a_i, b_i acceptable to the investor for selective assets belonging to W^{Free} and promoting a leveraged long-short portfolio.

Equations [4.8]–[4.13] define a single objective non-linear constrained fractional programming model which is difficult to solve using analytical methods and hence the need for metaheuristic methods.

However, to tackle the non-linear constraints represented by [4.9] together with the linear constraints (bounded and unbounded) represented by [4.10]–[4.13], it is essential that metaheuristic methods adopt specialized methods which may involve transformation of the original problem model. The constraint handling methods adopted by metaheuristic strategies are discussed in the following section.

4.3.1. *Constraint handling*

With regard to application of metaheuristic methods for combinatorial optimization problems, one of the major hurdles faced by the methods is in tackling the constraints enforced on the problems. The metaheuristic methods need to generate *feasible solution* sets wherein solution sets have to essentially satisfy all the constraints imposed on the model, before they eventually arrive at a near-optimal or acceptable solution. Thus *constraint handling* is a major problem in the application of metaheuristic methods for *constrained optimization problems*. Several methods to tackle the problem of constraint handling have been discussed in the literature. In this book, however, we choose to restrict the discussion to the application of two of these methods namely *Repair strategy* and *Penalty Function Strategy*.

Repair strategy

In this strategy the population of chromosomes/individuals whose genes/components represent the candidate solution sets to the optimization problem considered are checked to see if they represent feasible solution sets to the problems. If they are observed to violate one or more of the constraints specified then they are deemed "infeasible" chromosomes / individuals. The repair strategy now proceeds to "repair" the infeasible chromosomes / individuals with the help of well designed repair procedures, quite often tailor-made to the problem in hand, to transform them into feasible solution sets. The repair procedure may not be universal and quite often is specific to the problem in hand and by and large turns out to be complex. Hence this aspect of the strategy is viewed as its disadvantage for it might be difficult to evolve a repair procedure for certain problems. Nonetheless, many works ([MIC 96], for example) have shown that the repair strategy despite its complexness excels other strategies by way of speed and performance. Repair strategies have also been successfully applied to specific problem models in the discipline of portfolio optimization and fuzzy portfolio optimization [CHA 00, PAI 09, PAI 11, PAI 12a, PAI 17].

In this chapter for the Risk-budgeted portfolio optimization model discussed, we shall demonstrate how Repair strategy helps to tackle the linear constraints represented by [4.10]–[4.13].

Penalty function strategy

Penalty function strategy is based on similar methods adopted in conventional constrained optimization, where solutions that are infeasible are penalized using what are called *penalty coefficients*.

Thus given a constrained optimization problem, which is a minimization problem as described below:

$$\min (f(\bar{x})), \quad \bar{x} = (x_1, x_2, \ldots x_n)$$
$$g_k(\bar{x}) \le 0, \quad k = 1, 2, \ldots K$$
$$h_m(\bar{x}) = 0, \quad m = 1, 2, \ldots M \quad \quad [4.14]$$
$$x_i \in dom(x_i)$$

where $\bar{x} = (x_1, x_2, \ldots x_n)$ are the decision variables with $dom(x_i)$ as the domain of the decision variable x_i, $f(\bar{x})$ is the minimization objective function, $g_k(\bar{x})$ are the inequality constraints and $h_m(\bar{x})$ are the equality constraints, the penalty function strategy transforms the constrained optimization problem model into an unconstrained optimization problem model by reconstructing the objective function as shown below:

$$\phi(\bar{x}, r) = f(\bar{x}) + r \cdot \sum_{m=1}^{M} (h_m(\bar{x}))^2 + r \cdot \sum_{k=1}^{K} G_k \cdot (g_k(\bar{x}))^2 \quad \quad [4.15]$$

where G_k is the Heaviside operator such that

$$G_k = \begin{cases} 0, & g_k(\bar{x}) \le 0 \\ 1, & g_k(\bar{x}) > 0 \end{cases} \quad \quad [4.16]$$

and r is a positive multiplier that controls the magnitude of the penalty terms.

In the case of a constrained optimization problem, which is a maximization problem, the transformation could be effected by employing the *principle of duality* as shown below:

$$\max (f(\bar{x})) = -\min (-f(\bar{x})) \quad \quad [4.17]$$

Joines and Houck's penalty function method

Joines and Houck [JOI 94] proposed a penalty function-based constraint handling strategy employing *dynamic penalties*. In this method the penalty coefficient increases with the increasing count of generations. Thus in the tth generation, the penalized objective function is given by,

$$\phi(\overline{x},t) = f(\overline{x}) + (C.t)^{\alpha} \left(\sum_{m=1}^{M} \left(h_m(\overline{x}) \right)^{\beta} + \sum_{k=1}^{K} G_k \cdot \left(g_k(\overline{x}) \right)^{\beta} \right) \qquad [4.18]$$

here (C, α, β) are constants and the penalty term $(C.t)^{\alpha}$ increases constantly with each generation count. However, Joines and Houck indicated that the quality of the solution set is dependent on the choice of (C, α, β), while concluding that $(C = 0.5, \alpha = 2, \beta = 2)$ are a reasonable choice for the constants. The increasing penalty term $(C.t)^{\alpha}$ with each generation results in a situation where the infeasible chromosomes / individuals during the last few generations receive *death penalty* and thus the method tends to converge early.

In this chapter for the Risk-budgeted portfolio optimization model discussed, we shall demonstrate how Joines and Houck's penalty function method helps to tackle the non-linear risk budgeting constraint represented using [4.9].

4.3.2. *Transformed Risk-budgeted portfolio optimization model*

To tackle the non linear risk-budgeting constraint, Joines and Houck's Penalty function method is employed, which transforms the original objective function (maximization) to its dual (minimization), using the *principle of duality*. The revised formulations of the objective function and the risk budgeting constraints are as follows:

$$-\min \left(-\frac{\overline{p}.\overline{w}}{\sqrt{\overline{w}'.V.\overline{w}}} + \psi(\overline{w}, \overline{m}, t) \right) \qquad [4.19]$$

where $\psi(\overline{w}, \overline{m}, t)$ termed as the *constraint violation function* is given as,

$$\psi(\overline{w}, \overline{m}, t) = (C.t)^{\alpha} \left(\sum_{k=1}^{N} G_k \cdot \left(\varphi_k(w_k, m_k) \right)^{\beta} \right),$$

$$\varphi_k(w_k, m_k) = w_k.m_k - x\% \ of \ \sigma_P \quad \text{and}$$

G_k is the Heaviside Operator such that

$$G_k = 0, \quad for \quad \varphi_k(w_k, m_k) \leq 0, \quad and$$
$$= 1, \quad for \quad \varphi_k(w_k, m_k) > 0$$

$$\overline{m} = (m_1, m_2, \ldots m_N)' = \frac{(V.\overline{w})}{\sqrt{\overline{w}'.V.\overline{w}}} \qquad [4.20]$$

The transformed objective function represented by [4.19]–[4.20] together with the linear constraints represented by [4.10]–[4.13] now defines the transformed Risk-budgeted portfolio optimization model.

However, the transformed model is still a non-linear fractional programming optimization model with unbounded linear constraints though. The model is difficult to be solved using traditional methods and hence the need for metaheuristic methods, which is *Differential Evolution with Hall of Fame* (DE HOF), a refined version of the Differential Evolution algorithm.

4.4. Differential Evolution with Hall of Fame

The Differential Evolution algorithm was detailed in Chapter 2, section 2.5 and demonstrated over optimization of Beale function.

Differential Evolution with Hall of Fame (DE HOF) is a Differential Evolution algorithm augmented with a mechanism termed *Hall of Fame*. Hall of Fame is a repository that preserves one or more of the best individuals in each generation to promote super specialization. Thus in each generation the best-fit individuals compete with those in the Hall of Fame and the *best among the best* finds an entry into it. The inclusion of Hall of Fame in Evolutionary Algorithms in general, extends elitism in time. The Evolution Strategy algorithm with Hall of Fame was already discussed in Chapter 2, section 2.4. Thus when the termination criterion specified for the Differential Evolution algorithm (or for that matter an Evolutionary Algorithm in general) is met with, the chromosome/individual positioned in the Hall of Fame is chosen as the "optimal" solution to the problem concerned. Figure 4.1 illustrates the mechanism of Hall of Fame when imposed over the Differential Evolution algorithm. To recall, the Deterministic Selection operator (see Chapter 2, section 2.5.1) is invoked by DE when the better of the parent and offspring individuals in a population are selected to form the next generation of individuals (NEXTGEN). The Hall of Fame mechanism is included at this point where the best among the individuals in NEXTGEN compete with those in the Hall of Fame to gain entry into it. Assuming that the Hall of Fame is set to accommodate only one individual (size 1), if the fitness function value of the best individual in NEXTGEN, BEST, is better than that of the individual in the Hall of Fame, then BEST ousts the individual concerned in the Hall of Fame and leaves a copy of itself in the Hall of Fame. Otherwise, the individual reigning Hall of Fame is left undisturbed. NEXTGEN proceeds to the next generation cycle and the competition with Hall of Fame continues as before, until the termination criterion is met with. The individual in the Hall of Fame is finally declared the "optimal" solution. It is also possible to have more than one individual in the Hall of Fame (size k) and then select one among the k individuals in the Hall of Fame as the "optimal" solution.

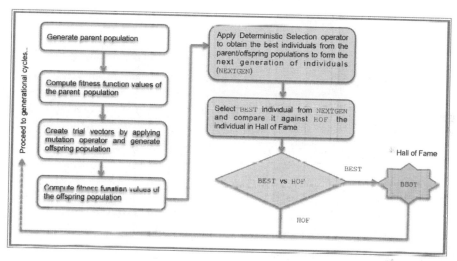

Figure 4.1. *Hall of Fame inclusion in the Differential Evolution process*

4.5. Repair strategy for handling unbounded linear constraints

In this section we detail the repair strategy employed to tackle the unbounded linear constraints represented by [4.11]–[4.12] subject to the constraint on fully invested portfolio [4.10] and accompanied by a constraint [4.13] with free bounds imposed on selective assets to promote leveraged long-short portfolio mix. The objective of the repair strategy is, given a chromosome/individual representing a set of random weights of the portfolio, to *repair* or *standardize* the weights in such a way that all the linear constraints represented by [4.10]–[4.13] are satisfied thereby transforming it into a feasible solution vector to the problem model. A population of such standardized chromosomes represent a feasible solution set to the problem which eventually at the end of the stipulated generation cycles evolve themselves to yield the optimal solution sets.

Let $\mathbf{W}$ represent a random vector of N weights of the portfolio comprising N assets, generated between *(-c, +c)*, for some *c*. Let W^+, W^{Spl} and W^{Free} represent the weight sets of the assets belonging to the three asset classes whose constraints are defined by [4.11], [4.12] and [4.13], respectively. Let *p*, *s* and *f* be the number of assets in each of these asset classes respectively, such that $p + s + f = N$. The following steps illustrate the working of the repair strategy:

Step 1: If weights w_i, $w_i \in W^+$ or $w_i \in W^{Spl}$ are less than their respective lower bounds, a non zero lower bound (0.001, for example) and 0 respectively, upgrade the respective weights to their respective lower bounds. Let $W^{+'}$ and $W^{Spl'}$ represent the upgraded weight sets. It needs to be emphasized that for the risk-budgeted portfolio optimization model considered, the portfolio demands   leveraging and hence the repair strategy only focuses on satisfying lower bounds with no concern whatsoever   for satisfying any upper bounds, subject to the important constraint of $\sum_{i=1}^{N} w_i = 1$.

Step 2: Find sum of weights $SUM = \sum_{w_i \in W^{+'}} w_i + \sum_{w_j \in W^{Spl'}} w_j + \sum_{w_k \in W^{Free}} w_k$ to ascertain if the fully invested constraint represented by [4.10] is satisfied.

>**if** *(SUM >1)* **then**
>
>>Find the excess weights $EXCESS = SUM - 1$;
>>
>>Obtain the proportion of weights to be decremented for each asset as $DECR\_WEIGHT = EXCESS / N$;
>>
>>Decrement weights as $w_i - DECR\_WEIGHT$,
>>
>>$w_i \in \left(W^{+'} \cup W^{Spl'} \cup W^{Free}\right), \quad \forall w_i$;
>>
>>**go to** Step 3;
>
>**else**   **if** *(SUM < 1)*
>
>**then**
>
>>Compute the deficit $DEFICIT = 1 - SUM$;
>>
>>Compute the proportion of weights to be incremented as $INCR\_WEIGHT = DEFICIT / N$;
>>
>>Increment weights as $w_i + INCR\_WEIGHT$

$$w_i \in \left(W^{+'} \cup W^{Spl'} \cup W^{Free}\right), \quad \forall w_i;$$

exit (Success); /* return repaired weights*/

else   exit (Success); /* return repaired weights*/

end

end

Step 3: Initialize R, the set of weights which are to be upgraded to satisfy their respective lower bounds to null, that is $R = \phi$.

Step 4: Check if, due to decrementing of weights, any of the weights $\{w_t\}$ belonging to $W^{+'}$ or $W^{Spl'}$ are violating their respective lower bounds.

If so, upgrade the weights to their respective lower bounds and update R which denotes the set of such upgraded weights, that is $R = R \cup \{w_t\}$. Let the rest of the weights be denoted as Q, that is $Q = \left(W^{+'} \cup W^{Spl'} \cup W^{Free}\right) - R$. Go to Step 5.

If not, go to Step 6.

Step 5: Since the weights have been upgraded in Step 2, find the new sum of weights

$$SUM = \sum W^{+'} + \sum W^{Spl'} + \sum W^{Free}.$$

if $(SUM > 1)$

then

Find the excess weights $EXCESS = SUM - 1$;

Obtain the proportion of weights to be decremented from each weight in Q as $DECR\_WEIGHT = EXCESS / |Q|$, where $|Q|$ denotes the number of asset weights in Q;

Decrement weights as $w_i - DECR\_WEIGHT$, $\forall w_i \in Q$;

go to Step 4;

else go to Step 6;

end

Step 6: **if** (SUM < 1)

> **then**
>
> > Compute the deficit $DEFICIT = 1\text{-}SUM$;
> >
> > Compute the proportion of weights to be incremented as
> >
> > $INCR\_WEIGHT = DEFICIT / N$;
> >
> > Increment weights as $w_i + INCR\_WEIGHT$
> >
> > $$w_i \in \left(W^{+'} \cup W^{Spl'} \cup W^{Free}\right), \quad \forall w_i;$$
>
> > **exit (Success)**; /* return repaired weights*/
>
> **else exit (Success)**;   /* return repaired weights*/
>
> **end**

The weight vector repaired satisfies all the linear constraints represented by [4.10]–[4.13] and hence represents a feasible solution to the transformed problem model represented using [4.19]–[4.20], [4.10]–[4.13]. DE HOF ensures that every parent/offspring population of chromosomes/individuals are repaired as detailed above so that they represent a feasible solution set. In other words, DE HOF in a departure from what most other versions of DE do, maneuvers its search process only through feasible solution space and not candidate solution space during the generation cycles, thereby resulting in faster convergence.

EXAMPLE.– The repair strategy explained above is illustrated over a toy weight set.

Let W = [-0.9856, -1.5673, 1.2546, 0.8653, 2.9567, -1.6894, -2.4685] represent a random weight vector of seven assets $\{a_1, a_2, a_3, a_4, b_1, b_2, c_1\}$ comprising a portfolio. The weight vector was randomly generated between the open interval (-3, 3). Let us suppose that $\{a_1, a_2, a_3, a_4\}$ are positive premia assets which have to satisfy the constraint represented by [4.11], $\{b_1, b_2\}$ are leveraged long-short assets with free bounds satisfying [4.13] and $\{c_1\}$ is a special asset that is optional but leveraged and satisfying constraint represented by [4.12]. Adopting the notations employed in the repair strategy discussed above,

$$W^+ = [-0.9856, -1.5673, 1.2546, 0.8653], \quad W^{Free} = [2.9567, -1.6894],$$
$$W^{Spl} = [-2.4685], \quad N = 7, p = 4, s = 1 \text{ and } f = 2$$

Step 1: Upgrading the weights in W^+ and W^{Spl} which are less than their respective lower bounds yields $W^{+'}= [0.001, 0.001, 1.2546, 0.8653]$ and $W^{Spl'} = [0]$. The upgraded weight set is given by $[0.001, 0.001, 1.2546, 0.8653, 2.9567, -1.6894, 0]$

Step 2: Check if the fully invested constraint represented by [4.10] is satisfied by the upgraded weight set and adjust the weights so that the constraint is satisfied. The computations undertaken are as listed below:

$SUM = 3.3892, \quad EXCESS = 3.3892 - 1 = 2.3892,$

$DECR\_WEIGHT = 2.3892/7 = 0.3413$

The decremented weight vector is given as

$[-0.3403, -0.3403, 0.9133, 0.5240, 2.6154, -2.0307, -0.3413]$

Step 3: Observing that assets $\{a_1, a_2, c_1\}$ are violating their lower bounds, the computations behind the weight set upgrading are as listed below:

R representing the upgraded weights of the assets $\{a_1, a_2, c_1\}$ is given by,

$R = [0.001, 0.001, 0]$

Q, representing the weights of the other assets is given by

$Q = [0.9133, 0.5240, 2.6154, -2.0307]$

Step 4: SUM of the upgraded weights now partitioned as R and Q is given by,
$SUM = 2.0239, EXCESS = SUM - 1 = 1.0239,$

$DECR\_WEIGHT = 1.0239/|Q| = 1.0239/4 = 0.2560$

The upgraded Q after decrementing the weights in Q is given by

$Q = [0.6573, 0.2680, 2.3594, -2.2867].$

It can be seen that none of the weights belonging to $W^{+'}$ and which are a part of Q violate their lower bounds, therefore the upgraded weights are gathered as $[0.001, 0.001, 0.6573, 0.2680, 2.3594, -2.2867, 0]$.

Since the sum of weights equals 1 the repair strategy exits with success.

It can be easily verified that the assets belonging to the respective asset classes satisfy their respective constraints. It can also be observed how the leveraged long-short mix of the portfolio is promoted by assets $\{b_1, b_2\}$.

4.6. DE HOF-based Risk-budgeted portfolio optimization

The DE HOF in principle works similar to the Differential Evolution algorithm discussed in section 2.5 and illustrated in Figure 2.8, for an unconstrained optimization instance though. The specific DE strategy adopted by DE HOF is *DE/rand/1/bin*, which to recall, randomly generates the target vector ("*rand*") and chooses one difference vector ("*1*") for the mutation operator and employs binomial crossover operator ("*bin*"). The inclusion of the Hall of Fame mechanism to extend elitism with time has been discussed in section 4.4 and illustrated in Figure 4.1. The tasks that turn DE HOF distinct to the problem model discussed, is in its ability to handle the multiple constraints that define the problem model. Thus DE HOF needs to equip itself with mechanisms and strategies to handle the constraints embedded in the problem model, while holding on to its search principle. It is in aspects such as these that metaheuristics in general, turn distinct and unique to the problems for which they are applied.

With regard to the Risk-budgeted portfolio optimization problem model, DE HOF had to adopt two strategies to tackle the non-linear/linear constraints imposed on the original formulation of the problem. The penalty function strategy was adopted to tackle the non-linear risk-budgeting constraint. Thus, following Joines and Houck's method, the non-linear constraint was absorbed into the objective function thereby eliminating non-linearity in the constraints, which otherwise could have been difficult to handle. The rest of the constraints which are linear, multiple though, were handled by devising an appropriate Repair strategy, as explained in section 4.5. With the constraints tackled effectively, DE HOF proceeds to obtain the optimal solution to the Risk-budgeted portfolio optimization problem model as illustrated in Figure 4.2.

DE HOF operators

The operators employed by DE HOF to solve the problem model concerned are:

– Mutation (see [2.5] of Chapter 2, section 2.5).

– Crossover (see [2.6] of Chapter 2, section 2.5).

– Deterministic Selection (see Chapter 2, section 2.5).

The termination criterion is fixed as the number of generations.

DE HOF fitness function value computation

DE HOF computes the fitness function values of its parent and offspring population from the objective function of the problem model. For the Risk-budgeted portfolio optimization problem, [4.19]–[4.20] define the transformed objective function which adopted penalty functions to tackle the non-linear risk-budgeting constraint.

With each individual in the population representing a weight vector which is repaired to represent a feasible solution set, the fitness values can be easily computed by substituting $\bar{w}$ in the objective function with the repaired weights, setting penalty function parameters such as (C, α, β) and t, obtaining $\bar{p}$ and V, the premia and variance-covariance matrix of returns for the portfolio concerned and computing $\bar{m}$, the marginal contributions to risk.

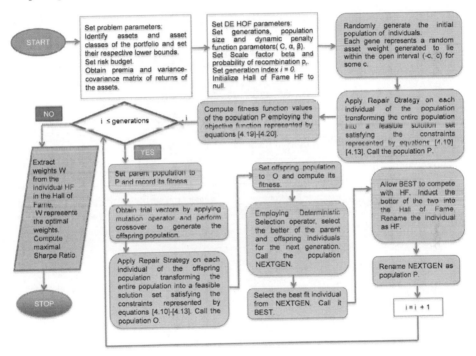

Figure 4.2. *Differential Evolution with Hall of Fame (DE HOF) process flow chart (for a color version of this figure, see www.iste.co.uk/pai/metaheuristics.zip)*

EXAMPLE.– The computation of fitness function values of an individual by DE HOF is demonstrated over a toy weight vector.

For five assets comprising a portfolio (N = 5), let $\bar{w}$ = [0.2410   0.2272   0.2272   0.0078   0.2969] be a standardized column weight vector representing an individual in a population generated during generation cycle $t = 100$. Let the premia of asset returns be given by $\bar{p} = [0.0887 \quad 0.0868 \quad 0.0766 \quad 0.0841 \quad 0.0828]$, the variance-covariance matrix of asset returns be given by

$$V = \begin{bmatrix} 0.0227 & 0.0191 & 0.0193 & 0.0221 & 0.0198 \\ 0.0191 & 0.0184 & 0.0173 & 0.0190 & 0.0178 \\ 0.0193 & 0.0173 & 0.0199 & 0.0191 & 0.0185 \\ 0.0221 & 0.0190 & 0.0191 & 0.0224 & 0.0197 \\ 0.0198 & 0.0178 & 0.0185 & 0.0197 & 0.0229 \end{bmatrix}, \text{ the risk budget } x\% = 12.5\% \text{ and}$$

penalty function parameters $(C, \alpha, \beta) = (0.5, 2, 2)$.

The list of computations undertaken to obtain the fitness function values for the specific weight vector $\bar{w}$ is shown below.

Portfolio risk $\sqrt{\bar{w}'.V.\bar{w}} = 0.1391$

$$\text{MCR } \bar{m} = (m_1, m_2, ... m_N)' = \frac{(V.\bar{w})}{\sqrt{\bar{w}'.V.\bar{w}}} = \begin{bmatrix} 0.1456 \\ 0.1306 \\ 0.1348 \\ 0.1438 \\ 0.1436 \end{bmatrix}$$

$$\varphi_k(w_k, m_k) = w_k.m_k - x\% \text{ of } \sigma_P$$
$$= \begin{bmatrix} 0.0177 & 0.0123 & 0.0132 & -0.0163 & 0.0252 \end{bmatrix}$$

yielding the penalty coefficients $G = [\ 1\ 1\ 1\ 0\ 1\ ]$.

The penalty term $(C.t)^{\alpha} = 2500$ and $\psi(\bar{w}, \bar{m}, t) = 3.1895$ finally yield the fitness function value for the specific weight vector $\bar{w}$ as $\left(-\dfrac{\bar{p}.\bar{w}}{\sqrt{\bar{w}'.V.\bar{w}}} + \psi(\bar{w}, \bar{m}, t) \right) = 2.5877$.

The computations are repeated over each individual comprising a population to arrive at their respective fitness values before they are put to use during deterministic selection or while competing with Hall of Fame, etc.

4.7. Case study global portfolio: results and analyses

We consider a global portfolio of 28 assets, whose descriptions and their premia $\bar{p}$ have been listed in Table 4.1. The composition of assets belong to equity indices, bonds, currencies and commodities. The variance-covariance matrix of daily returns $[V]_{28 \times 28}$ for the portfolio are also obtained (not shown here).

The investor decides to go in for Risk-budgeted portfolio optimization aiming for a leveraged long-short portfolio. The objective is to maximize the Sharpe Ratio of the portfolio. The problem constraints and parameters decided upon by the investor have been listed in Table 4.2. As can be observed, the investor's preferences fits the transformed Risk-budgeted portfolio optimization mathematical model defined by [4.19]–[4.20] as the penalized objective function and [4.10]–[4.13] as the linear constraints.

4.7.1. *Finding the optimal Risk-budgeted portfolio using DE HOF*

The DE HOF algorithm was executed to obtain the optimal portfolio. Table 4.3 lists the DE HOF parameters for the specific problem concerned.

The characteristics of the optimal portfolio obtained during a specific run of DE HOF, have been listed in Table 4.4 and Table 4.5. Table 4.4 shows the Risk/Return characteristics of the optimal portfolio. Considering the Sharpe Ratio of 1.5085, with a portfolio risk of 0.0151 and a portfolio return of 0.0228, DE HOF had indeed been successful in obtaining a leveraged portfolio of expected standards. Table 4.5 shows the optimal weights and the marginal contributions to risk of each asset.

Constraint satisfaction

The optimal portfolio obtained by DE HOF can be seen to satisfy all the constraints imposed on it. Thus the fully invested constraint [4.10] can be seen satisfied in Table 4.5 with the sum of weight equaling 1. The unbounded constraints imposed on equity indices and bonds with a lower bound of 0.001 [4.11] can be seen satisfied in their respective optimal weights. The special asset which was kept optional (lower bound was 0), viz. commodities in the portfolio, had its weight set to 0 and thus satisfied its constraint represented by [4.12]. The currencies given free bounds with regard to leveraging and long-shorting them, seem to have been longed while satisfying their constraints represented by [4.13].

The non-linear risk-budgeting constraint [4.9] to tackle which, Joines and Houck's dynamic penalty functions were used, can be seen satisfied in Table 4.5. Observe how each asset's Absolute Contribution to Risk satisfies the ceiling of 12.5% of the portfolio risk (see last column of Table 4.5), imposed on them and the sum of the Absolute Contributions to Risk equals the portfolio volatility of 0.0151.

4.7.2. Consistency of performance of DE HOF

As explained in Chapter 2, section 2.4.4 and section 2.5.5, metaheuristic methods need to be empirically tested for their consistency of performance, considering the fact these are stochastic search methods with the initial population and some metaheuristic operators inherently built on random mechanisms. Since DE HOF adopting the DE/rand/1/bin strategy is no different from the rest, the algorithm was repeatedly executed for several runs to observe its results. Table 4.6 shows the results for 10 sample runs. It can be seen that the Sharpe Ratios obtained, whose maximization was the single objective of the optimal portfolios, were consistent in all the runs.

S. No.	Description	Premia
1	Euro Stoxx	0.0887
2	Amsterdam	0.0868
3	DAX	0.0766
4	CAC 40	0.0841
5	IBEX 35	0.0828
6	FTSE 100	0.0845
7	S&P 500 mini	0.0724
8	Nasdaq	0.0629
9	Toronto	0.0569
10	Nikkei	0.065
11	Hang Seng	0.078
12	Taiwan	0.0719
13	Singapore	0.0706
14	2-year US Govt. Bonds	0.0058
15	5-year US Govt. Bonds	0.0196
16	10-year US Govt. Bonds	0.0328
17	30-year US Govt. Bonds	0.0438
18	2-year German Govt. Bonds	0.0079
19	5 year German Govt. Bonds	0.0165
20	10 year German Govt. Bonds	0.0228
21	Long German Bonds	0.0274
22	Japanese Govt. Bonds	0.0109
23	Gilt (UK Govt.)	0.0298
24	Dollar index	0
25	Euro/Dollar	0
26	Swiss Frank/Dollar	0
27	British Pound/Dollar	0
28	Commodities	0

Table 4.1. *Case study global portfolio: Assets comprising the portfolio and their respective premia*

4.7.3. *Convergence characteristics of DE HOF*

The convergence characteristics of DE HOF were studied by observing its P Measure. P Measure as a reliable metric for studying the convergence of Differential Evolution algorithms was discussed in Chapter 2, section 2.5.5. Those generations in which the population of individuals contributed a best-fit individual to the Hall of Fame and the P Measure values of the populations concerned, were recorded. Figure 4.3 illustrates the trace of P Measure values captured for five different runs of the DE HOF algorithm. It can be clearly seen that while the P Measure values remain chaotic until about 400 generations, the values thereafter begin crowding round a small region before slumping and remaining close to zero from then on. This behavior indicates that the individuals in the population have begun crowding round the optimal solution, thereby resulting in their radii reaching 0. In all, DE HOF displayed convergence in less than 600 generations for the problem considered.

Parameter	Description	Remarks
Portfolio size	28 assets	
Composition of assets in the portfolio	Equity Indices: 13	Asset Serial Numbers: 1-13
	Bonds: 10	Asset Serial Numbers: 14-23
	Currencies: 4	Asset Serial Numbers: 24-27
	Commodities: 1	Asset Serial Number: 28
Risk Budget	12.5%	
Portfolio objective	Maximize Sharpe Ratio	Equations [4.19]-[4.20]
Nature of the portfolio	Leveraged, fully invested and long-short	
Basic constraint	Fully invested portfolio	Equation [4.10] $$\sum_{i=1}^{28} w_i = 1$$
Investor defined asset classes and constraints imposed on them	Leveraged weights for Equity Indices and Bonds (Asset Serial Nos. : 1-23) Mandatory investment.	Equation [4.11] $w_i^+ > 0, i = 1, 2, ...23$ Lower bound set as 0.001
	Leveraged weights for commodities. (Asset Serial No. : 28) Optional investment.	Equation [4.12] $w_i^{Spl} \geq 0, i = 28$
	Leveraged long-short weights for Currencies (Asset Serial Nos.: 24-27)	Equation [4.13] $-a_i \leq w_i^{Free} \leq b_i, i = 24, ...27$ with free bounds

Table 4.2. *Case study global portfolio: Problem parameters and Portfolio Constraints defined by the investor*

Parameter	Description
Population size	300
Individual length	28
Generations	1000
Scale factor β_S	0.5
Probability of recombination p_r	0.87
(C, α, β)	(0.5, 2, 2)

Table 4.3. *Case study global portfolio: DE HOF control parameters*

Maximal Sharpe Ratio	Portfolio risk	Portfolio return
1.5085	0.0151	0.0228

Table 4.4. *Case study global portfolio: Risk/Return Characteristics of the optimal portfolio obtained by DE HOF*

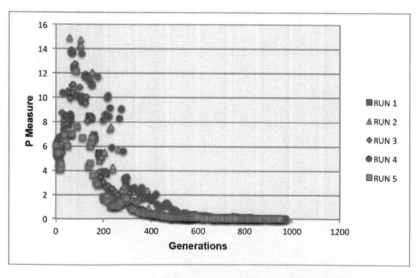

Figure 4.3. *Case study global portfolio: Convergence characteristics of DE HOF- Trace of P Measure values in five sample runs of 1,000 generations each (for a color version of this figure, see www.iste.co.uk/pai/metaheuristics.zip)*

Asset Serial No.	Asset Description	Optimal weights (w_i)	Marginal contribution to risk (m_i)	$w_i.m_i$	Whether Risk Budgeting constraint is satisfied? ($w_i.m_i$) - (12.5% of portfolio risk) ≤ 0 ?
1	Euro Stoxx	0.0010	0.0682	0.0001	-0.0018
2	Amsterdam	0.0255	0.0633	0.0016	-0.0003
3	DAX	0.0010	0.0624	0.0001	-0.0018
4	CAC 40	0.0010	0.0678	0.0001	-0.0018
5	IBEX 35	0.0010	0.0644	0.0001	-0.0018
6	FTSE 100	0.0214	0.0619	0.0013	-0.0006
7	S&P 500 mini	0.0358	0.0523	0.0019	-0.0000
8	Nasdaq	0.0010	0.0572	0.0001	-0.0018
9	Toronto	0.0046	0.0422	0.0002	-0.0017
10	Nikkei	0.0010	0.0491	0.0000	-0.0018
11	Hang Seng	0.0193	0.0566	0.0011	-0.0008
12	Taiwan	0.0073	0.0553	0.0004	-0.0015
13	Singapore	0.0304	0.0520	0.0016	-0.0003
14	2-year US Govt. Bonds	0.0797	0.0037	0.0003	-0.0016
15	5-year US Govt. Bonds	0.0012	0.0132	0.0000	-0.0019
16	10-year US Govt. Bonds	0.0929	0.0201	0.0019	0.0000
17	30-year US Govt. Bonds	0.0010	0.0290	0.0000	-0.0019
18	2-year German Govt. Bonds	0.1166	0.0050	0.0006	-0.0013
19	5 year German Govt. Bonds	0.0010	0.0118	0.0000	-0.0019
20	10 year German Govt. Bonds	0.0010	0.0173	0.0000	-0.0019
21	Long German Bonds	0.0010	0.0311	0.0000	-0.0019
22	Japanese Govt. Bonds	0.3597	0.0052	0.0019	-0.0000
23	Gilt (UK Govt.)	0.0938	0.0197	0.0018	-0.0000
24	Dollar index	0.0639	-0.0001	0.0000	-0.0019
25	Euro/Dollar	0.0087	0.0018	0.0000	-0.0019
26	Swiss Frank/Dollar	0.0074	0.0016	0.0000	-0.0019
27	British Pound/Dollar	0.0217	0.0022	0.0000	-0.0018
28	Commodities	0	0.0264	0	-0.0019
	Total	$\sum_{i=1}^{28} w_i = 1$		$\sum_{i=1}^{28} w_i.m_i = 0.0151$	

Table 4.5. *Case study global portfolio: Weight characteristics of the Optimal Risk-Budgeted Portfolio obtained by DE HOF with portfolio risk = 0.0151 and portfolio return = 0.0228*

DEHOF Runs	Sharpe Ratio	Portfolio Risk	Portfolio Return
RUN 1	1.5069	0.0159	0.0240
RUN 2	1.5084	0.0152	0.0229
RUN 3	1.5082	0.0147	0.0222
RUN 4	1.5087	0.0148	0.0224
RUN 5	1.5052	0.0162	0.0244
RUN 6	1.5072	0.0160	0.0241
RUN 7	1.5077	0.0159	0.0239
RUN 8	1.5077	0.0159	0.0240
RUN 9	1.4998	0.0177	0.0226
RUN 10	1.4995	0.0169	0.0253

Table 4.6. *Case study global portfolio: risk/return characteristics of the optimal portfolios obtained by DE HOF during various runs*

4.8. MATLAB® demonstrations

In this section we demonstrate MATLAB® functions and programs associated with the optimization of Risk-Budgeted portfolios as listed below. The coding style has been kept simple and direct to favor novices in MATLAB.

A. Generating the random initial population between (-c, c) for any integer c.

B. Repair strategy.

C. Computing fitness functions using the penalized objective function.

D. Generation cycles of DE HOF during Risk budgeted portfolio optimization.

A. *Generating the random initial population between (-c, c) for any integer c*

Since the Risk-budgeted portfolio optimization problem demands a leveraged long-short portfolio with the constraint defined by [4.13] permitting free bounds on its long-short portfolio mix, DE HOF first generates a random initial population of individuals whose genes (portfolio weights) have values between (-c, c) for some integer c. Figure 4.4 illustrates the MATLAB® program fragment to generate the random initial population for c = 3, that is (-3, 3).

B. *Repair strategy*

As was discussed in section 4.5, Repairing weights is a very crucial phase in DE HOF's working since it serves to standardize weights represented by each individual in the population (parent or offspring) and transform the populations to represent feasible solution sets that satisfy the linear constraints imposed on them ([4.10]–[4.13]).

```
. . .
default_low_bound = -3;
default_up_bound = 3;
popln_size = 300;
individual_length = 28; % portfolio size
. . .
% generate initial random population of individuals
initial_popln = default_low_bound +
        (default_up_bound-default_low_bound)
            *rand(popln_size, individual_length);
. . .
```

Figure 4.4. *MATLAB® program fragment to enable DE HOF*
generate initial random population with bounds (-3, 3) (for a color
version of this figure, see www.iste.co.uk/pai/metaheuristics.zip)

The six-step Repair strategy, discussed in section 4.5, was implemented by breaking down its tasks and encasing them in three MATLAB® functions, namely satisfy_lowbounds, weightstdzn and std_excesswgts, that are collectively executed in a sequence, to complete the weight repairing job. Thus Step 1, was encased in the function satisfy_lowbounds, Step 2 in the function weightstdzn and steps 3, 4, 5 and 6, in function std_excesswgts, with function weightstdzn calling function std_excesswgts as a sub function to tackle the steps assigned.

Figure 4.5 illustrates the function satisfy_lowbounds, where weight_mat is a weight matrix of size [row_mat, col_mat] representing the population of individuals which need to be standardized, low_bounds is the vector of lower bounds for each of the asset weights and assetsindx is the list of asset indices whose weights need to satisfy their mandatory lower bounds. Thus for the global portfolio discussed in section 4.7 and whose composition was listed in Table 4.2, the assets representing equity indices, bonds and commodities were assigned lower bounds which need to be satisfied before the rest of the weight standardization process takes place. satisfy_lowbounds examines such of these weights of the assets specified and upgrades their weights.

Figures 4.6 and 4.7 show the functions weightstdzn and std_excesswgts respectively. The actions performed in Step 2 of the Repair strategy can be clearly seen in the function weightstdzn. std_excesswgts is invoked to standardize weights in each individual of the population (weight_vec) using steps 3–6. Figure 4.8 illustrates how the Repair strategy is invoked on a population of individuals, initial_popln for example to obtain the standardized population of individuals initial_popln_stdz that satisfies all the linear constraints represented by [4.10]–[4.13] and hence represents a feasible solution set.

```
function upgraded_weight_mat =
satisfy_lowbounds(weight_mat, low_bounds,
assetsindx)

[row_mat, col_mat]=size(weight_mat);
len = length(assetsindx);
for j=1:len
    j_indx = assetsindx(j);
    for i=1:row_mat
    if (weight_mat(i,j_indx) < low_bounds(j_indx))
        weight_mat(i,j_indx) = low_bounds(j_indx);
    end
    end
end
    upgraded_weight_mat = weight_mat;
end
```

Figure 4.5. *MATLAB® function for handling Repair strategy (Step 1) (for a color version of this figure, see www.iste.co.uk/pai/metaheuristics.zip)*

```
% Step 2 of Repair strategy
function std_weight_mat = weightstdzn(weight_mat,
                          low_bounds, assetsindx)
[row_mat, col_mat]=size(weight_mat);

for i=1:row_mat

    Sum_Wgts = sum(weight_mat(i,:));
    if (Sum_Wgts >1)
        weight_mat(i,:)=
        std_excesswgts(weight_mat(i,:),low_bounds,
                          assetsindx);
    elseif (Sum_Wgts <1)
        Incr_amt = (1-Sum_Wgts)/col_mat;
        weight_mat(i,:)= weight_mat(i,:)+Incr_amt;
    else
        continue
    end
end
std_weight_mat = weight_mat;
end
```

Figure 4.6. *MATLAB® function for handling Repair strategy (Step 2, partially) (for a color version of this figure, see www.iste.co.uk/pai/metaheuristics.zip)*

C. *Computing fitness functions using the penalized objective function*

The non-linear risk-budgeting constraint was tackled using Joines and Houck's dynamic penalty function method and absorbed into the objective function as shown in [4.19]–[4.20]. As already known, objective functions serve to act as fitness functions and help to determine the best-fit/worst-fit individuals to ensure survival of the fittest and thus keep the evolutionary process in progress.

```
function std_weight_vec =
  std_excesswgts(weight_vec, low_bounds,assetsindx)
[row_mat, col_mat]=size(weight_vec);

% Step 2 Contd.
% find excess weights and shear off equal portions of
% the excess from  each of the weights

Sum_Wgts =sum(weight_vec);
Decr_amt = (Sum_Wgts-1)/col_mat;
weight_vec= weight_vec-Decr_amt;

% Steps  3, 4 and 5 of Repair Strategy
% partition weights as R and Q
R=[];
c_R=0;
len= length(assetsindx);
for j=1:len
 j_indx= assetsindx(j);
 if (weight_vec(1,j_indx)< low_bounds(j_indx))
    weight_vec(1,j_indx)= low_bounds(j_indx);
    c_R = c_R+1;
   R(c_R) = j_indx;
 end
end

% Q and R work to adjust excess weights
exit_flag = true;
while (exit_flag == true)
   exit_flag = false;
   Q = setdiff([1:col_mat], R);
   L = sum(weight_vec);
   F = L-1;
   len_Q= length(Q);
   Decr_amt=F/len_Q;
```

Figure 4.7. *MATLAB® function for handling Repair strategy (Step 2 Contd. and steps 3, 4 and 5) (for a color version of this figure, see www.iste.co.uk/pai/metaheuristics.zip)*

Figure 4.9 illustrates the MATLAB® function to compute the constraint violation function represented by $\psi(\overline{w},\overline{m},t)$ in [4.20] for the population of individuals weight_mat, whose fitness is to be computed. C_param, beta_param, alpha_param indicate the dynamic penalty function parameters (C, α, β), gencount the generation count t, covar_mat the variance-covariance matrix V and riskbudget, the risk budget needed as input to compute the penalty functions $\varphi_k(w_k,m_k)$ for the risk-budgeting constraint with penalty coefficients G_k. The portfolio risk σ_P and the marginal contributions to risk m_i are computed within the function. The function returns the constraint violation function values ψ and the penalties G (only to know which of those individuals satisfied the risk budgeting constraint and thereby reported zero penalties).

```
for j = 1: len_Q
    weight_vec(1, Q(j)) = weight_vec(1,Q(j))-
                                    Decr_amt;
    if (ismember(Q(j), assetsindx))
        if ( weight_vec(1, Q(j)) <
                low_bounds(Q(j)))
        weight_vec(1, Q(j)) =
                        low_bounds(Q(j));

    exit_flag = true;
        c_R = c_R+1;
        R(c_R) = Q(j);
        end
    end
  end
end % end while

% Step 6 of Repair Strategy
Sum_Wgts =sum(weight_vec);
if(Sum_Wgts <1)
 Incr_amt = (1-Sum_Wgts)/col_mat;
  weight_vec = weight_vec+Incr_amt;
end

std_weight_vec = weight_vec;
end
```

Figure 4.7. *Contd.*

Figure 4.10 illustrates the MATLAB® function comp_fitness which calculate the fitness values for the population of individuals using [4.19]. The constraint violation function ψ computed by function compute_constrvioln_fn (Figure 4.9) is used as input psi_fun, to obtain the fitness values.

```
...
initial_popln_levrg =
satisfy_lowbound(initial_popln, low_bounds,
                            assetsindx);

initial_popln_stdz =
weightstdzn(initial_popln_levrg, low_bounds,
                            assetsindx) ;

...
```

Figure 4.8. *MATLAB® code fragment demonstrating Repair strategy working on the initial random population of individuals*

```
function  [G, psi]  = compute_constrvioln_fn(
     weight_mat, covar_mat, riskbudget, C_param,
     beta_param, alpha_param, gencount)

[row_mat, col_mat]= size(weight_mat);

for i=1:row_mat

  % Select each individual from the population
  x_individual = weight_mat(i,:);

  % Compute portfolio risk
  portfolio_risk = sqrt(x_individual * covar_mat *
                                     x_individual');

  % Compute Marginal contribution to risk
  mcr =  (covar_mat * x_individual')
                                /portfolio_risk;

  % Compute function phi
  phi = (x_individual.*mcr')-(riskbudget/100)
                          *portfolio_risk;

  % Compute penalties g
  g = 1-(phi <=0);
  G(i,:) = g;

  % Compute penalty term
  penalty_term=
          power(C_param*gencount,alpha_param);

  % Compute  constraint violation function psi
  psi(i) =penalty_term *sum( g.*power(phi,
                  beta_param));
end
```

Figure 4.9. *MATLAB® function to compute constraint violation function represented by [4.20] for a population (for a color version of this figure, see www.iste.co.uk/pai/metaheuristics.zip)*

D. *Generation cycles of DE HOF during Risk-budgeted portfolio optimization*

Figure 4.11 illustrates the MATLAB® code fragment that implements the generation cycles of DE HOF. The code fragment shows a partial implementation of DE HOF's process flow chart shown in Figure 4.2.

initial_popln prior to its entry into the generation cycle loop and before being set as the parent population, is assumed to have been repaired with all its fitness values and penalty terms ready. The segment of code to undertake this has not been shown in Figure 4.11.

```
function popln_fitness = comp_fitness(popln_mat,
            premia_dat, covariance_dat,  psi_fun)

[popln_size,~]=size(popln_mat);

for i = 1: popln_size

 weight = popln mat(i,:);
 objfunc_val(i) =  -((premia_dat * weight')/
 sqrt(weight*covariance_dat * weight'))+ psi_fun(i);

end
popln_fitness = objfunc_val;
end
```

Figure 4.10. *MATLAB® function to compute fitness function values of the population of individuals, using [4.19] (for a color version of this figure, see www.iste.co.uk/pai/metaheuristics.zip)*

The entry into Hall of Fame was made strict by ensuring that only that individual whose fitness was better than the one existing in the Hall of Fame and whose penalty terms were all zeros (all asset weights comply with the risk-budgeting constraint) was deemed qualified to compete with the individual in the Hall of Fame. The code segment to this effect has been shown in the program.

```
. . .

% Beginning of generation cycles
while (gen_indx <= total_generations)

% Set parent population, fitness and constraint violation
% functions

 feas_parent_popln = initial_popln;
 feas_parent_popln_fitness = initial_popln_fitness;
 GP = GI;
 psi_p = psi_i;

% perform mutation to generate trial vectors
 trial_vector_popln = DE_mutation(feas_parent_popln, beta,
 popln_size);
```

```
% generate offspring population using the parent and
% trial vector  populations
offsprng_popln_raw = DE_bin_Crossover(feas_parent_popln,
        trial_vector_popln, pr_recombi, chromosm_length);

% undertake weight repair of offspring population
offsprng_popln_lev =
satisfy_lowbounds(offsprng_popln_raw,
                              bounds,bound_asset_indx);
offsprng_popln = weight.stdzn(offsprng_popln_lev, bounds,
                              bound_asset_indx);

% compute constraint violation function for the offspring
% population
[GO, psi_o]  = compute_constrvioln_fn( offsprng_popln,
  cv, risk_budget, C_dp, beta_dp, alpha_dp, gen_indx );

% compute fitness of the offspring population
offsprng_popln_fitness =
          comp_fitness(offsprng_popln,premia, cv, psi_o);

% set the population for the next generation
[next_gen pool, next_gen_pool fitness,  Penalty, Psi_fun]
    - DE_selection_penalty(feas_parent_popln, GP, psi_p,
        feas_parent popln_fitness, offsprng_popln,
        GO,  psi_o, offsprng_popln_fitness, popln size);
% Individuals compete to enter Hall of Fame

for i=1:popln_size
    if (isequal(Penalty(i,:), zeros(1, portfolio_size)))
        if (next_gen_pool_fitness(i)< HOF_fitness)
            HOF_fitness = next_gen_pool_fitness(i);
            HOF_individual = next_gen_pool(i,:);
        end
      else continue;
    end

  gen_indx = gen_indx + 1;
 % move  to the next generation
  initial_popln = next_gen_pool;
  initial_popln_fitness= next_gen_pool_fitness;
  GI = Penalty;
  psi_i= Psi_fun;
end                             % end of a generation cycle
. . .
```

Figure 4.11. *MATLAB® code fragment illustrating the generation cycles of DE HOF (for a color version of this figure, see www.iste.co.uk/pai/metaheuristics.zip)*

Project

A risk aggressive investor decides to invest in 20 high beta stocks and five bonds. He decides to opt for a Risk-budgeted portfolio optimization model hoping that risk budgets would help "cushion" the adverse effects of risk while helping him gain handsome returns. He decides on the following objective function and constraints:

(i) maximize Sharpe Ratio of the portfolio.

(ii) impose a Risk Budget of 15.5% with regard to the absolute contribution to risk of the assets chosen.

(iii) opt for a 60/40 fully invested portfolio with 60% of his capital invested on equities and 40% on bonds.

(a) Formulate the mathematical model reflecting the investor's choices.

(b) If you chose to tackle the asset class constraints listed in (iii) using Repair strategy, how would your strategy work to ensure that a random set of weights repairs itself to satisfy the constraints?

(c) Transform the mathematical model using Joines and Houck's Dynamic Penalty function.

(d) Implement DE HOF with suitable modifications in MATLAB®, for the transformed problem model, to arrive at the optimal portfolio. What was the optimal portfolio arrived at by DE HOF? Was the investor happy with the Sharpe Ratio obtained? Is it a 60/40 portfolio as he wished? Tabulate the results for various runs.

(e) Would DE HOF have yielded better results if experimented with other DE strategies? (see Chapter 2, section 2.5.3) Explore and tabulate the results.

Suggested Further Reading

Pai and Michel's [PAI 11] paper on "*Metaheuristic Optimization of Risk Budgeted Global Asset Allocation Portfolios*" details the implementation of the Risk-budgeted portfolio optimization model formulated as a single criterion objective function problem after absorbing the non-linear risk budgeting constraint with the help of Joines and Houck's dynamic penalty functions, as discussed in this chapter.

Alternatively, it is also possible to handle complex constraints by transforming them into objective functions and solving the problem model as a *Multi-objective optimization* problem model. The presence of multiple objectives conflicting with one another naturally results in multiple trade-off optimal solutions. Classical methods can at best find one solution in one run. In contrast, Metaheuristics due to their population-based search processes have exhibited the potential to explore multiple optimal solutions to such problems and therefore have turned out to be ideal candidates to solve multi-objective optimization problems.

Pai [PAI 14] attempted *Multi-objective Differential Evolution* (MODE)-based solution for the Risk-budgeted portfolio optimization problem model discussed in this chapter by framing the non-linear Risk Budgeting constraint as another objective function. While the quality of portfolios obtained by MODE was on par with those obtained by DE HOF with regard to the maximal Sharpe Ratios obtained, the convergence characteristics of MODE were superior to those of DE HOF.

Yann Collette and Patrick Siarry's book on *Multiobjective Optimization Principles and Case Studies* [COL 04], Deb's book on *Multi-Objective Optimization using Evolutionary Algorithms* [DEB 03] and Coello *et al.'s* book on *Evolutionary Algorithms for solving Multi-Objective Problems* [COE 07] are good textbooks to know more about multi-objective metaheuristic optimization.

While Risk based portfolio construction methods such as Maximum Diversification, Minimum Variance, Equal-Weighted portfolios and Risk Parity, to list the most popular, have been followed by the investment and finance industry, a generic and a unifying analytical framework that subsumes the aforementioned strategies has been proposed by Emmanuel Jurczenko *et al.*, [JUR 13, JUR 15]. Of their works, the one entitled *Generalized Risk-Based Investing*, was awarded the INQUIRE-EUROPE First Prize during the 2013 Autumn Seminar.

Heuristic Optimization of Equity Market Neutral Portfolios

This chapter discusses metaheuristic optimization of equity market neutral portfolios, a popular mode of portfolio construction. A naively posed problem model to illustrate the portfolio construction technique is discussed first. A risk-budget constrained formulation of the problem model and its implementation using a refined version of Differential Evolution with Hall of Fame (*DE/Rand5/Dir4*) algorithm is discussed next. The experimental results and analyses of the risk budgeted equity market neutral portfolio are then detailed. Finally, MATLAB® demonstrations of the functions and code fragments that illustrate the working of DE/Rand5/Dir4 based optimization for the risk-budgeted equity market neutral portfolio problem are presented.

5.1. Market neutral portfolio

Market neutral investing is a portfolio construction technique which encourages the selection of *both long and short positions from the same asset class* so that the risk would be neutralized. An asset class could be a specific sector or industry or country etc. While those stocks which are expected to appreciate in value are held long, those stocks which are expected to depreciate in value are held short. If the securities held, long and short that is, behave as intended and if the long positions outperform those of the short positions, then the spread between the long and short position returns will yield positive portfolio returns. In a general case however, based on the movements of the markets, the gains or losses made by the long positions can be approximately offset by similar size losses or gains made by the short positions.

The objective of market neutral portfolios ultimately is to construct a portfolio whose performance is independent of the broad market moves. A market neutral strategy "... is designed to be riskless in terms of its exposure to the relevant market benchmark..." [JAC 05]. However, it retains the individual asset returns and risks which due to the long and short nature of the assets, offset themselves to some degree with the spreads between them deriving returns. Nonetheless, extreme market conditions can impede the expected performance of the portfolio and therefore just as it is with other investment strategies, an insightful implementation of the strategy is called for.

Equity market neutral portfolio

An *equity market neutral portfolio* is a market neutral portfolio confined to the asset class of equities alone. Thus the portfolio is a mix of long positions and short positions that are equities and hence homogenous in nature, carefully selected so that they exhibit low correlations to the broader market and to one another. Equity market neutral portfolios exhibit superior risk-to-reward ratios either by increasing returns or decreasing volatilities. Equity market neutral portfolios can also be leveraged to earn higher returns through market protection and investment exposure. In fact it can be expected that leveraged equity market neutral portfolios may turn out to be much less riskier than their unleveraged long-only portfolio counterparts.

EXAMPLE.– Consider an equity market neutral portfolio with 20 stocks in a specific sector, 10 of which are longed since these stocks are expected to outperform and 10 of which are shorted since these stocks are expected to underperform. The longed stocks yield returns when the prices rise and the shorted stocks yield returns when the prices decline. Now whichever direction the market moves, it matters little, for the gains of one will offset the losses of the other and the spread between the returns is the yield of the portfolio.

The return of an equity market neutral portfolio can be measured as the weighted return of the long / short positions comprising it. The portfolio risk is measured as the standard deviation of the asset returns. An equity market neutral portfolio's weights should *sum to zero* to ensure that net equity exposure is zero. Also, equity market neutral portfolios target zero portfolio beta to ensure riskless exposure while yielding an expected return that is greater than the risk free lending rate.

Thus for an equity market neutral portfolio P if $W = (w_1, w_2, w_3, ... w_N)$ are the asset weights, w_i^+, w_i^- are the weights of the long and short positions comprising the portfolio P respectively and μ_i are the asset returns, then the portfolio return is given by

$$\sum_{i=1}^{N} w_i . \mu_i ,$$

[5.1]

the portfolio risk σ_P is given by

$$\sigma_P = \sqrt{W.V.W'}$$

[5.2]

where V is the variance-covariance matrix of asset returns.

The net equity exposure constraint is given by

$$\sum_{i=1}^{N} w_i = \sum_{j} w_j^+ + \sum_{k} w_k^- = 0, \quad j \neq k$$

[5.3]

and the portfolio beta constraint is given by

$$\left| \sum_{i=1}^{N} \beta_i \, w_i \right| < c$$

[5.4]

where c is a constant close to zero.

Selection of long and short positions for equity market neutral portfolio

The selection of long and short positions that revolves round the volatility of the stocks, is very crucial to market neutral investing. A variety of strategies exist and there is no consensus on which of these is the best.

A common selection method is to use *accounting variables* such as dividend payout ratio, dividend yield, market value, the company's assets, net income volatility, debt ratio etc. to assess the volatility of the stocks. In the absence of accounting variables, *market based variables* could be adopted. Thus one could go long on low risk stocks and go short on high risk stocks, or adopting a *contrarian* approach could go long on stocks that have lost value and short on stocks that have gained much already. A *risk differential* approach that involves shorting high volatility stocks and longing low volatility stocks, with the volatilities determined from the historic returns of the stocks could also be adopted. A *contrarian* approach with regard to historic returns would be to go short on stocks that over performed their betas and go long on stocks that underperformed their betas.

In this chapter, adopting a risk differential approach and subscribing to Blitz and Vliet's [BLI 07] work, the long and short positions were determined by a straightforward ranking of the volatilities of stock based on historical returns of the stocks. Blitz and Vliet asserted the volatility effect where "…low risk stocks exhibit significantly higher risk-adjusted returns than the market portfolio, while high risk stocks significantly underperform on a risk-adjusted basis…." Hence, the stocks were ranked based on their historic return volatilities and while the top percentile of stocks (low volatilities) were kept long, the bottom percentile of stocks (high volatilities) were kept short.

EXAMPLE 1.– *Equity market neutral portfolio over S&P BSE200 index*

Consider the historic return data set of equity stocks belonging to S&P BSE200 index (Bombay Stock Exchange, India, March 1999–March 2009). We compute the historic volatilities of the stocks as the square root of the diagonal of the variance-covariance matrix of daily returns and rank them according to their volatilities. Table 5.1 shows the stocks belonging to the top 15 percentile of the stocks (low volatilities). The betas estimated for the stocks and their daily mean returns (%) have also been shown in the table. The stocks categorized as L, indicate the long positions that are selected for the market neutral portfolio. Table 5.2 shows the bottom 15 percentile of the stocks (high volatilities) selected for the short positions labeled as S, for the equity market neutral portfolio. The betas of the shorted stocks and their daily returns (%) are also shown in the table. The equity market neutral portfolio comprises 38 assets as long and short positions.

EXAMPLE 2.– *Equity market neutral portfolio over Nikkei225 index*

For the historical data set for Nikkei225 index (Tokyo Stock Exchange, Japan, March 1999–March 2009) we consider an equity market neutral portfolio made up of top 15 percentile of its stocks ranked according to historic volatility, labeled as long positions and bottom 15 percentile of stocks labeled as short positions, with a total of 58 assets comprising the portfolio. Table 5.3 shows the historic volatilities and betas of the long positions and Table 5.4 shows the same for the short positions.

5.2. Optimizing a naïve equity market neutral portfolio

We define a naïve equity market neutral portfolio problem model whose objective is to maximize the expected portfolio return subject to the constraints that the net market exposure must be zero, the portfolio beta should be close to zero, with bounds laid on the weights of the long and short positions constituting the portfolio and budget constraints imposed on the long and short positions. The long (L) and short (S) positions for the portfolio were selected as the top x percentile and bottom x percentile of the stocks ranked according to their historic volatilities respectively, as discussed in the earlier section. The problem model is defined by the following mathematical formulation:

Serial Number	Stock	Beta value	Historical volatility	Mean daily returns (%)
1	ASIAN_PAINTS_LTD	0.38	29.92	0.09
2	NESTLE_INDIA_LIMITED	0.30	30.64	0.06
3	COLGATE_PALMOLIVE_(INDIA)	0.49	32.97	0.06
4	CASTROL_(INDIA)_LIMITED	0.48	34.31	0.01
5	GLAXOSMITHKLINE_PHARMACEUTIC	0.54	35.15	0.04
6	HINDUSTAN_UNILEVER_LIMITED	0.55	35.33	0.02
7	BOSCH_LIMITED	0.40	35.59	0.11
8	ITC_LTD	0.60	37.38	0.06
9	INDIAN_HOTELS_CO_LIMITED	0.76	40.01	0.03
10	CIPLA_LTD	0.64	40.04	0.10
11	HDFC_BANK_LIMITED	0.70	40.16	0.14
12	HERO_HONDA_MOTORS_LIMITED	0.56	40.88	0.10
13	MADRAS_CEMENTS_LIMITED	0.77	40.92	0.08
14	RELIANCE_INDUSTRIES_LIMITED	0.95	41.19	0.12
15	TATA_TEA_LTD	0.83	41.29	0.04
16	AMBUJA_CEMENTS_LIMITED	0.81	41.47	0.08
17	ABB_LTD_INDIA	0.79	41.51	0.08
18	PIRAMAL_HEALTHCARE_LIMITED	0.71	41.71	0.08
19	INDIAN_OIL_CORPORATION_LTD	0.79	42.50	0.09

Table 5.1. Long positions selected as top 15 percentile of the stocks ranked according to their historic volatilities, for the equity market neutral portfolio over S&P BSE 200 Index (March 1999–March 2009)

$$Max\left(\sum_{i=1}^{N} w_i.\mu_i\right) \quad \text{(Maximize expected portfolio return)} \qquad [5.5]$$

subject to

$$0 < w_i^+ \le 1 \qquad \text{(bound constraints on long positions)} \qquad [5.6]$$

$$-1 \le w_i^- < 0 \qquad \text{(bound constraints on short positions)} \qquad [5.7]$$

$$\sum_{i=1}^{N} w_i = 0 \qquad \text{(net market exposure constraint)} \qquad [5.8]$$

$$\sum_{i \in L} w_i^+ = 1 \qquad \text{(budget constraint on long positions)} \qquad [5.9]$$

$$\sum_{i \in S} w_i^- = -1 \qquad \text{(budget constraint on short positions)} \qquad [5.10]$$

and $\left| \sum_{i=1}^{N} \beta_i . w_i \right| \le c \qquad \text{(portfolio beta constraint)} \qquad [5.11]$

Serial Number	Stock	Beta value	Historical volatility	Mean daily returns (%)
1	UNITECH_LIMITED	0.93	67.90	0.26
2	PANTALOON_RETAIL_INDIA_LTD	1.04	68.15	0.22
3	GTL_LTD	1.24	68.52	0.10
4	JSW_STEEL_LIMITED	1.32	68.79	0.12
5	NEYVELI_LIGNITE_CORPORATION	1.38	71.60	0.17
6	ESSAR_SHIPPING_PORTS_&_LOGS	1.18	73.26	0.15
7	MERCATOR_LINES_LIMITED	1.16	73.38	0.27
8	IFCI_LIMITED	1.46	73.70	0.11
9	UNITED_BREWERIES_HOLDINGS_LT	1.05	74.84	0.16
10	PRAJ_INDUSTRIES_LIMITED	1.09	80.89	0.29
11	SHRIRAM_TRANSPORT_FINANCE	0.72	83.06	0.29
12	VIDEOCON_INDUSTRIES_LTD	0.86	83.50	0.23
13	FINANCIAL_TECHN_(INDIA)_LTD	1.38	88.42	0.27
14	ISPAT_INDUSTRIES_LTD	1.49	96.05	0.19
15	ESSAR_OIL_LTD	1.30	100.95	0.22
16	WELSPUN-GUJARAT_STAHL_LTD	1.35	118.18	0.36
17	GUJARAT_NRE_COKE_LTD	1.22	119.92	0.41
18	IVRCL_INFRASTRUCTURES_&_PROJ	1.57	173.14	0.42
19	UNITED_PHOSPHORUS_LTD	4.20	480.99	0.77

Table 5.2. *Short positions selected as bottom 15 percentile of the stocks ranked according to their historic volatilities, for the equity market neutral portfolio over S&P BSE 200 Index (March 1999–March 2009)*

The single objective optimization problem with linear constraints can be easily solved using linear programming to obtain the optimal equity market neutral portfolio. We discuss optimization of two equity market neutral portfolios invested over S&P BSE200 (March 1999–March 2009) and Nikkei225 (March 1999–March 2009) respectively, in the examples that follow, to illustrate the theory. The MATLAB® Toolbox implementation of the optimization model using its linear programming function has been discussed in section 5.6.

EXAMPLE 3.– *Optimal equity market neutral portfolio over S&P BSE200 index: Portfolio A*

Portfolio A alludes to an equity market neutral portfolio over S&P BSE200 index (March 1999–March 2009) with the top 15 percentile of stocks ranked according to their historic return volatility chosen as long positions L and the bottom 15 percentile of the ranked stocks chosen as short positions S comprising the portfolio, following Blitz and Vliet's observation [BLI 07]. Table 5.1 lists the 19 stocks that are labeled as long positions L and Table 5.2 the 19 stocks that are labeled as short positions S, which make up the portfolio of 38 stocks. The objective and constraints to be satisfied by Portfolio A are represented using [5.5]–[5.11]. For [5.6] and [5.7] representing the bound constraints for L and S respectively, the lower and upper bounds were set as 0.001 and -0.001 respectively, that is $0.001 \le w_i^l \le 1$ and $-1 \le w_i^- \le -0.001$. The constant c for the portfolio beta constraint was set to 0.1.

Table 5.5 illustrates the optimal weights obtained using linear programming for Portfolio A and the characteristics of the optimal portfolio. It can be seen in Table 5.5 that all the constraints imposed on Portfolio A, represented by [5.6]–[5.11] are satisfied. The annualized risk of the optimal equity market neutral portfolio is 60.127% and the expected portfolio annual return is -11.763%.

EXAMPLE 4.– *Optimal equity market neutral portfolio over S&P BSE200 index: Portfolio B*

Portfolio B alludes to another equity market neutral portfolio over S&P BSE200 index (March 1999–March 2009) with a larger composition of top 25 percentile of the stocks ranked according to their historic return volatility labeled as long positions L and the bottom 25 percentile of the ranked stocks labeled as short positions S comprising the portfolio. Thus the portfolio comprised 64 stocks, 32 labeled as L and the remaining labeled as S. Repeating the exercise that was undertaken for Portfolio A with the same constraints, resulted in an optimal portfolio whose summarized characteristics have been tabulated in Table 5.6.

Serial Number	Stock	Beta value	Historical volatility	Mean daily returns (%)
1	CHUBU_ELECTRIC_POWER_CO_INC	0.34	22.99	0.013
2	KANSAI_ELECTRIC_POWER_CO_INC	0.34	23.38	0.010
3	TOBU_RAILWAY_CO_LTD	0.60	25.03	0.026
4	TOKYO_ELECTRIC_POWER_CO_INC	0.33	25.61	0.015
5	ODAKYU_ELECTRIC_RAILWAY_CO	0.58	25.68	0.036
6	ASAHI_BREWERIES_LTD	0.48	27.17	0.002
7	TOKYO_GAS_CO_LTD	0.32	27.77	0.026
8	KEIO_CORP	0.62	28.36	0.018
9	EAST_JAPAN_RAILWAY_CO	0.41	29.35	0.005
10	KIRIN_HOLDINGS_CO_LTD	0.60	29.57	0.000
11	OSAKA_GAS_CO_LTD	0.41	29.70	0.014
12	AJINOMOTO_CO_INC	0.54	29.72	-0.011
13	KIKKOMAN_CORP	0.70	29.96	0.017
14	KAO_CORP	0.42	29.98	0.007
15	NISSHIN_SEIFUN_GROUP_INC	0.69	30.20	0.026
16	ALL_NIPPON_AIRWAYS_CO_LTD	0.61	30.22	0.023
17	PANASONIC_ELECTRIC_WORKS_CO	0.78	30.82	-0.007
18	TAKEDA_PHARMACEUTICAL_CO_LTD	0.61	31.02	0.012
19	SHISEIDO_CO_LTD	0.58	31.35	0.015
20	WEST_JAPAN_RAILWAY_CO	0.47	31.37	0.002
21	KEISEI_ELECTRIC_RAILWAY_CO	0.81	32.04	0.030
22	MEIJI_SEIKA_KAISHA_LTD	0.78	33.04	0.006
23	DAI_NIPPON_PRINTING_CO_LTD	0.83	33.24	-0.008
24	SEKISUI_HOUSE_LTD	0.81	33.71	-0.007
25	TOHO_CO_LTD	0.69	34.04	0.020
26	SHIZUOKA_BANK_LTD/THE	0.80	34.10	-0.001
27	YAMATO_HOLDINGS_CO_LTD	0.73	34.25	-0.004
28	TOYOTA_MOTOR_CORP	0.90	34.47	0.021
29	KURARAY_CO_LTD	0.85	34.78	0.008

Table 5.3. *Long positions selected as top 15 percentile of the stocks ranked according to their historic volatilities, for the equity market neutral portfolio over Nikkei225 index (March 1999–March 2009)*

EXAMPLE 5.– *Optimal equity market neutral portfolio over Nikkei225 index: Portfolio C*

Portfolio C represents an equity market neutral portfolio over Nikkei 225 index (March 1999–March 2009) with a composition of long and short positions, which are the top 25 percentile and bottom 25 percentile of the historic volatility ranked stocks. Comprising 98 stocks (49 stocks each labeled as L and S) the optimal equity market portfolios satisfying [5.5]–[5.11] and experimented over various bounds imposed on the weights of long and short positions have been tabulated in Table 5.7. It can be clearly seen how the bounds on weights affects the performance characteristics of the portfolio.

Serial Number	Stock	Beta value	Historical volatility	Mean daily returns (%)
1	NITTO_BOSEKI_CO_LTD	1.22	51.17	0.029
2	NIPPON_SHEET_GLASS_CO_LTD	1.20	51.37	0.026
3	FUJIKURA_LTD	1.36	51.91	0.007
4	PIONEER_CORP	1.13	52.14	-0.076
5	SUMITOMO_TRUST_&_BANKING_CO	1.29	52.15	0.041
6	KONAMI_CORP	0.92	52.99	0.055
7	OKUMA_CORP	1.48	53.21	0.030
8	FURUKAWA_CO_LTD	1.34	53.35	0.023
9	TOKYO_ELECTRON_LTD	1.27	53.85	0.033
10	MEIDENSHA_CORP	1.36	53.89	0.048
11	SUMITOMO_OSAKA_CEMENT_CO_LTD	1.17	53.90	0.050
12	TOHO_ZINC_CO_LTD	1.38	54.17	0.042
13	ADVANTEST_CORP	1.33	54.19	0.005
14	HITACHI_ZOSEN_CORP	1.25	54.59	0.002
15	SUMITOMO_HEAVY_INDUSTRIES	1.40	54.98	0.056
16	MITSUI_ENGINEER_&_SHIPBUILD	1.36	55.29	0.074
17	TAIYO_YUDEN_CO_LTD	1.30	55.95	0.033
18	SHINKO_SECURITIES_CO_LTD	1.48	56.11	0.069
19	JAPAN_STEEL_WORKS_LTD	1.40	56.30	0.134
20	FAST_RETAILING_CO_LTD	0.82	56.62	0.154
21	TOKYU_LAND_CORP	1.47	56.77	0.087
22	ISUZU_MOTORS_LTD	1.33	57.47	0.024
23	MIZUHO_TRUST_&_BANKING_CO	1.26	57.49	0.047
24	FURUKAWA_ELECTRIC_CO_LTD/THE	1.42	58.02	0.038
25	CSK_HOLDINGS_CORP	1.16	61.42	-0.057
26	CLARION_CO_LTD	1.19	62.18	-0.021
27	CHIYODA_CORP	1.47	67.80	0.072
28	SOFTBANK_CORP	1.23	70.40	0.103
29	PACIFIC_METALS_CO_LTD	1.40	74.76	0.178

Table 5.4. *Short positions selected as bottom 15 percentile of the stocks ranked according to their historic volatilities, for the equity market neutral portfolio over Nikkei225 index (March 1999–March 2009)*

5.3. Risk-budgeted equity market neutral portfolio

Risk budgeting is a popular investment strategy where a ceiling is imposed on the risk limits of assets or the asset classes of the portfolio and was elaborately discussed in Chapter 4, section 4.1. The risk-budgeted equity market neutral portfolio is a market neutral portfolio which along with the chief constraints of net market exposure being zero, portfolio beta getting close to zero and with bounds and budget constraints imposed on the long and short positions comprising the portfolio, includes the additional constraint of imposing risk budgets on the high risk assets of the portfolio selected by the investor. With the inclusion of high volatility assets that are shorted to earn more returns in the equity market neutral portfolio, the inclusion of risk budgets on these high risk assets serves to cushion the risk while aiding to earn more returns.

The mathematical formulation of the risk-budgeted equity market neutral portfolio model incorporates [5.5]–[5.11]. However, [5.7] which is the bounds constraint for the short positions applies only for those high volatility assets that are not risk budgeted. The risk-budgeted assets are governed by the following exclusive constraints besides those insisted upon by the naïve equity market neutral portfolio. The risk budgeting constraints governing the specific high risk assets are:

$$\left(w_i^H\right)^2 . \sigma_i^2 \leq x\% \ of \quad \sigma_B^2 \qquad \text{(risk-budget constraint)} \qquad [5.12]$$

where W_i^H denotes the weights of the high risk assets selected by the investor, σ_i^2 is the individual asset risk, σ_B^2 is the portfolio risk and x% indicates the risk budget chosen by the investor.

Since the high risk assets W_i^H that are risk budgeted need to be shorted too, the following constraint is emphasized,

$$-1 \leq w_i^H \leq 0 \qquad \text{(shorting of high risk assets)} \qquad [5.13]$$

Thus if w_i^+, w_i^- and w_i^H indicate the weights of long positions L, short positions S and risk budgeted high risk positions H respectively, of a portfolio P where $P = L \cup S \cup H$, then [5.5]–[5.13] define the mathematical model for the Risk-budgeted equity market neutral portfolio problem. However, since the mathematical model is a non-linear optimization problem we proceed to solve the problem by tackling the constraints using penalty functions.

Optimal weights w_i^+ (Long positions L)	Optimal weights w_i^- (Short positions S)
0.001	-0.001
0.001	-0.001
0.001	-0.4597
0.001	-0.001
0.001	-0.001
0.001	-0.001
0.001	-0.001
0.001	-0.001
0.001	-0.001
0.001	-0.001
0.001	-0.001
0.001	-0.5233
0.001	-0.001
0.982	-0.001
0.001	-0.001
0.001	-0.001
0.001	-0.001
0.001	-0.001
0.001	-0.001

Net market exposure constraint $\sum_{i=1}^{N} w_i$		Equals 0 (Satisfied)
Portfolio beta constraint $\left\lvert \sum_{i=1}^{N} \beta_i . w_i \right\rvert$		Equals 0.1 (Satisfied)
Budget constraint on long positions L $\sum_{i=1}^{N} w_i^+$		Equals 1 (Satisfied)
Budget constraint on short positions S $\sum_{i=1}^{N} w_i^-$		Equals -1 (Satisfied)
Bounds constraint on long positions L $0.001 \leq w_i^+ \leq 1$		Satisfied
Bounds constraint on short positions S $-1 \leq w_i^- \leq -0.001$		Satisfied

Annualized risk (%)	60.127
Expected portfolio annual return (%)	-11.763

Table 5.5. *Characteristics of optimal equity market neutral portfolio (Portfolio A) for S&P BSE200 (March 1999–March 2009) dataset comprising long and short positions listed in Table 5.1 and Table 5.2 respectively and satisfying the mathematical model represented by [5.5]–[5.11]*

Net market exposure constraint $\sum_{i=1}^{N} w_i$	Equals 0 (Satisfied)
Portfolio beta constraint $\left\| \sum_{i=1}^{N} \beta_i . w_i \right\|$	Equals 0.1 (Satisfied)
Budget constraint on long positions L $\sum_{i=1}^{N} w_i^{+}$	Equals 1 (Satisfied)
Budget constraint on short positions S $\sum_{i=1}^{N} w_i^{-}$	Equals -1 (Satisfied)
Bounds constraint on long positions L $0.001 \leq w_i^{+} \leq 1$	Satisfied
Bounds constraint on short positions S $-1 \leq w_i^{-} \leq -0.001$	Satisfied

Annualized risk (%)	61.004
Expected portfolio annual return (%)	31.178

Table 5.6. *Summarized characteristics of optimal equity market neutral portfolio (Portfolio B) for S&P BSE200 (March 1999–March 2009) dataset, satisfying the mathematical model represented by [5.5]–[5.11]*

Penalty function strategy, discussed in Chapter 4, section 4.3.1, is a potential method to tackle constraints, in conventional optimization. Transforming the non linear mathematical model using penalty functions by absorbing the portfolio beta constraint and the risk budgeting constraint into the objective function, yields the following optimization model with linear constraints:

$$Max\left(\sum_{i=1}^{N} W_i . \mu_i - \Phi\left(\bar{W}, \bar{\beta}, \bar{\sigma}, c, x\right) \right) \qquad [5.14]$$

where $\Phi\left(\bar{W}, \bar{\beta}, \bar{\sigma}, c, x\right)$ is the constraint violation function given as

$$\Phi\left(\bar{W}, \bar{\beta}, \bar{\sigma}, c, x\right) = G_1 . \psi\left(\bar{W}, \bar{\beta}, c\right)^2 + \sum_{i \in H} G_{2,i} . \gamma_i \left(\bar{W}, \bar{\sigma}, x\right)^2 \qquad [5.15]$$

where

$$\psi(\bar{W},\bar{\beta},c)=\left|\sum_{i=1}^{N}\beta_i.W_i\right|-c \ \text{ and}$$

[5.16]

G_1 is the Heaviside operator given by

$$G_1 = \begin{cases} 0, & for \quad \psi(\bar{W},\bar{\beta},c)\leq 0 \\ 1, & otherwise \end{cases}$$

[5.17]

$$\gamma_i(\bar{W},\bar{\sigma},x)=(w_i^H)^2.\sigma_i^2-\frac{x}{100}.\sigma_B^2\leq 0,$$

[5.18]

and $G_{2,i}$ is the Heaviside operator given by

$$G_{2,i} = \begin{cases} 0, & for \quad \gamma_i(\bar{W},\bar{\sigma},x)\leq 0 \\ 1, & otherwise \end{cases}$$

[5.19]

subject to the constraints,

$0<w_i^+\leq 1$ (bound constraints on long positions L)   [5.20]

$-1\leq w_i^-<0$ (bound constraints on short positions S)   [5.21]

$-1\leq w_i^H<0$ (bound constraints on high volatility assets H)   [5.22]

$$\sum_{i=1}^{N}w_i=0 \qquad \text{(net market exposure constraint)}$$

[5.23]

$$\sum_{i\in L}w_i^+=1 \qquad \text{(budget constraint on long positions)}$$

[5.24]

$$\sum_{i\in S}w_i^-=-1 \qquad \text{(budget constraint on short positions)}$$

[5.25]

The transformed risk budgeted equity market neutral portfolio problem model adopts metaheuristics viz. a refined version of Differential Evolution with Hall of Fame (DE HOF) already discussed in Chapter 4, section 4.4 and section 4.6, to solve the problem and arrive at the optimal weights of the portfolio. The penalized objective function ([5.14]–[5.19]) serves to play the role of fitness function and thereby participates in the metaheuristic process to find the best solutions that need to be inducted into the Hall of Fame, a mechanism that executes elitism. The constraints ([5.20]–[5.25]) are handled using weight repair strategies akin to the ones discussed in Chapter 4, section 4.3.1 and section 4.5, but devised exclusively for the specific problem model. DE HOF employs *Rand5/Dir4* strategy to undertake mutation and *tournament selection* to select individuals for the next generation and hence is different from the version discussed earlier. This version will be referred to in this chapter as *DE/Rand5/Dir4* strategy.

Bound constraints on long /short positions	Annualized Risk(%)	Expected portfolio annual return (%)
$0.0001 \leq w_i^+ \leq 1$ $-1 \leq w_i^- \leq -0.0001$	46.56	20.10
$0.001 \leq w_i^+ \leq 1$ $-1 \leq w_i^- \leq -0.001$	41.99	16.21
$0.001 \leq w_i^+ \leq 1$ $-1 \leq w_i^- \leq -0.0001$	43.89	18.28
$0.001 \leq w_i^+ \leq 1$ $-1 \leq w_i^- \leq -0.0009$	42.19	16.44
$0.01 \leq w_i^+ \leq 1$ $-1 \leq w_i^- \leq -0.0001$	39.73	-4.29

Table 5.7. *Summarized characteristics of optimal equity market neutral portfolio (Portfolio C) for Nikkei225 (March 1999–March 2009) dataset, satisfying the mathematical model represented by [5.5]–[5.11] for various bound constraints*

5.4. Metaheuristic risk-budgeted equity market neutral portfolios

The metaheuristic optimization of risk-budgeted equity market neutral portfolios using DE/Rand5/Dir4 strategy is explained in this section. Figure 5.1 illustrates the process flow chart of the strategy as applied to the problem model defined by [5.14]–[5.25].

DE/Rand5/Dir4 adopts a version of RAND/DIR strategy [FEO 06] to generate trial vectors during mutation. RAND/DIR strategies adopt information about the objective function while calculating the direction of differentiation and are considered similar to gradient descent based strategies used in conventional optimization. The objectives of these strategies are fundamentally to reduce exploration of search space and render them more stable. However, there is no guarantee that these algorithms will work efficiently for all problems, justifying the *No Free Lunch theorem* with regard to optimization [WOL 97]. The version of RAND/DIR strategy used by the differential evolution algorithm for the risk budgeted equity market neutral portfolio problem is *Rand5/Dir4* and hence the name DE/Rand5/Dir4 for the strategy.

5.4.1. *Rand5/Dir4 strategy*

In this strategy five random individuals built from four different random directions are used to generate the trial vectors. The five random individuals serve to explore the search space entirely and better and the inclusion of the information provided by the objective function in the strategy helps to determine precisely the descent direction. The trial vector t is given by,

$$t = V^* + \phi.(3V^* - V_1 - V_2 - V_3 - V_4) \qquad [5.26]$$

where for the scaling factor β_S, $\phi = \beta_S/4$, is known as the constant of differentiation. Of the five random individuals extracted from the population, V^* is that individual which has the "best" (min /max) objective function value and V_1, V_2, V_3, V_4 are the rest of the four individuals. Since the constant of differentiation ϕ considerably affects the convergence rate, Vitaliy Feoktistov [FEO 06] proposed the following range to the choice of ϕ:

$$\phi \in (-1,0) \cup (0,1+) \qquad [5.27]$$

Once the trial vectors are generated for a population of individuals then the crossover operations proceed as appropriately decided upon for the problem model.

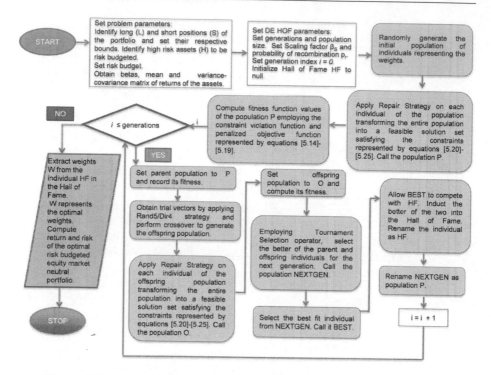

Figure 5.1. *Process flow chart of DE/Rand5/Dir4 strategy with tournament selection, for equity market neutral portfolio optimization (for a color version of this figure, see www.iste.co.uk/pai/metaheuristics.zip)*

5.4.2. Tournament selection

The Deterministic Selection operator discussed in Chapter 2 section 2.5.1 ensures selection of the best fit amongst the parent and offspring population of individuals by undertaking a one-on-one comparison of their respective fitness function values (objective function values). However, Vitaliy Feoktistov [FEO 06] and Andrzej Osyczka [OSY 02] suggested selection approaches that were not only based on the individuals' objective function values but also on how good a feasible solution the individuals stood for, by involving their respective constraint violation functions too! Osyczka [OSY 02] named this approach as *tournament selection* approach between the competing individuals.

Let P and O represent the parent and offspring individual belonging to their respective populations in a generation. Let Obj_P and Obj_O represent the objective function values and Φ_P and Φ_O the constraint violation functions of the individuals P and O, respectively. **Algorithm Tournament_Selection** illustrates the selection approach adopted by DE/Rand5/Dir4 for this problem. Unlike deterministic selection, tournament selection creates a new generation of individuals each of which either lies in the feasible region or at worst is closer to the feasible region, during each generation cycle.

```
Algorithm Tournament_Selection( P, O, Obj_P, Obj_O,

                                          Φ_P , Φ_O )

if      (Φ_P  =    Φ_O  =  0),   (i.e.)  if  both  the
        individuals  P  and  O    lie  in  the  feasible
        region   and   hence   represent        feasible
        solutions
then    select  the  better  of  Obj_P and Obj_O and move
        the    respective  individual  concerned  P  or
        O,  to  the  next  generation;
end

if      (Φ_P ≠ 0  and  Φ_O ≠ 0),  (i.e.)  if both the
        individuals  P  and  O  do  not  lie  in  the
        feasible  region  and  hence  do  not  represent
        feasible  solutions
then    select  the  better  of  Φ_P  and  Φ_O  that  lies
        closer  to  the  feasible  region,  (i.e.)  if Φ_P
        < Φ_O  then  select  individual  P  and  if  Φ_O < Φ_P
        then  select  individual  O  and  move  the
        individual     concerned     to     the     next
        generation.    Comparisons  of  the  respective
        objective  function  values  viz.,  Obj_P and Obj_O
        are  not  done  for  this  case;

end

if      (Φ_P ≠ 0  and  Φ_O = 0)  or  (Φ_O ≠ 0  and  Φ_P = 0),
        (i.e.)  if     any  one  individual  lies  in  the
        feasible  region  and  the  other  does  not
then    select  that  individual  which  is    the
        feasible  solution  and  move  it  to  the  next
        generation.  Comparisons  of  the  respective
        objective  function  values  viz.,  Obj_P and Obj_O
        are  not  done  for  this  case;
end

end Tournament_Selection
```

5.4.3. *Constraint handling*

For the problem model defined using [5.14]–[5.25], the non-linear risk budgeting constraint and the portfolio beta constraint tackled using penalty functions, becomes a component of the fitness function only to be exploited by DE/Rand5/Dir4 during its search for optimal solutions. With regard to the linear constraints concerning the long and short positions in the portfolio and defined by [5.20]–[5.25] however, a repair strategy needs to be evolved to enable the transformation of the population set to a feasible solution set. The repair strategy discussed in Chapter 4, section 4.3.1 and section 4.5 can be tweaked to handle the constraints concerned.

We consider the portfolio to have two "pockets" – long positions in one pocket satisfying constraints defined by [5.20] and [5.24] and short positions (inclusive of high risk assets that are to be risk budgeted) in the other pocket satisfying constraints defined by [5.21], [5.22] and [5.25]. Once these constraints are satisfied the net market exposure constraint defined by [5.23] automatically gets satisfied, since the constraints defined over long and short positions complement one another. Therefore it is enough if the weight repair strategy is designed to satisfy the set of constraints imposed on long positions, which comprises positive weights. Running the same strategy on short positions but finally complementing the weights arrived at to yield negative weights should serve to yield the desired results with regard to short positions. Thus the weight repair strategy is invoked twice, once over long positions and the last over short positions with the output weights complemented in the case of the latter.

The weight repair strategy for long positions to enable them to satisfy constraints defined by [5.20] and [5.24] is described below:

Let $\mathbf{W}$ represent a random vector of N weights of the portfolio comprising N assets, generated between *(-c, +c)*, for some c. Let W^+ and W^- denote the long and short positions in the portfolio the latter including W^H which are the risk budgeted high risk short positions. The repair strategy works on the long position weights W^+ as follows:

Step 1: If weights $w_i \in W^+$ are less than their respective lower bounds, a non-zero lower bound ε_i (0.001, for example), upgrade the respective weights to their respective lower bounds. Let R denote the set of such upgraded weights and Q the rest which already satisfied their lower bounds and hence were not upgraded.

Step 2:   Let SUM be the sum of weights in Q and let F the free proportion of weights be $F = 1 - \sum_{i \in L} \varepsilon_i$. Distribute F over asset weights in Q, proportional to their respective weight holdings as follows:

$$TERM = F/SUM;$$

$$w_i' = \varepsilon_i + w_i * TERM;$$

Let $W^{+'}$ denote the set of upgraded weights of long positions L that satisfy their respective lower bounds and add up to 1.

Step 3: Check if weights belonging to $W^{+'}$ exceed their upper bounds δ_i (typically 1).

if all weights of $W^{+'}$ satisfy their respective upper bounds

then output $W^{+'}$ as the standardized weight set; **exit (Success)**;

else

Reset such of these weights to their upper bound 1 and label these as set R. Let Q indicate the rest of the weights that satisfy their upper bounds;

go to Step 4;

end

Step 4: Compute SUM, the sum of weights in Q and F the free proportion of weights as $F = 1 - \sum_{w_i \in Q} \varepsilon_i . |Q| - \sum_{w_i \in R} \delta_i . |R|$ where $|Q|$ and $|R|$ indicate the lengths of Q and R respectively. Distribute F over Q proportional to their respective holdings as

$$TERM = F/SUM;$$

$$w_i'' = \varepsilon_i + w_i' * TERM;$$

if $w_i'' \in Q$ $\forall w_i''$, satisfy their respective upper bounds
then go to Step 6

else go to Step 5;

end

Step 5: If there exists any $w_i" \in Q$ that exceeds their respective upper bounds, level off such weights to their upper bounds, remove them from Q, add them to R and **go to** Step 4;

Step 6: Output weights in R and Q as the upgraded weight set $W^{+"}$ and **exit** (***Success***); $W^{+"}$ satisfies its upper and lower bounds and sums up to 1.

In the case of weight standardization of short positions, the strategy repeats itself considering the absolute weights $|W^-|$ as W^+, going through Steps 1-6 as described above, before finally delivering the complement of $W^{+"}$ i.e. $-W^{+"}$ as the standardized weight set $W^{-"}$.

EXAMPLE.– Let $\mathbf{W} = [0.9, 1.1, -0.5, 0.7, -1, -1.5]$ represent a random weight vector of six assets $\{l_1, l_2, l_3, , s_1, s_2, s_3\}$ comprising a portfolio, three of which viz. $\{l_1, l_2, l_3\}$ are long positions labeled as L and the rest viz. $\{s_1, s_2, s_3\}$ are short positions labeled as S. The weight vector was randomly generated between the open interval $(-3, 3)$. The objective is to demonstrate the standardization of the weight vector W so that it satisfies the constraints listed in [5.20] to [5.25]. The strategy works in two stages, once over the long positions alone and next over the short positions alone, before the standardized weight set satisfies its objectives.

Adopting the notations employed in the repair strategy discussed above,

$$W^+ = [0.9, 1.1, -0.5,] , \quad W^- = [0.7, -1, -1.5] \text{ and } \varepsilon_i = 0.001, \quad \delta_i = 1$$

The strategy first proceeds to standardize W^+ as follows:

Step 1: Upgrading the weights in W^+ which are less than their respective lower bounds yields $[0.9, 1.1, 0.001]$ and therefore $R = \{0.001\}$ and $Q = \{0.9, 1.1\}$.

Step 2: $SUM = 2$ and $F = 1 - \sum_{i \in L} \varepsilon_i = 0.997$. Therefore $TERM = 0.4985$ and the updated weights are

$$w_i' = \varepsilon_i + w_i * TERM$$
$$= 0.001 + [0.9, 1.1, 0.001] * 0.4985 = [0.4496, 0.5494, 0.001]$$

Hence $W^{+'} = [0.4496, 0.5494, 0.001]$. It can be observed that $W^{+'}$ satisfies its lower bounds and the weights sum up to 1.

Step 3: Checking for weights that satisfy or violate their upper bounds in $W^{+'}$ yields a favorable result where all weights satisfy their upper bounds. Hence the strategy exits with success with $W^{+'}$ as the standardized weight set. It can be observed that the long position weights satisfy all their respective constraints defined by [5.20] and [5.24].

In the next stage the strategy proceeds to standardize W^- just as it did for W^+ but only after considering their absolute weights viz. [|0.7|, |-1|, |-1.5|] and defining $\varepsilon_i = 0.001$, $\delta_i = 1$, as follows:

Step 1: Upgrading the absolute weights in W^- which are less than their respective absolute lower bounds yields $R = \phi$ and $Q = \{ 0.7, 1, 1.5 \}$.

Step 2: $SUM = 3.2$ and $F = 1 - \sum_{i \in L} \varepsilon_i = 0.997$. Therefore $TERM = 0.3116$ and the updated weights are

$$w_i' - \varepsilon_i + w_i * TERM$$
$$- 0.001 + [0.7, 1, 1.5] * 0.3116 = [0.2191, 0.3126, 0.4683]$$

Hence $W^{-'} = [0.2191, 0.3126, 0.4683]$. It can be observed that $W^{-'}$ satisfies its absolute lower bounds and the weights sum up to 1.

Step 3: Checking for weights that satisfy or violate their absolute upper bounds in $W^{-'}$ yields a favorable result where all weights satisfy their absolute upper bounds. At this point the complement of the weights in $W^{-'}$ is obtained which yields [-0.2191, -0.3126, -0.4683]. Hence the strategy exits with success with $W^{-'}$ as the standardized weight set. It can be observed that the short position weights shown in $W^{-'}$ satisfy all their respective constraints defined by [5.21] / [5.22] and [5.25].

Conjoining $W^{+'}$ and $W^{-'}$ yields the final standardized weight set [0.4496, 0.5494, 0.001, -0.2191, -0.3126, -0.4683] which also satisfies the net market exposure constraint specified in [5.23].

Thus, employing the weight repair strategy over each individual in the population set yields a population of individuals that satisfy constraints represented by [5.20] to [5.25] and hence lie in the feasible region.

5.5. Experimental results and analyses

In this section we explore the application of metaheuristic equity market neutral portfolio model with risk budgets defined over selective high risk assets, to two categories of portfolios defined over S&P BSE200 index (March 1999–March 2009, Bombay Stock Exchange, India) and Nikkei 225 index (March 1999–March 2009, Tokyo Stock Exchange, Japan).

The long and short positions comprising the portfolios were selected using Blitz and Vliet's [BLI 07] approach as discussed in section 5.1. Of the three naïve EMNP portfolios detailed in section 5.2, viz. Portfolio A, Portfolio B and Portfolio C, we consider Portfolio B and Portfolio C for the experiments discussed in this section, with risk budgets imposed on selective high risk stocks in each portfolio.

To recall, Portfolio B comprised top/bottom 25 percentile of stocks ordered according to their historic volatilities respectively (Long/Short positions), of S&P BSE 200 data set and Portfolio C the same with regard to Nikkei 225 dataset.

Optimal risk-budgeted equity market neutral portfolio for S&P BSE200: Portfolio B

Portfolio B comprised 32 long positions (L) which are the top 25 percentile of historic volatility ranked stocks and 32 short positions (S) which are the bottom 25 percentile of historic volatility ranked stocks. Amongst stocks belonging to S, a risk budget of 20% of the portfolio risk was imposed on the top five high volatility stocks (H). Thus ESSAR_OIL_LTD, WELSPUN_GUJARAT_STAHL_LTD, GUJARAT_ NRE_COKE_LTD,   IVRCL_INFRASTRUCTURES_&_PROJECTS   and UNITED_ PHOSPOROUS_LTD were the five risk budgeted assets in Portfolio B.

The bounds for the long, short and risk-budgeted positions were as follows, where W^+, W^- and W^H are their weights respectively:

$$0.0001 \leq W^+ \leq 1$$
$$-1 \leq W^- \leq -0.0001$$
$$-1 \leq W^H \leq -0.0001$$

The objective was to obtain the optimal portfolio using the model defined by [5.14]–[5.25] using DE/Rand5/Dir4 strategy with tournament selection.

Table 5.8 illustrates the control parameters of the DE/Rand5/Dir4 strategy for Portfolio B.

Parameter	Description
Population size	640
Individual length	64
Generations	10000
Scale factor β_s	0.5
Probability of recombination p_r	0.87
Constant of differentiation ϕ	$\beta_s/4$

Table 5.8. *DE/Rand5/Dir4 strategy for optimizing Portfolio B: Control parameters*

Table 5.9 illustrates the optimal risk/return characteristics of the risk-budgeted Portfolio B obtained by DE/Rand5/Dir4 strategy during five sample runs.

The convergence characteristics of DE/Rand5/Dir4 strategy were observed by studying the fitness function values of the best individual that is inducted into the Hall of Fame during the specific generations concerned. Figure 5.2 illustrates the trace of the fitness values of the HOF individual during the generation cycles of a specific run. It can be clearly seen that the fitness function values have begun settling down as early as 1,000 generations signaling the convergence of the metaheuristic strategy.

Runs	Annualized Portfolio Risk(%)	Expected Portfolio Annualized Return (%)
RUN 1	62.5424	34.6842
RUN 2	63.3969	34.9091
RUN 3	63.2923	34.8015
RUN 4	63.1317	34.5642
RUN 5	63.0551	34.5263

Table 5.9. *Risk-budgeted portfolio B: Risk/return characteristics of the optimal portfolios obtained by DE/Rand5/Dir4 strategy during various runs*

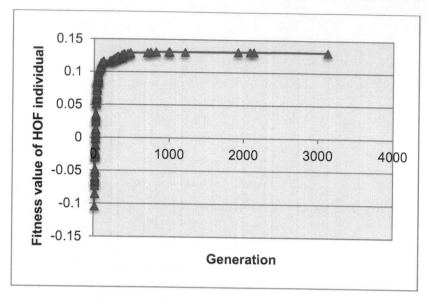

Figure 5.2. *Convergence characteristics of DE/Rand5/Dir4 strategy during risk-budgeted equity market neutral portfolio optimization over S&P BSE200 dataset*

Optimal risk-budgeted equity market neutral portfolio for Nikkei225: Portfolio C

Portfolio C comprised 49 long positions (L) which are the top 25 percentile and 49 short positions (S) which are the bottom 25 percentile of stocks ranked according to their order of historic volatilities. Amongst stocks belonging to S, a risk budget of 20% of the portfolio risk was imposed on top 2 high volatility stocks (H). Thus SOFTBANK_CORP and PACIFIC_METALS_CO_LTD were the two risk-budgeted assets in Portfolio C.

The bounds for the long, short and risk-budgeted positions were as follows, where W^+, W^- and W^H are their weights respectively:

$$0.0001 \leq W^+ \leq 1$$

$$-1 \leq W^- \leq -0.0001$$

$$-1 \leq W^H \leq -0.0001$$

The objective was to obtain the optimal portfolio using the model defined by [5.14]–[5.25] and employing DE/Rand5/Dir4 strategy.

Table 5.10 illustrates the control parameters of the DE/Rand5/Dir4 strategy for Portfolio C.

Parameter	Description
Population size	980
Individual length	98
Generations	5000
Scale factor β_S	0.5
Probability of recombination p_r	0.87
Constant of differentiation ϕ	$\beta_S / 4$

Table 5.10. *DE/Rand5/Dir4 strategy for optimizing Portfolio C: Control parameters*

Table 5.11 illustrates the optimal risk/return characteristics of the risk budgeted Portfolio C obtained by DE/Rand5/Dir4 strategy during five sample runs.

Runs	Annualized Portfolio Risk (%)	Expected Portfolio Annualized Return (%)
RUN 1	44.8497	18.6927
RUN 2	44.7701	18.7534
RUN 3	44.7216	18.6279
RUN 4	44.9096	18.7470
RUN 5	44.9476	18.8314

Table 5.11. *Risk-budgeted Portfolio C: Risk/return characteristics of the optimal portfolios obtained by DE/Rand5/Dir4 strategy during various runs*

The convergence characteristics of DE/Rand5/Dir4 strategy observed by studying the fitness function values of the best individual that is inducted into the Hall of Fame during the specific generations yielded the graph shown in Figure 5.3. It can be clearly seen that the fitness function values have begun settling down as early as 1,500 generations signaling the convergence of the metaheuristic strategy.

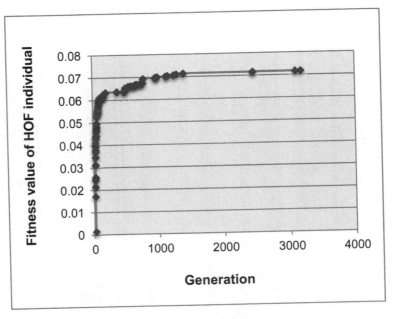

Figure 5.3. *Convergence characteristics of DE/Rand5/Dir4 strategy during risk-budgeted equity market neutral portfolio optimization over Nikkei225 dataset*

5.6. MATLAB® demonstrations

In this section we demonstrate MATLAB® functions and programs associated with the optimization of equity market neutral portfolios, as listed below. The coding style has been kept naïve and direct to favor novices in MATLAB®.

A. Optimization of naïve equity market neutral portfolios

B. Implementation of Rand5/Dir4 operator

C. Repair strategy

D. Computing constraint violation functions

E. Computing fitness function

F. DE/Rand5/Dir4 generational cycle

A. *Optimization of naïve equity market neutral portfolios*

The optimization of naïve equity market neutral portfolios described by [5.5]–[5.11] using linear programming and discussed in section 5.2, can be easily accomplished using MATLAB® `linprog` function available in its Optimization Toolbox. Chapter 1 section 1.3 B already introduced the application of `linprog` for unconstrained portfolio optimization. However, since naïve equity market neutral portfolios command constrained optimization with linear inequality and equality constraints, the parameters of the `linprog` function need to be appropriately defined. Figure 5.4 shows the MATLAB® program fragment invoking `linprog` to optimize the portfolio. `x_star` and `max_ret_fun_val` represent the optimal weights and the maximal objective function value returned by `linprog`.

B. *Implementation of Rand5/Dir4 operator*

The Rand5/Dir4 operator adopted by the Differential Evolution strategy for the equity market neutral portfolio optimization problem model has been discussed in section 5.4.1. Figure 5.5 illustrates the MATLAB® function that performs the operation on a population of individuals. Following [5.26], for each individual in the population five random individuals (`differential_vec_indx`) different from it are selected. Of the five, that individual with the maximal objective function value (`f_val`) is chosen as V* and the rest of them are chosen to represent V_1, V_2, V_3 and V_4 in the equation. In this function `F_val` represents the scaling factor that was chosen to be 0.5. `mutated_popln` yields the trial vectors for the population of individuals `popln`.

C. *Repair strategy*

Linear constraint handling using weight repair strategy for the equity market neutral portfolio optimization problem model discussed in section 5.3.1, is demonstrated in Figure 5.6. Steps 1–2 of the strategy which discuss standardization of lower bounds followed by Steps 3–5 which discuss standardization of upper bounds can be seen implemented in the code shown.

Given `weight_mat` to be the weight matrix of individuals, it is assumed that the weights of the long positions are followed in sequence by those of the short positions (or vice-versa).

```
...
% extract mean and variance-covariance of asset
% returns where source_data is the historical dataset
% of asset returns
mean_data = mean(source_data);
cov_data = cov(source_data);

% set bounds for long positions and short
% position weights
Long_low_bound = 0.0001;
Long_up_bound = 1;
Short_low_bound = -1;
Short_up_bound =-0.0001;

% set limits for portfolio beta constraint
beta_lmt = 0.1

% set linprog function parameters to model
% equations [5.5]-[5.11]
f=-1*mean_data';

% frame equality constraints represented by Aeq and
% beq
Aeq= [ones(1, L_col) zeros(1,S_col); zeros(1, L_col)
                                 ones(1, S_col) ];
beq=[1 -1];

% set bounds for the variables
lb= [zeros(1, L_col)+ Long_low_bound
zeros(1,S_col)+Short_low_bound];
ub= [ones(1, L_col)    zeros(1, S_col)+Short_up_bound];

% set inequality constraints
% beta_assets is the  beta values of the assets
Aineq =[Beta_assets; -Beta_assets];
bineq=[beta_lmt   beta_lmt];

% invoke linprog function
[x_star,max_ret_fun_val,exitflag] =
                linprog(f,Aineq,bineq,Aeq,beq, lb,ub)

...
```

Figure 5.4. *MATLAB® code fragment demonstrating application of* linprg
*function for naïve equity market neutral portfolio optimization (for a color
version of this figure, see www.iste.co.uk/pai/metaheuristics.zip)*

Begin_col and   End_col denote the starting and ending positions or
indices of the long and short positions in the weight vector. Low_bound and
Up_bound denote the lower and upper bounds of the weights of the long

positions/short positions. Signal is a flag that when set to 0, undertakes weight repair of the short positions alone and when set to 1 undertakes weight repair of the long positions alone. Thus the same function can be reused for both long position and short position standardization, with appropriate amendments to the weights before and after weight standardization in the case of short positions. The function EMNP_eqconstr_wgtstd is invoked twice over each individual in the population, once to standardize long position weights and the next to standardize short position weights so that the individual ultimately satisfies the set of linear constraints represented by [5.20]–[5.25] thereby transforming the entire population of individuals into a feasible solution set.

```
% differential evolution  Rand5/Dir4 Operator

function mutated_popln = DE_Rand5Dir4_Operator(popln,
f_val,  F_val, popln_size, individual_length)

% initialization
differential_vec_indx(1:5) = 0;
V_star(1,1:individual length) = 0;
V(1:4,1:individual_length) = 0;
mutated_popln(1:popln_size, 1:individual_length) =0;

for i = 1 : popln_size

% prepare rand_indx, random number indices for each
% population individual to enable it choose five
% random individuals from the population, without
% repeating itself.

    rand_indx = randperm(popln_size);
    for t=1:popln_size
        if (rand_indx(t)==i)
            elimx = t;
        end
    end
    rand_indx(elimx)=[];

    % select five random individuals from the
    % population

    for u=1:5
    differential_vec_indx(u) = rand_indx(u);
    end
```

Figure 5.5. MATLAB® function for Rand5/Dir4 mutation operator (for a color version of this figure, see www.iste.co.uk/pai/metaheuristics.zip)

```
% Obtain V* the best individual with the maximal
% objective function and  represent the rest as
% V1, V2, V3 and V4 as defined in equation [5.26]

  [~, max_obj_indx] = max(
            [f_val(differential_vec_indx(1)),
             f_val(differential_vec_indx(2)),
             f_val(differential_vec_indx(3)),
         f_val(differential_vec_indx(4)),
           f_val(differential_vec_indx(5))] );

  j=1;
  for z=1:5
      if (differential_vec_indx(z) ==
          differential_vec_indx(max_obj_indx))
          V_star(1,:) =
          popln(differential_vec_indx(z), :);
      else
          V(j,:) =
              popln(differential_vec_indx(z),:);
          j=j+1;
      end
  end


  % obtain trial vector for each of the parent
  % vector individual

  mutated_popln(i,:) = V_star(1,:) + F_val/4 *
  (3*V_star(1,:) - V(1,:)-V(2,:)-V(3,:)-V(4,:));

  end
end
```

Figure 5.5. *Contd.*

```
% Repair strategy to standardize weights of
% long/short positions to satisfy their linear
% constraints

function std_weight_mat =
EMNP_eqconstr_wgtstd(weight_mat,
                 Begin_col, End_col, Low_bound,
                 Up_bound, signal)

[row_mat, col_mat]=size(weight_mat);

if (signal ==0)     % short positions
  weight_mat(1:row_mat,
       Begin_col:End_col)=abs(weight_mat(1:row_mat,
                                 Begin_col:End_col) );
end
```

Figure 5.6. *Weight repair strategy: Standardization of weights to satisfy linear constraints for long/short positions (for a color version of this figure, see www.iste.co.uk/pai/metaheuristics.zip)*

D. *Computing constraint violation functions*

The portfolio beta and risk budgeting constraints were tackled using constraint violation functions ([5.15]–[5.19]) that were absorbed into the objective function ([5.14]) to obtain the penalized objective function.

The computation of constraint violation function is demonstrated in Figure 5.7. `weight_mat` represents the population of individuals which having undergone weight repair (through function `EMNP_eqconstr_wgtstd`) are already feasible solution sets. The covariance of the assets in the portfolio, their individual betas and the specific high volatility assets on whom risk budgets have been imposed are input to the function as `covar_mat`, `betas_assets` and `Highvolassets` respectively. `G1` and `G2` represent the penalty terms computed and `psi` the constraint violation function values for the entire population. The code demonstrates a risk budget of 20% of the portfolio risk on the high volatility assets.

```
% standardize  lower bounds for long /short positions
% for each population individual

  for i=1: row_mat

    % R: those weights which are less than their
    % lower bounds

    R=[];
    c_R=0;
    for j=Begin_col:End_col
        if (weight_mat(i,j)< Low_bound)
            weight_mat(i,j)= Low_bound;
            c_R = c_R+1;
            R(c_R) = j;
        end
    end

    % Q:  weights which satisfy their lower bounds
    Q = setdiff([Begin_col:End_col], R);

    % F: free proportion of weights
    F = 1 - Low_bound *(End_col-Begin_col+1);

    SUM = sum(weight_mat(i,Q));
    if (SUM==0)
            if (length(Q) ~=0)
            term = F / length(Q);
            weight_mat(i,Q)= Low_bound+ term;
            else
            term = F / length(R);
            weight_mat(i,R)= Low_bound+ term;
            end
    else
            term = F / SUM;
            weight_mat(i,Q)  = Low_bound+
    weight_mat(i,Q)* term;
    end

  end
```

Figure 5.6. *Contd.*

```
% standardize upper bounds for long / short
% positions for each population  individual
for i = 1: row_mat
    kr = 1;
    R = [];
    ex_flag = true;
    Q = setdiff([Begin_col:End_col], R);
    while (ex_flag == true)
            ex_flag = false;
            for j = 1: length(Q)
                if ( weight_mat(i, Q(j)) <= Up_bound )
                continue;
                else
                ex_flag = true;
                R(kr) = Q(j);
                kr = kr+1;
                end
            end
            Q = setdiff([Begin_col:End_col], R);
            if (ex_flag == true)
            SUM = sum(weight_mat(i,Q));
            F = 1   ( length(Q)*Low_bound) -
                            (length(R)*Up_bound);
            if (SUM==0)
            term = F;
            weight_mat(i,Q(1))= term;
            else
            term = F/SUM;
            weight_mat(i,Q) = Low_bound+
                        weight_mat(i,Q)* term;
            end
            weight_mat(i,R)=Up_bound;
            end
    end
end
if (signal ==0)
 weight_mat (1:row_mat, Begin_col:End_col) =
      -weight_mat(1:row_mat, Begin_col:End_col);
end
std_weight_mat = weight_mat;

end
```

Figure 5.6. *Contd.*

E. *Computing fitness function*

Fig. 5.8 illustrates the computation of fitness function values from the penalized objective function shown in [5.14], for the population of individuals `popln_mat`. `mean_dat` represents the mean returns of the assets in the portfolio and `psi_fun` the constraint violation function values ([5.15]–[5.19]) obtained through function `EMNP_compute_constr_violn_fn`. The outputs are given by `popln_fitness` and `popln_obj_val`, denoting the fitness function values (penalized objective function values) and the objective function values respectively. With the tournament selection operator (**Algorithm Tournament_ Selection**) discussed in section 5.4.2 demanding a selection based on objective function values when the competing parent and offspring individuals both lie in the feasible region, it is essential to remember the objective function values as much as the fitness function values for the population of individuals during each generation cycle.

F. *DE/Rand5/Dir4 generation cycle*

Figure 5.9 illustrates the MATLAB® code fragment for the generation cycles of DE/Rand5/Dir4 strategy for the equity market neutral portfolio optimization problem model. The operations undertaken in a generation cycle viz. setting parent population, executing mutation to generate trial vectors, performing cross over to generate offspring population, weight repairing to enable the offspring population transform themselves into feasible solution set, selecting the best individuals from the parent and offspring populations through tournament selection to the next generation, inducting the best individual amongst the next generation individuals to the Hall of Fame, as described in the process flow chart of DE/Rand5/Dir4 strategy shown in Figure 5.1, can be clearly seen in the code fragment, encapsulated within the body of the `while` loop.

It is assumed that the initial random population of individuals transformed into a feasible solution set viz. `initial_popln`, along with the other parameters connected with it viz. `initial_popln_fitness`, `psi_i`, `initial_G1`, `initial_G2` and `initial_popln_obj_val` (self descriptive variables) are made available before the `while` loop of the generation cycles begins execution (not shown in code). `DE_Rand5Dir4_Operator`, `DE_bin_ Crossover`, `EMNP_eqconstr_wgtstd`, `EMNP_compute_constr_ violn_fn`, `EMNP_comp_fitness` and `EMNP_DE_selection` are the sequence of functions executed by DE/Rand5/Dir4 strategy during the generation cycle.

```
function  [psi, G1,G2]  =
EMNP_compute_constr_violn_fn( weight_mat,
           covar_mat, betas_assets, Highvolassets )
[row_mat, col_mat]= size(weight_mat);
No_Highvolassets = length(Highvolassets);

for i=1:row_mat
   x_chromo = weight_mat(i,:);
   portfolio_risk  =  (x_chromo * covar_mat *
                                      x_chromo');
   % penalty function G1
   portfolio_beta_term = sum(betas_assets.*
                                    x_chromo);
   g1_term = abs(portfolio_beta_term) - 0.1;
   g1_result = power(g1_term,2);
   if (g1_term <=0 )
       G1(i)=0;
   else
       G1(i)=1;
   end

   % penalty function G2
   for k=1: No_Highvolassets
     RiskLmt_ShortHighvol(k)=
     (x_chromo (1, Highvolassets(k)) ^2)   *
     covar_mat (Highvolassets(k), Highvolassets(k)) ;

     g2_term(i,k) - RiskLmt_ShortHighvol(k)-
                                (portfolio_risk/5) ;
     g2_result(i,k)= power(g2_term(i,k), 2);
     if (g2_term <=0 )
        G2(i,k)=0;
     else
        G2(i,k)=1;
     end
   end

   % compute constraint violation function
    psi(i)= (G1(i)*g1_result +
    sum(G2(i,1:No_Highvolassets)
           .*g2_result(i,1:No_Highvolassets)) );
end
end
```

Figure 5.7. *Computation of Constraint Violation function for the equity market neutral portfolio optimization problem (for a color version of this figure, see www.iste.co.uk/pai/metaheuristics.zip)*

```
function [popln fitness, popln obj val] =
    EMNP_comp_fitness_function(popln_mat,mean_dat,
                                            psi_fun)
[popln_size, chro_len]=size(popln_mat);

for i =1:popln_size

    weight = popln_mat(i,:);
    func_val(i) = (weight* mean_dat');
    fitness_val(i)= func_val(i)- psi_fun(i);

end
popln_fitness = fitness_val;
popln_obj_val = func_val;
end
```

Figure 5.8. *Computation of fitness function for the equity market neutral portfolio optimization problem (for a color version of this figure, see www.iste.co.uk/pai/metaheuristics.zip)*

```
...
% DE generation cycles begin

while (gen_indx <= total_generations)

    feas_parent_popln = initial_popln;
    feas_parent_popln_fitness =
                            initial_popln_fitness;
    psi_p = psi_i;
    feas_parent_G1= initial_G1;
    feas_parent_G2 = initial_G2;
    feas_parent_obj_val = initial_popln_obj_val;

    % perform mutation

    trial_vector_popln = DE_Rand5Dir4_Operator(
        feas_parent_popln, feas_parent_popln_fitness,
        beta, popln_size, chromosm_length);
```

```
% perform cross over

  offsprng_popln_raw =
      DE_bin_Crossover(feas_parent_popln,
         trial_vector_popln, pr_recombi,
                              chromosm_length);

% undertake weight repair of long/short positions

 offsprng_popln_longstd =
      EMNP_eqconstr_wgtstd(offsprng_popln_raw,  1,
         L_col, Long_low_bound, Long_up_bound, 1);
 offsprng_popln_shortstd =
      EMNP_eqconstr_wgtstd(offsprng_popln_longstd,
         L_col+1,  L_col+S_col,   -Short_up_bound, -
         Short_low_bound,0);
 offsprng_popln = offsprng_popln_shortstd;

% compute constraint violation functions

[psi_o,offsprng_G1, offsprng_G2]   =
      EMNP_compute_constr_violn_fn( offsprng_popln,
         cov_data, Beta_assets, Highvolat_assets);

% compute fitness functions

 [offsprng_popln_fitness, offsprng_obj_val] =
        EMNP_comp_fitness_function(offsprng_popln,
           mean_data, psi_o);

% tournament selection of individuals for the
% next generation

[next_gen_pool, next_gen_pool_obj_val,  Psi_fun,
 G1_nextgen,G2_nextgen,  next_gen_pool_fitness] =
 EMNP_DE_selection(feas_parent_popln,  psi_p,
 feas_parent_G1,feas_parent_G2,
 feas_parent_obj_val, feas_parent_popln_fitness,
 offsprng_popln,  psi_o, offsprng_G1,
 offsprng_G2, offsprng_obj_val,
          offsprng_popln_fitness,  popln_size);
```

```
    % induct best individual into Hall of Fame
    for i=1:popln_size
        if (Psi_fun(i)== 0)
            if (next_gen_pool_fitness(i) >
                                 HOF_fitness)
            HOF_fitness =
                    next_gen_pool_fitness(i)
            HOF_individual =  next_gen_pool(i,:);

            HOF_genarray(i1) = gen_indx;
            HOF_fitarray(i1) = HOF_fitness;
            i1=i1+1;
            end
        else continue;
        end
    end

    % increment generation cycle counter
    gen_indx = gen_indx + 1;

    % reset initial population and parameters
    initial_popln = next_gen_pool;
    initial_popln_fitness= next_gen_pool_fitness;
    psi_i= Psi_fun;
    initial_G1=G1_nextgen;
    initial_G2 = G2_nextgen;
    initial_popln_obj_val = next_gen_pool_obj_val;


 end     % while loop for DE generation cycles ends


% record the individual in the Hall of Fame as the
% optimal solution

x_star = HOF_individual; % optimal weights

...
```

Figure 5.9. *MATLAB*® *code fragment demonstrating the generation cycles of DE/Rand5/Dir4 strategy for equity market neutral portfolio optimization (for a color version of this figure, see www.iste.co.uk/pai/metaheuristics.zip)*

It can be seen that the weight repair function `EMNP_eqconstr_wgtstd` is invoked twice for standardizing the weights of long and short positions in that order, by setting the flag `signal = 1` and `signal = 0`, respectively. Inducting a better individual into the Hall of Fame is not just made on the basis of the fitness function values but also on the pre requisite qualification that the individual should necessarily belong to the feasible region (`Psi_fun(i) == 0`).

Project

An investor decides to explore investing in an equity market neutral portfolio dictating her preferences (whimsical though!) as follows:

She decides to invest in long (L_A) and short positions (S_A) in the same sector A, carefully matching them against one another so as to hedge the sector and the market in which the assets lie. However, she doesn't stop with this but decides to go one step further and include another set of long (L_D) and short positions (S_B) carefully matched, but selected from another sector B. The important thing to note is that she ensures that sector A and sector B themselves are negatively correlated in the market, in other words have opposite behavior. Thus if sector A stock prices rise then those in sector B have to essentially fall. For example, if she chose Oil as Sector A then she might choose Airlines or Real Estate as Sector B, since it is well known that Oil sector has negative correlations with Airlines or Real Estate.

Assume she decided to impose the following objectives and constraints:

(i)   maximize Sharpe Ratio of the portfolio

(ii)   impose a risk budget of 15.5% of the portfolio risk on those short positions with high betas

(iii) ensure that net market exposure of the portfolio is zero, and

(iv)   obeys portfolio beta constraint.

  (a) Formulate the mathematical model reflecting the investor's choices.

  (b) Transform the mathematical model using Penalty Functions.

  (c) Implement DE/Rand5/Dir4 with appropriate modifications in MATLAB®, to arrive at the optimal portfolio. What was the optimal portfolio arrived at by DE/Rand5/Dir4? Was the investor happy with the Sharpe Ratio obtained? Tabulate the results for various runs.

(d)   Would Differential Evolution have yielded better results if experimented with other DE strategies? Vitaliy Feoktistov [FEO 06] discusses four categories of strategies viz. RAND, RAND/DIR, RAND/BEST and RAND/BEST/ DIR.Rand5/Dir4 discussed in this chapter was one example of the RAND/DIR category. Explore the possibilities of including other appropriate strategies that will refine the behavior of Differential Evolution with regard to the solution of the problem posed.

Suggested Further Reading

Pai and Michel's [PAI 12a] work on *"Differential Evolution based Optimization of Risk Budgeted Equity Market Neutral Portfolios"* details the implementation of the risk-budgeted equity market neutral portfolio optimization model in an alternative fashion. Penalty functions were used only to tackle the portfolio beta constraint. The non-linear risk budget constraints and other linear constraints were tackled using weight repair strategies specially formulated to tackle the respective constraint sets. The Differential Evolution strategy with Hall of Fame, that was employed to optimize the problem, adopted only conventional mutation operator to generate its trial vectors and used only deterministic selection to gather the best of the parent and offspring individuals for the next generation. A rigorous analysis of the problem model revealed the robustness of the DE HOF algorithm in solving the specific formulation of the risk-budgeted equity market neutral portfolio problem.

Vitaliy Feoktistov's book on *"Differential Evolution: In search of solutions"* [FEO 06] is a good read on Differential Evolution and its refinements.

It is also possible to formulate Market Neutral portfolio problem models with multiple objectives and constraints and construct multi-objective metaheuristic optimization strategies to solve them. Deb's book on *Multi-Objective Optimization using Evolutionary Algorithms* [DEB 03], Coello *et al.'s* book on *Evolutionary Algorithms for solving Multi-Objective Problems* [COE 07] and Collette and Siarry's work on *Multiobjective Optimization, Principles and Case Studies* [COL 04], are some good textbooks to know more about multi-objective metaheuristic optimization.

Metaheuristic 130-30 Portfolio Construction

This chapter details different approaches – traditional and metaheuristic – to construct 130 30 portfolios and a comparison of their performances vis-à-vis long only portfolios. The traditional approaches are demonstrated using MATLAB® Portfolio Optimization Object available in Its Financial Toolbox. The metaheuristic approach is implemented using Differential Evolution strategy, introduced earlier in this book. The essential MATLAB® functions and code fragments to illustrate the approaches concerned have been included in this chapter.

6.1. 130-30 portfolio

130-30 strategy is a portfolio construction method that employs *leveraging*, to short poor performing stocks to the tune of 30% of the portfolio value and then divert the funds to take up long positions in stocks that will perform well, to the tune of 130% of the portfolio value. Thus 130-30 portfolio is a long-short portfolio expected to yield higher returns for it is notionally expected to enhance investment exposure and ensure market protection at the same time. On that count, 130-30 portfolios have by and large performed better than their long-only counterparts.

EXAMPLE.– Suppose a fund manager has a capital of $100 million to be invested on his/her portfolio. In the event of a 130-30 portfolio construction, the manager would borrow $30 million to short $30 million worth of unattractive stocks or stocks that are expected to under perform. The proceeds of the short sales amounting to $30 million is now invested over and above the already ear marked $100 million, for taking up long positions on attractive stocks or stocks that are expected to perform well. Thus a total of $130 million is invested over long positions. The net investment on the 130-30 portfolio is given by a positive $130 million on long positions (+130), a negative $30 million on borrowing (-30), a negative $30 million on short sales (-30) and a positive $30 million on proceeds of the short sales (+30). As can be seen, the net result amounts to only $100 million. In a sense, the return of the 130-30 portfolio could be construed as the return on the $130 million long position investment minus the $30 million short position investment and the borrowing and shorting costs of course.

Although the label "130-30" is popular and has come to stay in vogue, there is no reason why a similar "140-40" or "150-50" or "160-60" to quote a few, cannot be considered to construct similar portfolios. Gordon Fowler Jr. [FOW 07] studied these alternative strategies and concluded that an optimal choice of the strategy could be made by observing the *information ratio* (IR) or the incremental information ratio of the portfolios created, where IR is given by,

$$IR = \frac{(R_{Portfolio} - R_{Index})}{S_{Active\,Return}}$$

[6.1]

Here $R_{Portfolio}$ is the return of the portfolio and R_{Index} is the return of the index or the benchmark. ($R_{Portfolio}$ - R_{Index}) which is the difference between the returns of the portfolio and the index concerned, is also known as *Active Return*. $S_{ActiveReturn}$ is the standard deviation of the Active Returns and is also known as *Tracking error*. However, in this book we shall restrict the discussion only to 130-30 strategies.

6.2. 130-30 portfolio optimization: mathematical formulation

Construction of a 130-30 portfolio involves optimization of a long-short portfolio that guarantees performance. Jacobs *et al.* [JAC 99] were critical of the approach where long-short portfolios are constructed by combining a *long-only portfolio* with a *short-only portfolio*. Terming it *long-plus-short portfolio*, they asserted that such a construction does not reap the real benefits of long-short portfolios, which manifest only when the portfolio is constructed as a *single integrated combination of long and short positions*. In other words, long-short portfolio construction is not a two-portfolio strategy but a "… one-portfolio strategy in which the long and short positions are determined jointly within an optimization that takes into account the expected returns of the individual securities, the standard deviation of those returns and the correlations between them, as well as the investor's tolerance for risk" [JAC 99].

The mathematical formulation of such a specific 130-30 portfolio optimization model that adopts integrated optimization of the long and short positions, is given below

$$\max\left(\frac{\bar{\mu}.\bar{w} - R_f}{\sqrt{\bar{w}'.V.\bar{w}}}\right) \text{ (maximize Sharpe Ratio)} \qquad [6.2]$$

where $\bar{w} = (W_1, W_2, ... W_N)'$ and $\bar{\mu} = (\mu_1, \mu_2, ... \mu_N)$ are the weight and expected return vectors of the N assets in the portfolio. V is the variance-covariance matrix of returns and R_f is the risk free rate of return, subject to

$$\sum_{i=1}^{N} W_i = 1 \qquad \text{(budget constraint on portfolio)} \qquad [6.3]$$

$$\sum_{j} W_j^+ \leq 1.3 \quad \text{(budget constraint on long positions)} \qquad [6.4]$$

$$0 \leq W_j^+ \leq 1.3 \quad \text{(leveraged bounds on long positions)} \qquad [6.5]$$

$$-0.3 \leq W_k^- \leq 0 \qquad \text{(bounds on short positions), and} \qquad [6.6]$$

$$\beta_{Portfolio} = \sum_{i=1}^{N} \beta_i.W_i - 1 \qquad \text{(portfolio beta constraint)} \qquad [6.7]$$

where W_j^+ and W_k^- are the long and short positions of the optimal portfolio respectively, β_i are the individual asset betas and $\beta_{Portfolio}$ is the portfolio beta. While equation [6.4] induces leveraging on long positions (130%), equations [6.3] and [6.4] indirectly induce a budget constraint of 30% on the short positions (and hence not shown explicitly). Equations [6.5] and [6.6] define the bounds on the long and short positions respectively. The portfolio beta constraint equated to 1 and shown in [6.7] ensures that the volatility of the portfolio matches with that of the market.

6.3. 130-30 portfolio optimization using MATLAB Financial Toolbox™

MATLAB® Portfolio Object available in its Financial Toolbox™ could be used to solve the portfolio optimization problem defined using [6.2]–[6.7]. Figure 6.1 shows the definition and invocation of the portfolio object defined for the problem with maximizing Sharpe Ratio as its objective function.

```
...

AEQ = AssetBetas;
bEQ = 1;
Leverage = 0.3;

% declare Portfolio object p
p = Portfolio('RiskFreeRate', r0, 'AssetMean', ExpRet,
              'AssetCovar', ExpCov);

% set constraints
q =   setBounds(p, -Leverage, 1 + Leverage);
q =   setBudget(q, 1, 1);
q =   setEquality(q, AEQ, bEQ);
q =   setOneWayTurnover(q, 1 + Leverage, Leverage);

% invoke method estimateMaxSharpeRatio to obtain the
% optimal weights of the portfolio p with maximal
% Sharpe Ratio

[qswgt, qslong, qsshort] = estimateMaxSharpeRatio(q)


% invoke method estimatePortMoments to obtain the risk
% and return of the constrained portfolio q

[qsrsk, qsret] = estimatePortMoments(q, qswgt)

% compute the annualized risk, return and Sharpe ratio
% of the  optimal constrained 130-30 portfolio

risk_MaxSharpeRatio =   qsrsk*sqrt(261);
return_MaxSharpeRatio = qsret*261;
SharpeRatio = (return_MaxSharpeRatio-r0) /
                            risk_MaxSharpeRatio;
```

Figure 6.1. *130-30 constrained portfolio optimization using MATLAB® Portfolio Object (for a color version of this figure, see www.iste.co.uk/pai/metaheuristics.zip)*

Here `r0` is the risk free rate and `ExpRet`, `ExpCov` are the expected returns and variance–covariance matrix of the asset returns defined prior (and hence not shown). The constraints defined by [6.3]–[6.7] are handled by the methods `setBounds`, `setBudget`, `setEquality` and `setOneWayTurnover`. Thus, with `Leverage = 0.3`, `setBounds(p, -Leverage, 1 + Leverage)` ensures that the bounds of the assets oscillate only between [-0.3, 1.3], fulfilling [6.5]–[6.6]. `setBudget(q, 1, 1)` sets a budget constraint of 1 on the portfolio thereby satisfying [6.3]. `setEquality(q, AEQ, bEQ)` where `AEQ` is set as `AssetBetas`, the vector of asset betas and `bEQ = 1`, defines the portfolio beta constraint defined by [6.7].

`estimateMaxSharpeRatio(q)` optimizes the constrained portfolio `q` to yield the optimal weights and the specific optimal weights of the long and short positions in the optimal 130-30 portfolio as `[qswgt, qslong, qsshort]` in that order. `estimatePortMoments(q, qswgt)` obtains the risk and return of the optimal 130-30 portfolio only to be presented as annualized risk, annualized return along with the corresponding Sharpe Ratio, as shown in the code that follows it.

6.3.1. *Experimental results*

In this section, we discuss the results of various experiments performed over 130-30 portfolios constructed over S&P BSE200 (Bombay Stock Exchange, India, March 1999–March 2009) and Nikkei 225 (Tokyo Stock Exchange, Japan, March 1999–March 2009) indices.

A heuristic selection of assets was undertaken by *k*-means clustering the stock universes concerned into *k* clusters and ensuring that one asset from each cluster was chosen to construct the portfolio, to favor diversification. To recall, such a portfolio was termed *k-portfolio* for ease of reference. The mean returns and the variance-covariance of asset returns in the respective original universes were chosen as the principal characteristics for clustering the assets. Chapter 3 elaborates on the heuristic selection of securities using *k*-means clustering to construct *k*-portfolios. All the experiments discussed in the following sections were undertaken over *k*-portfolios.

Experiment 1: *Optimal integrated 130-30 portfolio construction*

In this experiment an integrated optimization of a 130-30 portfolio with no assets earmarked as long only or short only, was undertaken. It was left to MATLAB® Portfolio Object to decide upon the appropriate optimal combination of long and short positions.

Table 6.1 illustrates the composition and characteristics of the optimal constrained 130-30 k-portfolio obtained for $k = 90$, for S&P BSE 200 and Table 6.2 the same for Nikkei 225 index. Although the k-portfolios considered for constructing 130-30 portfolios comprised 90 assets each, only those long and short positions in the optimal 130-30 portfolio that held non-zero weights have been listed in the tables concerned, along with their individual betas.

Thus for the k-portfolio invested over S&P BSE200 index ($k = 90$), the optimal 130-30 portfolio arrived at by using MATLAB® Portfolio Object using the code shown in Figure 6.1 and described in Table 6.1, yielded 27 long positions and four short positions. For an average risk free rate of 6.5% for Indian markets during the period considered, the annualized risk (%), annualized expected portfolio return (%) and Sharpe ratio turned out to be 35.92, 86.23 and 2.22, respectively. The 130-30 portfolio satisfied all the constraints, viz. budget constraint on the portfolio and long/short positions, the bound constraints and the portfolio beta constraint as described by [6.3]–[6.7].

For the k-portfolio invested over Nikkei 225 index ($k = 90$) the optimal 130-30 portfolio computed using MATLAB® Portfolio Object using the code shown in Figure 6.1 and as described in Table 6.2, yielded 12 long positions and two short positions. For an average risk free rate of 1.5% for the Japanese markets during the period considered, the optimal 130-30 portfolio yielded an annualized risk (%), annualized return (%) and Sharpe Ratio of 35.56, 40.06 and 1.1 respectively. All the constraints described by [6.3]–[6.7] that were imposed upon the 130-30 portfolio were seen satisfied.

Experiment 2: 130-30 portfolios versus long only portfolios

Advocates of long-short portfolio strategies have always argued in favor of these strategies vis-a-vis long-only portfolio strategies. For example, Grinold and Kahn [GRI 00] showed that fully leveraged long-short strategies perform better than long only strategies when the universe of assets is large, volatility of assets is low or the strategy has high active risk. However, the costs of short sales turning out to be impediments in the efficiency of the portfolios constructed, have been debated by Michaud [MIC 93] and others as well.

Nevertheless, the rising popularity of 130-30 portfolios which are leveraged long-short portfolios and the increasing frustrations over long-only portfolios with regard to their performances, have kept the arguments alive and in favor of 130-30 portfolios. Andrew Lo and Pankaj Patel [LO 07] and Johnson et al. [JOH 07] to quote a few, concluded that 130-30 strategy indeed performs better when compared to their equivalent long-only counterparts since the strategy adds value from both the long and the short sides.

Optimal integrated 130-30 Portfolio Composition					
LONG Positions			SHORT Positions		
Asset label	Optimal weight	Asset Beta	Asset label	Optimal weight	Asset Beta
CROMPTON GREAVES LIMITED	0.0218	1.126	UNITED BREWERIES HOLDINGS LT	-0.1511	1.053
JAIN IRRIGATION SYSTEMS LTD	0.0494	0.824	TATA MOTORS LTD	-0.0930	1.091
SHRIRAM TRANSPORT FINANCE	0.0890	0.718	TATA CHEMICALS LIMITED	-0.0299	1.048
SINTEX INDUSTRIES LIMITED	0.0229	0.729	ROLTA INDIA LIMITED	-0.0260	1.427
FINANCIAL TECHN (INDIA) LTD	0.0597	1.377			
NAGARJUNA CONSTRUCTION CO	0.0082	1.236			
PRAJ INDUSTRIES LIMITED	0.0881	1.092			
BEML LIMITED	0.0004	1.228			
ESSAR OIL LTD	0.0165	1.298			
ADANI ENTERPRISES LTD	0.0135	0.973			
AREVA T&D INDIA LTD	0.0433	1.017			
PANTALOON RETAIL INDIA LTD	0.0752	1.040			
INFOSYS TECHNOLOGIES LTD	0.0097	0.807			
GUJARAT NRE COKE LTD	0.0685	1.224			
SESA GOA LTD	0.0096	1.198			

SUN PHARMACEUTICAL INDUS	0.1250	0.601
BHARAT ELECTRONICS LIMITED	0.0447	1.071
UNITED PHOSPHORUS LTD	0.0132	4.197
APOLLO HOSPITALS ENTERPRISE	0.0330	0.789
UNITECH LIMITED	0.0891	0.927
IVRCL INFRASTRUCTURES & PROJ	0.0317	1.573
GODREJ INDUSTRIES LTD	0.0191	1.039
STERLITE INDUSTRIES INDIA LT	0.1095	1.225
HINDUSTAN ZINC LIMITED	0.0762	1.099
WELSPUN-GUJARAT STAHL LTD	0.0554	1.346
VIDEOCON INDUSTRIES LTD	0.0335	0.862
JAI CORP LTD	0.0937	0.731

Optimal integrated 130-30 Portfolio Characteristics

Budget constraints on long and short positions	1.3		-0.3
Budget Constraint on portfolio	1		
Portfolio Beta	1.01		
Annualized Risk(%)	35.92		
Expected Portfolio Annualized Return(%)	86.23		
Sharpe Ratio	2.22		

Table 6.1. *Optimal integrated 130-30 portfolio obtained using MATLAB® Portfolio Object, its composition and characteristics, for k = 90 equity assets from S&P BSE200 index (Bombay Stock Exchange, India, March 1999-March 2009)*

In this experiment, the integrated optimal 130-30 portfolios constructed over S&P BSE200 and Nikkei 225 indices and listed in Table 6.1 and 6.2, were compared over their respective equivalent long-only counter parts. Eliminating short sales, leveraging and portfolio beta constraints, the equivalent long-only portfolio optimization model considered for the comparison is as follows:

$$\max\left(\frac{\bar{\mu}.\bar{w} - R_f}{\sqrt{\bar{w}'.V.\bar{w}}}\right) \quad \text{(maximize Sharpe Ratio)} \quad [6.8]$$

where $\bar{w} = (W_1, W_2, ...W_N)'$ and $\bar{\mu} = (\mu_1, \mu_2, ...\mu_N)$ are the weight and expected return vectors of the N assets in the portfolio. V is the variance-covariance matrix of returns and R_f is the risk free rate of return.

Optimal integrated 130-30 Portfolio Composition					
LONG Positions			SHORT Positions		
Asset label	Optimal weight	Asset Beta	Asset label	Optimal weight	Asset Beta
BANK OF YOKOHAMA LTD/THE	0.0046	0.9516	PIONEER CORP	-0.1779	1.1296
FAST RETAILING CO LTD	0.3299	0.8171	CSK HOLDINGS CORP	-0.1221	1.1574
SUMITOMO METAL MINING CO LTD	0.1066	1.1252			
DOWA HOLDINGS CO LTD	0.0159	1.3004			
SOFTBANK CORP	0.1178	1.2337			
KONICA MINOLTA HOLDINGS INC	0.0958	1.2177			
JGC CORP	0.2719	1.0799			
HITACHI CONSTRUCTION MACHINE	0.1365	1.1941			
NISSAN CHEMICAL INDUSTRIES	0.0202	1.0682			
DAIKIN INDUSTRIES LTD	0.1197	1.0436			
SHIONOGI & CO LTD	0.0677	0.6936			
KOMATSU LTD	0.0135	1.1616			

Optimal integrated 130-30 Portfolio Characteristics		
Budget constraints on long and short positions	**1.3**	**-0.3**
Budget Constraint on portfolio	1	
Portfolio Beta	1	
Annualized Risk(%)	35.56	
Expected Portfolio Annualized Return(%)	40.06	
Sharpe Ratio	1.1	

Table 6.2. *Optimal integrated 130-30 portfolio obtained using MATLAB® Portfolio Object, its composition and characteristics, for k = 90 equity assets from Nikkei 225 index (Tokyo Stock Exchange, Japan, March 1999–March 2009)*

subject to

$$\sum_{i=1}^{N} W_i = 1 \qquad \text{(budget constraint on portfolio)} \qquad [6.9]$$

$$0 \le W_i \le 1 \qquad \text{(bound constraint)} \qquad [6.10]$$

The model is the same as the Sharpe Ratio-based Portfolio Optimization model described by [1.24] in Chapter 1. Obtaining the optimal solution to the problem model using MATLAB® Portfolio Object was also demonstrated in Chapter 1, section 1.3 D (Figure 1.10). Adopting the same procedure and code, Tables 6.3 and 6.4 illustrate the composition and characteristics of the optimal long-only portfolio for S&P BSE 200 and Nikkei 225 indices respectively.

As can be seen from Table 6.3, the equivalent long-only portfolio for S&P BSE200 index yields an annualized risk, annualized return and Sharpe ratio of 28.91%, 61.88% and 1.92, respectively. The same for Nikkei 225 index and listed in Table 6.4 yields 32.97%, 28.75% and 0.83, respectively. Going by the Sharpe Ratios alone, it is evident that the performance of 130-30 portfolios far exceed that of their equivalent long-only portfolios be it for S&P BSE 200 or Nikkei 225. The experiment conducted over other k-portfolios for various k, over both the indices also yielded similar performances by the respective 130-30 portfolios when compared to those of their long-only counterparts.

Experiment 3: Long plus short 130-30 portfolios

In this experiment, a long plus short approach was adopted to construct 130-30 portfolios. A definite number of specific assets were selected as long and short positions. In the experiment, the choices of the assets were made based on their betas. Thus the assets in the k-portfolio were ranked according to their increasing order of asset betas and the top x percentile of assets with low betas were considered for long positions and the rest for short positions. The rest of the constraints described by [6.3]–[6.7] were kept intact and the objective was to obtain the portfolio with maximal Sharpe Ratio. The budget constraints on the portfolio and long positions explicitly described by [6.3]–[6.4] had in fact implicitly described the following short position budget constraint:

$$\sum_k W_k^- \le -0.3 \quad \text{(budget constraint on short positions)} \quad [6.11]$$

Since the long and short positions are fixed in a long plus short portfolio, the method setInequality(p, AIN, bIN) was used to tackle the budget constraints on long and short positions described by [6.4] and [6.11] as inequality constraints. For the MATLAB® Portfolio Object p shown in the method AIN and bIN are the linear inequality matrix and vector respectively, to be provided as inputs to the method. Figure 6.2 illustrates the MATLAB® code fragment using Portfolio Object for optimizing long plus short 130-30 portfolios. Here LongAssets and ShortAssets indicate the indices of the long positions and the short positions in the k-portfolio considered where k = NumAssets. LongPositions and ShortPositions denote the (Boolean) vectors of dimension NumAssets, for the long and short positions. AssetBounds denotes the matrix of bounds for the long and short positions with the first row indicating the lower bounds for the long/short positions concerned (0/-0.3 respectively) and the second row indicating the upper bounds for the long/short positions concerned (1.3/0 respectively).

Optimal long-only Portfolio Composition		
Asset label	Optimal weight	Asset Beta
JAIN IRRIGATION SYSTEMS LTD	0.0454	0.824
SHRIRAM TRANSPORT FINANCE	0.0901	0.718
SINTEX INDUSTRIES LIMITED	0.0354	0.729
FINANCIAL TECHN (INDIA) LTD	0.0042	1.377
PRAJ INDUSTRIES LIMITED	0.0580	1.092
HERO HONDA MOTORS LIMITED	0.0188	0.556
AREVA T&D INDIA LTD	0.0139	1.017
PANTALOON RETAIL INDIA LTD	0.0433	1.040
GUJARAT NRE COKE LTD	0.0555	1.224
ASIAN PAINTS LTD	0.0409	0.384
SUN PHARMACEUTICAL INDUS	0.1585	0.601
UNITED PHOSPHORUS LTD	0.006	4.197

APOLLO HOSPITALS ENTERPRISE	0.0306	0.789
UNITECH LIMITED	0.0888	0.927
IVRCL INFRASTRUCTURES & PROJ	0.0196	1.573
STERLITE INDUSTRIES INDIA LT	0.0240	1.225
HINDUSTAN ZINC LIMITED	0.0432	1.099
WELSPUN-GUJARAT STAHL LTD	0.0359	1.346
JUBILANT ORGANOSYS LTD	0.0269	0.581
VIDEOCON INDUSTRIES LTD	0.0351	0.862
JAI CORP LTD	0.0919	0.731
CONTAINER CORP OF INDIA LTD	0.0339	0.541
Optimal long-only Portfolio Characteristics		
Budget constraint	1	
Annualized Risk(%)	28.91	
Expected Portfolio Annualized Return(%)	61.88	
Sharpe Ratio	1.92	

Table 6.3. *Optimal long-only portfolio obtained using MATLAB® Portfolio Object, its composition and characteristics, for k = 90 equity assets from S&P BSE200 index (Bombay Stock Exchange, India, March 1999–March 2009)*

Optimal long-only Portfolio Composition		
Asset label	**Optimal weight**	**Asset Beta**
FAST RETAILING CO LTD	0.3758	0.8171
SUMITOMO METAL MINING CO LTD	0.0734	1.1252
ODAKYU ELECTRIC RAILWAY CO	0.0605	0.5823
SOFTBANK CORP	0.0406	1.2337
JGC CORP	0.2454	1.0799
HITACHI CONSTRUCTION MACHINE	0.0798	1.1941
DAIKIN INDUSTRIES LTD	0.0512	1.0436
SHIONOGI & CO LTD	0.0733	0.6936
Optimal long-only Portfolio Characteristics		
Budget constraint	1	
Annualized Risk(%)	32.97	
Expected Portfolio Annualized Return(%)	28.75	
Sharpe Ratio	0.83	

Table 6.4. *Optimal long-only portfolio obtained using MATLAB® Portfolio Object, its composition and characteristics, for k = 90 equity assets from Nikkei 225 index (Tokyo Stock Exchange, Japan, March 1999–March 2009)*

```
. . .

% Set Long positions and Short positions vectors
LongPositions = zeros(1, NumAssets);
ShortPositions = zeros(1, NumAssets);
LongPositions(1, LongAssets) = 1;
ShortPositions(1, ShortAssets) =1;

% Set linear inequality matrix and vector for long
% and short position %budget constraints
AIN - [LongPositions; ShortPositions];
bIN = [1.3, -0.3];

% Set linear equality matrix and vector for
% portfolio beta constraint
AEQ = AssetBetas;
bEQ = 1;

% declare Portfolio object p
p = Portfolio('RiskFreeRate', r0, 'AssetMean', ExpRet,
'AssetCovar', ExpCov);

% set 130 30 portfolio constraints
p =   setBounds(p, AssetBounds(1,:),
                              AssetBounds(2,:));
p =   setBudget(p, 1, 1);
p =   setInequality(p, AIN, bIN);
p =   setEquality(p, AEQ, bEQ);

% invoke method estimateMaxSharpeRatio to obtain
% the optimal weights of the portfolio p with
% maximal Sharpe Ratio
portfoliowgt = p.estimateMaxSharpeRatio;

. . .
```

Figure 6.2. *Code fragment for long plus short 130-30 constrained portfolio optimization using MATLAB® Portfolio Object (for a color version of this figure, see www.iste.co.uk/pai/metaheuristics.zip)*

For a k-portfolio ($k = 90$) with a 60:30 choice of long and short positions based on their asset betas, Tables 6.5 and 6.6 illustrate the composition and characteristics of the optimal 130-30 portfolios constructed over S&P BSE200 and Nikkei 225 indices respectively. Only those long and short positions with non-zero weights have been listed. The optimal long plus short 130-30 portfolio for S&P BSE200 and illustrated in Table 6.5 shows an annualized risk, annualized return and Sharpe Ratio of 41.17%, 74.87% and 1.66, respectively and the same for Nikkei 225 index illustrated in Table 6.6 shows 36.32, 37.64 and 1.0 respectively.

204 Metaheuristics for Portfolio Optimization

As can be observed all the constraints are satisfied but the Sharpe Ratios of the long plus short 130-30 portfolios are no better than those of their integrated 130-30 portfolio counterparts.

6.4. Metaheuristic 130-30 portfolio optimization

In this section we demonstrate the application of a metaheuristic approach, viz. Differential Evolution with Hall of Fame (DE HOF) for the constrained optimization of 130-30 portfolios.

Metaheuristic approaches have always come in handy when traditional methods or solvers have found it difficult to solve complex constrained optimization problems, by providing acceptable or near optimal solutions to the problems concerned. In such a background, the integrated optimization of 130-30 portfolios described by [6.2]–[6.7] and discussed in section 6.3.1, Experiment 1, can turn difficult for solving using traditional methods of optimization due to its *integrated* nature of optimization which does not ear mark specific set of assets as long or short in the initial stage itself, but has to dynamically arrive at that optimal composition of long and short positions that will yield the maximal Sharpe Ratio. MATLAB® Portfolio Object, however, is endowed with the ability to solve this specific 130-30 portfolio optimization problem, with the help of its setOneWayTurnover method and this was what was demonstrated in section 6.3.1, Experiment 1, using the code fragment exhibited in Figure 6.1.

Notwithstanding the availability of MATLAB® solver for the solution of this specific problem, the objective of this section and the book in general, is to explore if metaheuristic approaches left to themselves would be able to arrive at an acceptable or near-optimal solution to this specific problem in question. We therefore proceed to explore if a robust metaheuristic optimization algorithm such as Differential Evolution with Hall of Fame (DE HOF) (introduced in Chapter 2, section 2.5 and applied to various other portfolio optimization models discussed in Chapters 4 and 5) can arrive at a respectable solution for the problem concerned.

6.4.1. *Transformation of 130-30 portfolio optimization model*

The 130-30 portfolio optimization model described using [6.2]–[6.7] has to be transformed to render it amenable for solving using a metaheuristic method. Chapter 4, section 4.3.1 elaborated on constraint handling methods adopted by metaheuristics strategies to tackle the problem in question. Two popular methods viz. *repair strategy* and *penalty function strategy* were introduced. Repair strategy to recall, was one where each individual in the population, representing a candidate solution, repairs itself by adjusting its genes to satisfy the constraints imposed and in the process transforms itself into a feasible solution vector. Penalty function strategy, on the other hand, was one where infeasible solutions are penalized using what are called penalty coefficients and the constrained optimization problem is transformed into an unconstrained optimization problem by employing penalized objective functions. Also, Joines and Houck's penalty function strategy [JOI 94] that employs dynamic penalties was also discussed and demonstrated in section 4.3.2. We follow the same techniques here to tackle constraints ([6.3]–[6.7]) of the 130-30 portfolio optimization problem model.

Joines and Houck's dynamic penalty functions were used to tackle the portfolio beta constraint represented by [6.7] and weight repair strategies were used to tackle the rest of the constraints described by [6.3]–[6.6]. The transformed mathematical model employing Joines and Houck's dynamic penalty function strategy is as shown below:

$$\max\left(\frac{\bar{\mu}.\bar{w}-R_f}{\sqrt{\bar{w}'.V.\bar{w}}}-\psi(\bar{w},\bar{\beta}_A,t)\right) \qquad \text{(maximize Sharpe Ratio)} \qquad [6.12]$$

where $\bar{w}=(W_1,W_2,...W_N)'$ and $\bar{\mu}=(\mu_1,\mu_2,...\mu_N)$ are the weight and expected return vectors of the N assets in the portfolio. V is the variance-covariance matrix of returns and R_f is the risk free rate of return. $\psi(\bar{w},\bar{\beta}_A,t)$ is the constraint violation function given by,

$$\psi(\bar{w},\bar{\beta}_A,t)=(C.t)^\alpha.G.\left(\varphi(\bar{w},\bar{\beta}_A)\right)^\beta,$$

$$\varphi(\bar{w},\bar{\beta}_A)=\left|\sum_{k=1}^{N}\beta_A^k.w_k-1\right| \quad \text{and}$$

$\quad\quad\quad G \quad$ is the Heaviside Operator such that $\qquad\qquad\qquad\qquad$ [6.13]

$\quad\quad\quad G=0, \quad for \quad \varphi(\bar{w},\bar{\beta}_A)\le\varepsilon, \quad$ and

$\quad\quad\quad\quad\; =1, \quad for \quad \varphi(\bar{w},\bar{\beta}_A)>\varepsilon$

where $\bar{\beta}_A=\left(\beta_A^1,\beta_A^2,\beta_A^3,...\beta_A^N\right)$ are the asset betas and ε is the tolerance limit which is a very small number.

Optimal long plus short 130-30 Portfolio Composition					
Optimal LONG Positions			Optimal SHORT Positions		
Asset label	Optimal weight	Asset Beta	Asset label	Optimal weight	Asset Beta
SHRIRAM TRANSPORT FINANC	0.0459	0.718	UNITED BREWERIES HOLDINGS LT	-0.2968	1.053
PRAJ INDUSTRIES LIMITED	0.2026	1.092	ZEE ENTERTAINMENT ENTERPRISE	-0.0032	1.115
ICICI BANK LTD	0.0049	1.015			
ADANI ENTERPRISES LTD	0.0195	0.973			
AREVA T&D INDIA LTD	0.1155	1.017			
PANTALOON RETAIL INDIA LTD	0.1646	1.040			
BHARATH HEAVY ELECTRICALS	0.0879	1.073			
BHARATH ELECTRONICS LTD	0.2156	1.071			
AXIS BANK LTD	0.1108	1.054			
BOMBAY DYEING & MFG CO LTD	0.0526	1.332			
CESC LTD	0.0445	1.027			
UNITECH LIMITED	0.0951	0.927			
GODREJ INDUSTRIES LTD	0.1203	1.039			
VIDEOCON INDUSTRIES LTD	0.0203	0.862			

Optimal long plus short 130-30 Portfolio Characteristics			
Budget constraints on long and short positions	1.3		-0.3
Budget Constraint on portfolio	1		
Portfolio Beta	1		
Annualized Risk(%)	41.17		
Expected Portfolio Annualized Return(%)	74.87		
Sharpe Ratio	1.66		

Table 6.5. *Optimal long plus short 130-30 portfolio obtained using MATLAB® Portfolio Object, its composition and characteristics, for k = 90 equity assets from S&P BSF200 index(Bombay Stock Exchange, India) with 60 long positions and 30 short positions in the k-portfolio*

The portfolio beta constraint is expressed as

$$\left| \sum_{k=1}^{N} \beta_A^k . w_k - 1 \right| \leq \varepsilon \qquad [6.14]$$

to incorporate the tolerance limit (ε) for the equality constraint. (C, α, β) are constants and the penalty term $(C.t)^{\alpha}$ increases constantly with each generation count t.

The rest of the constraints described by [6.3]–[6.6] are retained as they are, but for reasons of convenience, have been explicitly listed as shown below.

$$\sum_{i=1}^{N} W_i = 1 \qquad \text{(budget constraint on portfolio)} \qquad [6.15]$$

$$\sum_{j} W_j^+ \leq 1.3 \qquad \text{(budget constraint on long positions)} \qquad [6.16]$$

$$\sum_{k} W_k^- \leq -0.3, k \neq j, \qquad \text{(budget constraint on short positions)} \qquad [6.17]$$

$$0 \le W_j^+ \le 1.3 \qquad \text{(leveraged bounds on long positions)} \qquad [6.18]$$

$$-0.3 \le W_k^- \le 0 \qquad \text{(bounds on short positions)} \qquad [6.19]$$

Thus for the metaheuristic *integrated* optimization of 130-30 portfolios, the mathematical model represented by [6.12]–[6.13] as the penalized objective function and constraints described by [6.15]–[6.19] are considered for solving using Differential Evolution with Hall of Fame.

Optimal long plus short 130-30 Portfolio Composition					
LONG Positions			**SHORT Positions**		
Asset label	**Optimal weights**	**Asset Beta**	**Asset label**	**Optimal weights**	**Asset Beta**
FAST RETAILING CO LTD	0.2608	0.8171	PIONEER CORP	-0.2116	1.1296
SUMITOMO METAL MINING CO LTD	0.2313	1.1252	CSK HOLDINGS CORP	-0.0884	1.1574
SHIMZU CORP	0.0827	1.1275			
JGC CORP	0.3858	1.0799			
NISSAN CHEMICAL INDUSTRIES	0.1128	1.0682			
KYOCERA CORP	0.0325	1.0776			
DAIKIN INDUSTRIES LTD	0.1943	1.0436			
Optimal long plus short 130-30 Portfolio Characteristics					
Budget constraints on long and short positions	1.3		-0.3		
Budget Constraint on portfolio	1				
Portfolio Beta	1				
Annualized Risk(%)	36.32				
Expected Portfolio Annualized Return(%)	37.64				
Sharpe Ratio	1.0				

Table 6.6. *Optimal long plus short 130-30 portfolio obtained using MATLAB® Portfolio Object, its composition and characteristics, for k = 90 equity assets from Nikkei 225 index (Tokyo Stock Exchange, Japan) with 60 long only assets and 30 short only assets*

6.4.2. *Constraint handling*

Weight repair strategies are employed to tackle constraints described by [6.15]–[6.19] in two phases.

In the first phase, each population of individuals undergoes weight repair to ensure that the bound constraints and the portfolio budget constraint represented by [6.18]–[6.19] and [6.15] respectively, are satisfied. At the end of the procedure, all the respective long positions and short positions in each individual of the population satisfy their respective bound constraints and the summation of the weights of the individuals in the portfolio equals 1. We term this phase *Weight repair strategy Phase 1*.

In the second phase, the population of individuals repaired by the first phase, are further repaired to satisfy constraints described by [6.16] and [6.17] so that the long positions and short positions exclusive to the individual concerned, satisfy their respective budget constraints without violating the constraints already satisfied by Phase 1. We term this phase as *Weight repair strategy Phase 2*.

Generic weight repair strategies for Phase 1 and Phase 2 have been presented below.

Weight repair strategy Phase 1

Let W represent a random vector of N weights of the portfolio comprising N assets, generated between *(-0.3, 1.3)*. Let W^+ and W^- denote the positive weights (long positions L) and negative weights (short positions S) in the weight vector. The repair strategy to satisfy constraints ([6.18]–[6.19] and [6.15]) demonstrated on the specific weight vector, works as follows:

Step 1: If weights $w_i \in W^+$ or $w_i \in W^-$ are less than their respective lower bounds 0 and -0.3 respectively, upgrade the respective weights to their respective lower bounds. Let R denote the set of such upgraded weights and Q those that already satisfied their lower bounds and hence were not upgraded.

Step 2: Let SUM be the sum of absolute weights in Q and let F, the free proportion of weights be $F = 1 - \sum_{i \in R \cup Q} \varepsilon_i$, where ε_i indicates the lower bounds of the respective long and short positions in sets R and Q. Distribute F over asset weights in Q, proportional to their respective weight holdings as follows:

$$TERM = F / SUM;$$
$$w_i' = \varepsilon_i + |w_i| * TERM;$$

Let W' denote the set of these upgraded weights that satisfy their respective lower bounds and add up to 1.

Step 3: Check if weights of the long and short positions belonging to W' exceed their respective upper bounds δ_i (1.3 and 0 respectively).

>**if** all weights of W' satisfy their respective upper bounds
>**then** Output W' as the standardized weight set; **exit (Success);**
>**else**
>Level off such of these weights to their respective upper bounds δ_i and label these as set R. Let Q indicate the rest of the weights that satisfy their upper bounds.
>**go to** Step 4;
>**end**

Step 4: Compute *SUM*, the absolute sum of weights in Q and F the free portion of weights as $F = 1 - \sum_{i \in Q} \varepsilon_i - \sum_{j \in R} \delta_j$ where ε_i and δ_i are the respective lower bounds and upper bounds of weights in Q and R. Distribute F over Q proportional to their respective holdings as

>$TERM = F / SUM;$
>$w_i'' = \varepsilon_i + |w_i'| * TERM;$
>
>**if** $w_i'' \in Q$ $\forall w_i''$, satisfy their respective upper bounds
>**then**   **go to** Step 6
>**else go to** Step 5;
>**end**

Step 5: **if** there exists any $w_i'' \in Q$ that exceeds their respective upper bounds,

>**then** level off such weights to their upper bounds, remove them from Q, add them to R;
>**go to** Step 4;
>**end**

Step 6: Output weights in R and Q as the upgraded weight set W'' and **exit (Success);**

W'' records weights of long and short positions that satisfy their respective upper and lower bounds and have their total weight summing up to 1, thereby satisfying constraints described by [6.18]–[6.19] and [6.15], respectively.

EXAMPLE.– Let $W = [1.4, 0.9, -0.4, 0.1, -0.2, -0.5]$ represent a random weight vector of six assets. Going by the sign of their weights, the portfolio represented by the weight vector and denoted as $\{ l_1, l_2, s_1, l_3, s_2, s_3 \}$ has three long positions viz. L $= \{ l_1, l_2, l_3 \}$ and three short positions viz. $S = \{s_1, s_2, s_3\}$. To reemphasize, since it is integrated optimization, the long and short positions are not preset as it is done in long plus short strategies.

Adopting the notations employed in the repairing strategy discussed above,

$W^+ = [1.4, 0.9, 0.1]$, $W^- [-0.4, -0.2, -0.5]$ and $(\varepsilon_i, \delta_i) = (0,1.3)$ are the lower and upper bounds for long positions and $(\varepsilon_i, \delta_i) = (-0.3, 0)$ are the same for short positions.

Step 1: Upgrading the weights in W which are less than their respective lower bounds yields $[1.4, 0.9, -0.3, 0.1, -0.2, -0.3]$ and therefore $R = \{s_1, s_3\} = \{ -0.3, -0.3 \}$ and $Q = \{ l_1, l_2, l_3, s_2 \} = \{ 1.4, 0.9, 0.1, -0.2 \}$.

Step 2: SUM the sum of absolute weights in Q equals 2.6 and F the free portion of weights equals 1.9. Therefore $TERM- 1.9/2.6 - 0.731$ and the updated weights of Q given by $w_i' = \varepsilon_i + |w_i| * TERM$, result in

$W' = [0 + 1.4 * 0.731, \ 0 + 0.9 * 0.731,$

$\qquad -0.3, \ 0 + 0.1 * 0.731, \ -0.3 + |-0.2| * 0.731, \ -0.3]$

$\qquad = [1.0234, \ 0.6579, \ -0.3, \ 0.0731, \ -0.1538, \ -0.3]$

It can be observed that W' satisfies its lower bounds and the weights sum up to 1.

Step 3: Checking for weights that satisfy or violate their upper bounds in W' yields a favorable result where all weights satisfy their respective upper bounds. Hence the strategy exits with success with W' as the standardized weight set. It can be observed that the weights satisfy the constraints defined by [6.18]–[6.19] and [6.15].

Thus, employing the weight repair strategy over each individual in the population set yields a population of individuals that satisfy constraints represented by [6.18]–[6.19] and [6.15].

Weight repair strategy Phase 2

In the second phase, the standardized population of individuals W' which now satisfy constraints described by [6.18]–[6.19] and [6.15], are repaired to enable them satisfy the budget constraints of long/short positions described by [6.16]–[6.17] subject to the portfolio budget constraint defined by [6.15].

The following are the steps undertaken. *DEPOSIT* is a repository of weights that is initialized to 0 and used to adjust excess weights if any, between the long and short positions as a whole so that ultimately the portfolio budget constraint of weights summing up to 1 is satisfied.

Step 1: *Repairing long position weights to tackle their budget constraint of 1.3:*

The long positions L are first tackled.

if $0 \le \sum w_i'^+ \le 1.3$ where $w_i'^+ \in W'^+$ **then go to** Step 3;

else go to Step 2;

Step 2: Shear off excess weights and store them in *DEPOSIT* as *DEPOSIT* = $DEPOSIT + \left(\sum w_i'^+ - 1.3 \right)$. Adjust long position weights so that they now sum up to 1.3 while satisfying their individual bounds of [0, 1.3] as shown in Steps 3 and 4.

Step 3: Let *SUM* be the sum of the long position weights in W'^+ and let F, the free proportion of weights be $F = 1.3 - \sum_{i \in L} \varepsilon_i$, where ε_i indicates the lower bounds of the respective long positions. Distribute F over the long position weights, proportional to their respective weight holdings as follows:

$TERM = F / SUM;$

$w_i''^+ = \varepsilon_i + w_i'^+ * TERM;$

Here $w_i''^+$ denotes the set of upgraded weights of the long positions that satisfy their respective lower bounds and add up to 1.3.

Step 4: Check if weights of the long positions $w_i^{''+}$ exceed their respective upper bounds δ_i i.e. 1.3.

if $w_i^{''+}, \forall i$ satisfy their respective upper bounds

then output $W^{'''+} = w_i^{''+}$ as the standardized weight set for long

positions;

go to Step 7;

else

Level off such of these weights to their respective upper bounds δ_i and label these as set R. Let Q indicate the rest of the weights that satisfy their upper bounds;

go to Step 5;

end

Step 5: Compute SUM_Q, the sum of weights in Q and F the free portion of weights as $F = 1.3 - \sum_{i \in Q} \varepsilon_i - \sum_{j \in R} \delta_j$ where ε_i and δ_i are the respective lower bounds and upper bounds of weights in Q and R. Distribute F over Q proportional to their respective holdings as

$$TERM = F / SUM\_Q;$$
$$w_i^{'''+} = \varepsilon_i + w_i^{''+} * TERM, \quad w_i^{''+} \in Q;$$

if $w_i^{'''+} \in Q, \forall w_i^{''+}$, satisfy their respective upper bounds

then let $W^{'''+} = w_i^{'''+};$ **go to** Step 7;

else go to Step 6;

end

Step 6: If there exists any $w_i^{'''+} \in Q$ that exceeds their respective upper bounds, level off such weights to their upper bounds, remove them from Q, add them to R and **go to** Step 5;

Step 7: *Repairing short position weights to tackle their budget constraint of -0.3:*

Let W'^- indicate the short positions in the weight vector set W'.

Compute $SUM = \sum_i w_i'^-$ and $ABS\_SUM = \sum_i |w_i'^-|$ and

$DEPOSIT = DEPOSIT + SUM,$ where DEPOSIT now denotes the actual ceiling of weights to be satisfied by the short positions, which will turn out to be $\sim$ -0.3 due to the portfolio budget constraint already being satisfied in Phase 1.

Step 8: Let F the free proportion of weights be, $F = -0.3 - \sum\limits_{i \in S} \varepsilon_i$, where ε_i indicates the lower bounds of the respective short positions. Distribute F over the short position weights, proportional to their respective weight holdings as follows:

$$TERM = F / ABS\_SUM;$$
$$w_i''^{-} = \varepsilon_i + \left| w_i'^{-} \right| * TERM;$$

Here $w_i''^{-}$ denotes the set of upgraded weights of the short positions that satisfy their respective lower bounds and adds up to -0.3.

Step 9: Check if weights of the short positions $w_i''^{-}$ exceed their respective upper bounds δ_i $(= 0)$.

if $w_i''^{-}, \forall i$ satisfy their respective upper bounds

then output $W''^{-} = w_i''^{-}$ as the standardized weight set for short

positions;

go to Step 12;

else

Level off such of these weights to their respective upper bounds δ_i and label these as set R. Let Q indicate the rest of the weights that satisfy their upper bounds;

go to Step 10;

end

Step 10: Compute ABS_SUM_Q, the sum of absolute weights in Q and F the free portion of weights as $F = -0.3 - \sum\limits_{i \in Q} \varepsilon_i \cdot |Q| - \sum\limits_{j \in R} \delta_j \cdot |R|$ where $|Q|$ and $|R|$ indicate the lengths of Q and R respectively and ε_i and δ_i are the respective lower bounds and upper bounds of weights in Q and R respectively. Distribute F over Q proportional to their respective holdings as

$$TERM = F / ABS\_SUM\_Q;$$
$$w_i''^{-} = \varepsilon_i + \left| w_i''^{-} \right| * TERM, \ w_i''^{-} \in Q$$

if $w_i''^-\in Q,\quad \forall i$, satisfy their respective upper bounds

then set $W''^- = w_i''^-$ and

      go to Step 12;

else **go to** Step 11;

end

Step 11: **if** there exists any $w_i''^-\in Q$ that exceeds their respective upper bounds

    then level off such weights to their upper bounds, remove them from
        Q and add them to R;

        go to Step 10;

  end

Step 12: Conjoin the long position weights W''^+ and short position weights W''^- to form the weight vector W''' which is the feasible solution set that satisfies all its constraints described by equations [6.15]–[6.19]. Output the upgraded weight set W''' and **exit (Success)**;

Thus, employing the weight repair strategy over each individual in the population set with Phase 1 immediately followed by Phase 2, yields a population of individuals that satisfy constraints represented by [6.15]–[6.19] .

EXAMPLE.– Since outputs of Phase 1 become inputs to Phase 2, we shall consider the standardized weight set arrived at in the example discussed for Weight repair strategy Phase 1, $W' = [1.0234, 0.6579, -0.3, 0.0731, -0.1538, -0.3]$ to demonstrate the working of Phase 2. Going by the sign of their weights, the portfolio represented by the weight vector and denoted as $\{l_1, l_2, s_1, l_3, s_2, s_3\}$ has three long positions viz., L = $\{l_1, l_2, l_3\}$ three short positions viz. S = $\{s_1, s_2, s_3\}$. The steps undertaken to standardize them to satisfy the budget constraints imposed on long and short positions described by [6.16]–[6.17] are as follows:

Steps 1–2: Since $\sum w_i'^+ = (1.0234 + 0.6579+0.0731) = 1.7544$, exceeds 1.3, shearing off the excess weights yields $DEPOSIT = 1.7544\ -1.3 = 0.4544$.

Step 3: SUM the sum of long position weights equals 1.7544 and F the free portion of weights equals 1.3. Therefore $TERM = 1.3/1.7544 = 0.7410$ and the updated weights are given by

$$w_i^{''+} = [\ 1.0234 * 0.7410,\ 0.6579*0.7410, 0.0731*0.7410]$$

$$= [0.7583, 0.4875, 0.0542]$$

It can be observed that $\sum w_i^{''+} = 1.3$ and each of the weights satisfy their lower bounds.

Step 4: Checking for weights that satisfy or violate their upper bounds in $w_i^{''+}$ yields a favorable result where all weights satisfy their respective upper bounds. Hence the strategy delivers W''^+ as the standardized weight set for the long positions. It can be observed that the weights satisfy the constraints defined by [6.16]. The strategy proceeds to Step 7 to standardize the short position weights.

Step 7: Compute $SUM = (-0.3-0.1538-0.3) = -0.7538$, $ABS\_SUM = |-0.7538|$ and $DEPOSIT = DEPOSIT + SUM = 0.4544 - 0.7538 = -0.2994$ (which is approximately -0.3).

Step 8: $F = -0.3 - (-0.3*3) = 0.6$ and $TERM = 0.6/0.7538 = 0.7959$. The upgraded weights,

$$w_i^{''-} = (-0.3 +|-0.3|*0.7959, -0.3+|-0.1538|*0.7959,\ -0.3+|-0.3|*0.7959)$$

$$= (-0.06123, -0.1776, -0.06123)$$

It can be observed that $\sum w_i^{''-} = -0.3$ and each upgraded weight satisfies its lower bounds.

Step 9: Since all the weights satisfy their upper bounds, the strategy delivers the standardized weight set for short positions as $W''^- = w_i^{''-}$ and moves to Step 12.

Step 12: Conjoining W''^+ and W''^- yields the standardized weight vector W''' = (0.7583, 0.4875, -0.06123, 0.0542, -0.1776, -0.06123) which can be seen to satisfy all the constraints for the 130-30 portfolio described by [6.15]–[6.19].

EXAMPLE.– Steps 5 and 6 of Weight repair strategy Phase 2, illustrate the actions to be taken when the partially standardized weight set for long positions satisfying its lower bounds and budget constraint of 1.3 (undertaken in Steps 1–4) proceeds to satisfy its upper bounds subject to the budget constraint, if any violations have happened during the course of Step 3. The weight set shown in the previous example did not face such as situation and hence Steps 5–6 were not applicable. Besides in an integrated optimization of 130-30 portfolios there is no earmarking of assets as long or short initially and the strategy works to find out the optimal composition of long and short positions from the assets decided upon. Hence the upper and lower bounds of the long and short positions are kept loose fitting [0, 1.3] for long positions and [-0.3, 0] for short positions. Therefore there is always a strong likelihood of some steps getting short circuited during the execution of the generic weight repair strategies discussed.

Nonetheless, we now illustrate steps 5 and 6 over a hypothetical weight set $w_i^{"\,|} = (0.75, 0.5, 0.05)$ for three long positions L = {l_1, l_2, l_3} just after the standardized weight set was released as output by Step 3. For the sake of discussion let us suppose that the upper and lower bounds of the three long positions are as follows, where leveraging is permissible only on l_3. :

$$0 \le w_1 \le 0.5, \quad 0 \le w_2 \le 0.25, \quad 0 \le w_3 \le 1.3$$

$w_i^{"\,+} = (0.75, 0.5, 0.05)$ adhering to Step 3's actions, satisfies its respective lower bounds as well as its budget constraint of 1.3. However, long positions l_1, l_2 are seen to be violating their respective upper bounds. We therefore proceed to steps 4–6 as shown below:

Step 4: Long positions {l_1, l_2} are not satisfying their respective upper bounds. Leveling them off to their upper bounds results in R = {0.5, 0.25} and Q = {0.05}.

Step 5: Compute $SUM\_Q = 0.05$, $F = 1.3-(0)-(0.5+0.25) = 0.55$ and

$TERM = F / SUM\_Q = 11$.

The weights in Q are upgraded as $w_i^{"\,+} = (0+0.05*11) = 0.55$.

Gathering the weight set yields, $w_i^{"\,+} = (0.5, 0.25, 0.55)$ wherein each weight satisfies its respective upper and lower bounds, besides the budget constraint of 1.3. Since there are no violations, Step 6 is skipped and the standardized long position weights are delivered as $W^{"+} = w_i^{"\,+} = (0.5, 0.25, 0.55)$.

In the event of any of the weights in Q over shooting their upper bounds after their upgrading in Step 5, the weights are leveled off to their upper bounds, deleted from Q and pushed into R. The strategy cycles back to Step 5 repeating the process of upgrading the new Q and so on until there are no such upper bound violations happening in Q. At that stage the standardized weight set is gathered and delivered as $W^{"+} = w_i^{"\,+}$.

6.4.3. *Differential Evolution-based 130-30 portfolio construction*

In this section we describe the construction of optimal 130-30 portfolios using Differential Evolution with Hall of Fame (DE HOF).

DE HOF as was discussed in Chapter 4, section 4.4, is a population-based metaheuristic search process that begins with an initial random population of individuals representing a candidate solution set to the problem in hand, transforms them into a population of feasible solution sets by weight repair or some such strategies (a method fiercely adopted with regard to all metaheuristic approaches discussed in this book), obtains trial vectors and undertakes cross over to generate population of offspring individuals, employs appropriate selection mechanisms between parent and offspring populations to generate the new population of individuals for the next generation, promotes the best individual in the new generation to compete with that in the Hall of Fame and triggers a sequence of generation cycles until a termination criterion is met with at which stage the individual in the Hall of Fame is deemed to represent the "optimal" solution.

However, the specific differences in the DE HOF-based metaheuristic optimization process adopted for 130-30 portfolio construction are that, DE HOF:

1) employs a tweaked version of a mutation operator *Rand4/Best/Dir5* [FEO 06] to widen its search process;

2) employs dynamic scale factors beta, using a procedure that has been termed *dither.* Here the scale factor beta is randomly chosen between [0.5, 1] during *each generation* or *for each difference vector*. It has been observed that such a selection ensures significant improvement in the convergence behavior of the strategy. DE HOF for 130-30 portfolio optimization employs dither for each generation;

3) adopts specialized weight repair strategies to tackle the respective budget and bound constraints imposed on long and short positions of the 130-30 portfolio, which was detailed in section 6.4.2;

4) proceeds to work on a custom made fitness function suited to the 130-30 portfolio model, incorporating the penalized objective function as dictated by Joines and Houcke's penalty function strategy for the problem model.

Rand4/Best/Dir5 strategy

Chapter 2, section 2.5.3 discussed various DE strategies and Chapter 5, section 5.4 discussed Rand5/Dir4 strategy to tackle equity market neutral portfolios. Rand4/Best/Dir5 strategy is yet another strategy that increases search space exploration by employing five different directions in the formulation of the difference vector. The formula is given by,

$$t = V^{best} + \phi.\left(5.V^{best} - IND - V_1 - V_2 - V_3 - V_4\right) \qquad [6.20]$$

where ϕ known as the constant of differentiation is given by $\phi = \beta_S / 5$ and β_S the dynamic scale factor is randomly selected between $[0.5,1]$ for each generation, employing dither. IND is the target or the current individual in the population whose inclusion increases search space exploration. V^{best} which was traditionally chosen to be the "best" individual in the population, was tweaked to represent the "best" individual amongst the five random individuals that were selected, to compute trial vector t for the current individual IND. Thus, of the five random individuals selected, the best amongst them was labeled V_b and the rest were labeled as V_1, V_2, V_3 and V_4. By including IND the current individual along with V_1, V_2, V_3 and V_4, five directions get considered during the search.

The inherent characteristics of Rand5/Best/Dir4 strategy coupled with dither based scale factors ensured better convergence behavior by DE HOF for the specific 130-30 portfolio optimization problems considered.

Process flow chart

The process flow chart for the integrated optimization of 130-30 constrained portfolios described by [6.12]–[6.19] is shown in Figure 6.3. As can be seen, the best individual ensconced in the Hall of Fame when the termination criterion is met with, represents the optimal weights for the constrained 130-30 portfolio. The long positions and the short positions in the portfolio can be ascertained and the annualized risk, expected portfolio annualized return and the Sharpe Ratio of the portfolio, easily obtained using the weights. However, a significant observation to be made with regard to best individuals competing to enter the Hall of Fame is that only those individuals with maximum fitness values and whose constraint violation function values, viz. $\psi(\bar{w}, \bar{\beta}_A, t)$ are zero, which happens on account of their penalty terms G becoming 0, are alone considered eligible candidates. This additional restriction ensures that only those individuals which satisfy the portfolio beta constraint represented by [6.13] and are therefore feasible solutions in the complete sense, are deemed eligible to be promoted as the optimal solution and not all and sundry who merely report maximal fitness function values while violating their respective portfolio beta constraints. In other words, those individuals which are feasible solutions alone are eligible to compete for the Hall of Fame and upgrade themselves as optimal solutions.

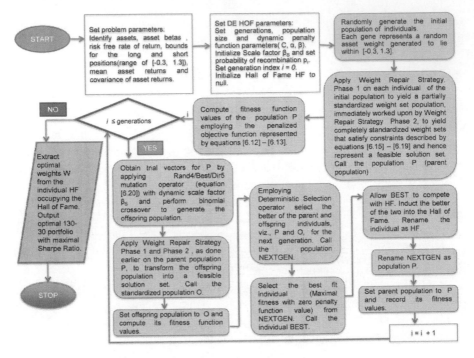

Figure 6.3. *Differential Evolution with Hall of Fame (DE HOF) employing Rand5/Best/Dir4 strategy with dithering of scale factors, for constrained 130-30 portfolio optimization (for a color version of this figure, see www.iste.co.uk/pai/metaheuristics.zip)*

6.4.4. Experimental results

The working of the DE HOF employing Rand5/Best/Dir4 strategy with dynamic scale factors was studied over a large portfolio of S&P BSE200 index (March 1999–March 2009) data set. The S&P BSE200 universe was k-means clustered (see Chapter 3 for details on Heuristic selection of Portfolios using k-means clustering) using the mean returns and variance-covariance matrix of returns of the stock universe as the characteristics for the clustering algorithm. The stock universe was clustered for $k = 90$ and a portfolio with one asset randomly selected from each cluster was included in the portfolio. To recall k-means clustered assets ensure intra cluster similarity and inter cluster dissimilarity and hence the choice of one asset from each cluster to enforce diversification of assets. Various choices of k-portfolios were considered for the experimental studies.

The betas of the assets concerned were computed. The average risk free rate (R_f) for Indian markets during the period concerned was set to 6.5%. The mean returns of the assets $[\bar{\mu}]_{1\times90}$ and variance-covariance matrix $(V)_{90\times90}$ of the assets were set. The leveraged bounds for the long positions and those for the short positions were set as shown in [6.18]–[6.19]. With all other constraints, viz. portfolio budget, budgets on long and short positions and portfolio beta constraint kept intact, the objective was to obtain an optimal constrained 130-30 portfolio for the k-portfolio considered by using DE HOF to solve the appropriate mathematical model described by [6.12]–[6.19] defined over it.

Table 6.7 illustrates the control parameters of DE HOF (*Rand4/Best/Dir5*) for the 130-30 portfolio optimization problem.

Parameter	Description
Population size	1000
Individual length	90 (k = 90)
Generations	8000
Dynamic Scale factor β_S following dithering in each generation	[0.5, 1]
Probability of recombination p_r	0.87
(C, α, β)	(0.5, 2, 2)

Table 6.7. *Control parameters of DE HOF (Rand4/Best/Dir5) for constrained 130-30 portfolio optimization*

Table 6.8 illustrates the characteristics of the optimal constrained 130-30 k-portfolio obtained for S&P BSE 200 data set, using DE HOF (*Rand4/Best/Dir5*) during a run. Several runs of the metaheuristic algorithm on a specific k-portfolio yielded highly consistent results with regard to the maximal Sharpe ratio. Table 6.9 illustrates the summarized results of five sample runs over two different selections of k-portfolios (k = 90) concerned, from the same cluster sets for S&P BSE 200 index.

The convergence aspects of DE HOF (*Rand4/Best/Dir5*) strategy was studied by observing the fitness function values (typically penalized objective function values) of the individuals that were inducted into the Hall of Fame during the course of the generation cycles. Figure 6.4 shows the graphs traced during five sample runs over a specific k-portfolio (k =90) of S&P BSE 200 index. It could be seen that the convergence was reached in around 3000 generations with the fitness function values stabilizing and thereafter not favoring induction of better entries into the Hall of Fame.

6.5. MATLAB® demonstrations

In this section, the following concepts distinctive to the DE HOF (*Rand4/Best/Dir5*) strategy discussed in this chapter, are demonstrated through MATLAB® functions or code fragments, so as to illustrate the computation or implementation of the concepts in a naïve way to favor novices in MATLAB.

A. Implementation of Rand4/Best/Dir5 operator

B. Implementation of weight repair strategy Phase 1

In this, the 130-30 portfolio proceeds to satisfy the individual bound constraints represented by equations [6.18]–[6.19] subject to the portfolio budget constraint represented by equation [6.15].

C. Implementation of weight repair strategy Phase 2

Here, the 130-30 portfolio proceeds to satisfy the budget constraints imposed on long and short positions described by equations [6.16]–[6.17].

D. Implementation of constraint violation function and fitness value function for 130-30 portfolio optimization

The function implemented is described by equations [6.12]–[6.14].

E. Generation cycle of DE HOF (*Rand4/Best/Dir5*) strategy during 130-30 portfolio optimization

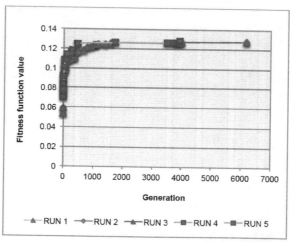

Figure 6.4. *Convergence characteristics of DE HOF (Rand4/Best/Dir5) strategy during sample runs, over a specific constrained 130-30 k-portfolio (for a color version of this figure, see www.iste.co.uk/pai/metaheuristics.zip)*

A. *Implementation of Rand4/Best/Dir5 operator*

Figure 6.5 shows the implementation of Rand4/Best/Dir5 as a function in MATLAB®. `V_b(1,1:individual_length)`, `V(1:4,1:individual_length)`, IND and `beta_val` represent the parameters V^{best}, V_1, V_2, V_3 and V_4, IND and β_S that describe [6.20] associated with the Rand4/Best/Dir5 strategy. `trialvector_popln` represents the population of trial vectors generated by Rand4/Best/Dir5 strategy for the parent population `popln` whose fitness function values are given by `fitness_val`.

B. *Implementation of weight repair strategy Phase 1*

Figure 6.6 illustrates the implementation of weight repair strategy Phase 1. The function `weight_std_130_30_boundsconstr` standardizes the population of weights `weight_mat` to enable them satisfy their respective lower and upper bounds represented by [6.18]–[6.19] and sum up to 1 ([6.15]), to ultimately yield the standardized weight set `std_weight_mat`. `low_up_bounds` is a 2 × N matrix where `low_up_bounds(1,:)` indicate the lower bounds of the assets in the portfolio and `low_up_bounds(2,:)` indicate the upper bounds of the assets in the portfolio. The MATLAB® code fragments implementing steps 1–2 and steps 3–6 of the weight repair strategy Phase 1, which standardizes weights to satisfy their lower and upper bounds respectively, subject to the portfolio budget constraint of the weights adding up to 1, have been illustrated through comment statements in the code.

Assets in the optimal 130-30 portfolio		Betas of the assets	Optimal weights (W_i)	
Long Positions	SHRIRAM TRANSPORT FINANCE	0.718	W_1	0.1182
	PRAJ INDUSTRIES LIMITED	1.092	W_2	0.1182
	PANTALOON RETAIL INDIA LTD	1.040	W_3	0.1182
	GUJARAT NRE COKE LTD	1.224	W_4	0.1182
	SUN PHARMACEUTICAL INDUS	0.601	W_5	0.1182
	BHARAT ELECTRONICS LIMITED	1.071	W_6	0.1182
	UNITECH LIMITED	0.927	W_7	0.1182
	STERLITE INDUSTRIES INDIA LTD	1.225	W_8	0.1182
	HINDUSTAN ZINC LIMITED	1.099	W_9	0.1182
	WELSPUN-GUJARAT STAHL LTD	1.346	W_{10}	0.1182

	JAI CORP LTD	0.731	W_{11}	0.1182
Short Positions	UNITED BREWERIES HOLDINGS LTD	1.053	W_{12}	-0.2383
	TATA CHEMICALS LIMITED	1.048	W_{13}	-0.0617

Maximal Sharpe Ratio	2.0187
Annualized risk(%)	41.928
Expected portfolio annualized return(%)	91.141
Portfolio beta constraint ([6.14])	Satisfied
Portfolio budget constraint ([6.15])	Satisfied
Long positions budget constraint ([6.16])	Satisfied
Short positions budget constraint (equation [6.17])	Satisfied
Bound constraints on long and short positions ([6.18]-[6.19])	Satisfied

Table 6.8. *The characteristics of the optimal constrained 130-30 k-portfolio (k = 90) for S&P BSE 200 index, obtained by DE HOF (Rand4/Best/Dir4) strategy during a specific run (long and short positions with non-zero weights in the optimal portfolio alone have been shown)*

		Annualized risk (%)	Expected portfolio annualized return (%)	Sharpe Ratio
k-portfolio 1	Run 1	41.928	91.1411	2.0187
	Run 2	41.928	91.1411	2.0187
	Run 3	38.915	85.056	2.0186
	Run 4	41.928	91.1411	2.0187
	Run 5	38.915	85.056	2.0186
k-portfolio 2	Run 1	39.219	85.240	2.0077
	Run 2	39.219	85.240	2.0077
	Run 3	41.003	86.694	1.9558
	Run 4	40.491	87.524	2.0011
	Run 5	40.491	87.524	2.0011

Table 6.9. *Summarized characteristics of optimal constrained 130-30 k-portfolios (k = 90) of S&P BSE 200 index, obtained by DE HOF (Rand4/Best/Dir5) strategy during sample runs*

C. Implementation of weight repair strategy Phase 2

The implementation of weight repair strategy Phase 2 is accomplished by breaking down the task into subtasks and coding MATLAB® functions for each of the sub tasks. Figure 6.7 illustrates the main function `weight_std_130_30_budgetconstr` that implements weight repair strategy Phase 2, employing three other sub functions viz. `group_assets_130_30`, `std_wgts_asset_130_30_longclass` and `std_wgts_asset_130_30_shortclass`.

`weight_std_130_30_budgetconstr` works on the standardized weight matrix `weight_mat`, which is the output of the weight repair strategy Phase 1 undertaken by function `weight_std_130_30_boundsconstr` (described in Sec. 6.5 B) that should immediately precede it. The inputs `long_low_up_bounds` and `short_low_up_bounds`, denote the lower/upper bounds of the long positions and short positions respectively. Each of these is a 2 × N matrix where `long_low_up_bounds(1,:)` and `short_low_up_bounds(1,:)` indicate the lower bounds of long and short positions and `long_low_up_bounds(2,:)` and `short_low_up_bounds(2,:)` indicate the upper bounds of the long and short positions in the portfolio. The final standardized weight set is output as `std_weight_mat`.

`group_assets_130_30` executes an important role of segregating the long and short positions, in other words, the positive and negative weights of each individual in the population. This is very essential since 130-30 portfolio optimization attempted using metaheuristics in this chapter, executes an integrated optimization of long-short portfolios and therefore the distribution of positive and negative weights is kept varying from individual to individual in a population, to decide on the optimal composition of long and short positions. Figure 6.8 illustrates the `group_assets_130_30` function. For every `individual` the cell array C of dimension 1 × 2, stores its long positions in C{1} and its short positions in C{2}.

`std_wgts_asset_130_30_longclass` function illustrated in Figure 6.9 takes care of steps 3–6 of weight repair strategy Phase 2, with regard to repairing of long position weights to enable them satisfy their budget of 1.3. M is the cell array that holds the long positions and TW is the budget (1.3 in this case) that the long positions have to satisfy. The function standardizes one individual at a time denoted as `weight_vector` with the lower and upper bounds of the individual assets input to it as `low_up_bounds`.

```
function trialvector_popln =
DE_Rand4BestDir5_Operator(popln, fitness_val,
                    beta_val, popln_size, individual_length)

% initialization
differential_vec_indx(1:5) - 0;
V_b(1,1:individual_length) = 0;
V(1:4,1:individual_length) = 0;
trialvector_popln(1:popln_size, 1:individual_length) =0;

for i = 1 : popln_size

    % set IND the current individual in the population
    % indicated by i
    IND = popln(i,:);

    % prepare rand_indx, random  indices for each
    % population individual,  to enable it choose five
    % random individuals from the population, without
    % repeating itself.

    rand_indx = randperm(popln_size);
    for t=1:popln_size
        if (rand_indx(t)==i)
            elimx = t;
        end
    end
    rand_indx(elimx)=[];

    % select five random individuals from the population
    for u=1:5
    differential_vec_indx(u) = rand_indx(u);
    end
```

Figure 6.5. *Rand4/Best/Dir5 function implementation in MATLAB®*
(for a color version of this figure, see www.iste.co.uk/pai/metaheuristics.zip)

```
% Obtain Vb the best individual with the maximal
% objective function and represent the rest as
% V1, V2, V3 and V4 as defined in equation [6.20]
[~, max_obj_indx] =
      max( [fitness_val(differential_vec_indx(1)),
            fitness_val(differential_vec_indx(2)),
            fitness_val(differential_vec_indx(3)),
            fitness_val(differential_vec_indx(4)),
            fitness_val(differential_vec_indx(5))]);
   j=1;
   for z=1:5
   if (differential_vec_indx(z) ==
              differential_vec_indx(max_obj_indx))
      V_b(1,:) = popln(differential_vec_indx(z), :);
   else
      V(j,:) = popln(differential_vec_indx(z),:);
      j=j+1;
   end
   end


   % obtain trial vector for each of the parent vector
   % individual
   trialvector_popln(i,:) = V_b(1,:) + beta_val/5 *
   (5*V_b(1,:) - IND - V(1,:)-V(2,:)-V(3,:)-V(4,:));
  end

end
```

Figure 6.5. *Contd.*

std_wgts_asset_130_30_shortclass illustrated in Figure 6.10 takes care of Steps 7–11 of the weight repair strategy Phase 2, repairing the short position weights to enable them satisfy their budget of -0.3. Every individual weight_vector whose long position weights were standardized to satisfy their budget constraint through the std_wgts_asset_130_30_longclass function, passes through this function to repair their respective short position weights to make them satisfy the budget of -0.3 The output weight_vector released by this function represents an individual that satisfies all its constraints represented by [6.15]–[6.19].

```
function std_weight_mat =
weight_std_130_30_boundsconstr(weight_mat, low_up_bounds)

[row_mat, col_mat]=size(weight_mat);
[~, up_bound] = size(low_up_bounds);


% Steps 1 and 2 of Weight Repair Strategy Phase 1
% standardize weights to satisfy their lower bounds while
% summing up to 1

for i=1: row_mat
    % R: those weights which are less than their
    % respective lower bounds
    R=[];
    c_R=0;
    for j=1:col_mat
    if (weight_mat(i,j)< low_up_bounds(1,j))
        weight_mat(i,j)= low_up_bounds(1,j);
        c_R = c_R+1;
        R(c_R) = j;
    end
    end

    % Q: those weights which satisfy their respective
    % lower bounds
    Q = setdiff([1:col_mat], R);
    F = 1 - sum(low_up_bounds(1,R))-
                            sum(low_up_bounds(1,Q));
    L = sum(abs(weight_mat(i,Q)));
    if (L==0)
        term = F / length(Q);
        weight_mat(i,Q)= low_up_bounds(1,Q)+ term;
    else
        term = F / L;
        weight_mat(i,Q) = low_up_bounds(1,Q)+
                            abs(weight_mat(i,Q))* term;
    end
end
```

```
% Steps 3-6 of Weight Repair Strategy Phase 1
% standardize upper bounds so that weights ultimately
% satisfy both upper and lower bounds and sum up to 1

for i = 1: row_mat
    kr = 1;
    r = [];
    ex_flag = true;
    q = setdiff([1:col_mat], r);
    while (ex_flag == true)
        ex_flag = false;

        for j = 1: length(q)
        if ( weight_mat(i, q(j)) <= low_up_bounds(2, q(j)))
        continue;
        else
        ex_flag = true;
        r(kr) = q(j);
        kr = kr+1;
        end
        end

        q = setdiff([1:col_mat], r);

        if (ex_flag == true)
        L = sum(abs(weight_mat(i,q)));
        F = 1 - ( sum(low_up_bounds(1,q))+ sum(
                            low_up_bounds(2,r)) );

        if (L==0)
        term = F;
        weight_mat(i,q(1))= term;
        else
        term = F/L;
        weight_mat(i,q) = low_up_bounds(1,q) +
                        (abs(weight_mat(i,q))* term);
        end
        weight_mat(i,r)=low_up_bounds(2,r);
        end

    end
      std_weight_mat = weight_mat;
end
```

Figure 6.6. *Weight repair strategy Phase 1 function implementation in MATLAB*®
(for a color version of this figure, see www.iste.co.uk/pai/metaheuristics.zip)

D. *Implementation of constraint violation function and fitness value function for 130-30 portfolio optimization*

The constraint violation function and fitness value functions formulated for the constrained 130-30 portfolio optimization problem model and described by [6.13]–

[6.14] and [6.12] respectively, are implemented as MATLAB® functions shown in figures 6.11 and 6.12 respectively. Function `ConstrViolnFun_130_30` considers the standardized weight population `weight_mat`, the asset betas `betas_assets`, the parameters C, α, β and generation count t as `C_param`, `alpha_param`, `beta_param` and `gencount`, respectively as inputs. `[psi, G1]` the output of the function represents the constraint violation function $\psi(\overline{w}, \overline{\beta}_A, t)$ and penalty term G of [6.13] respectively.

Function `CompFitness_130_30` computes the fitness function values for the standardized population of individuals `popln_mat`, with `return_dat`, `covariance_dat`, `riskfree` and `psi_fun`, representing the asset returns, variance-covariance matrix of asset returns, risk free rate and constraint violation function $\psi(\overline{w}, \overline{\beta}_A, t)$ respectively, as inputs as described in [6.12].

E. Generation cycle of DE HOF (Rand4/Best/Dir5) strategy during 130-30 portfolio optimization

Figure 6.13 illustrates the code fragment demonstrating a generation cycle of DE HOF (*Rand4/Best/Dir5*) strategy during 130-30 portfolio optimization. `dynamic_beta` ensures that each generation uses a dynamic scale factor β_S. Functions `DE_Rand4BestDir5_Operator` and `DE_bin_Crossover` serve to generate trial vectors and the respective offspring population. Functions `weight_std_130_30_boundsconstr` and `weight_std_130_30_budgetconstr` serve to repair weights of the offspring population in two phases, to satisfy all their constraints, viz. bounds, portfolio budget and long and short position budgets, to yield the output population `feas_mutat_popln` that represents a feasible solution set. Functions `ConstrViolnFun_130_30` and `CompFitness_130_30`, compute the constraint violation function values and fitness function values for the standardized offspring population `feas_mutat_popln`. Function `DE_selection_penalty_13030` selects the best fit amongst the parent population `feas_parent_popln` and offspring population `feas_mutat_popln`, to form the next generation of individuals `next_gen_pool`. The best individual amongst the new generation competes with that in the Hall of Fame. `HOF_individual` represents the individual which occupies the Hall of Fame. It can be seen here that only that individual which surpasses the existing `HOF_individual` with larger fitness values (since the objective function deals with maximization) and whose constraint violation function value is 0, `(Psi_fun(i)== 0)`, is designated to be labeled as the next `HOF_individual`. With `next_gen_pool` designated as the parent population for the next generation, the current generation cycle comes to a close, only to trigger the next generation cycle by repeating the evolutionary process all over again, until the termination criterion is met with. At this stage, `HOF_individual` indicates the optimal solution and the composition and characteristics of the optimal 130-30 portfolio can be extracted from it.

```
function std_weight_mat =
weight_std_130_30_budgetconstr(weight_mat,
                    long_low_up_bounds, short_low_up_bounds)

[row_mat, col_mat]= size(weight_mat);

% budgets for long positions
eta = 1.3;
gamma = 0;
for p = 1:row_mat

        H = group_assets_130_30(col_mat, weight_mat(p,:));

        % adjust weights representing long positions
        deposit_wgts =0;
        h=1;
        sum_wgts = sum(weight_mat(p,H{h}));

        % check if sum of weights of long positions lie
        % within limits
        if (sum_wgts <= eta ) && (sum_wgts >= gamma)
        continue;
        else
        deposit_wgts = deposit_wgts + (sum_wgts-eta);
        MP = eta;
        weight_mat(p,:) =
        std_wgts_asset_130_30_longclass(weight_mat(p,:),
                        H{h}, sum_wgts, MP, long_low_up_bounds);
        end

        % adjust weights representing short positions
        if (deposit_wgts ==0) continue;
        else
        h = 2;
        sum_wgts = sum(weight_mat(p,H{h}));
        abs_sum_wgts = sum(abs(weight_mat(p,H{h})) );
        deposit_wgts = deposit_wgts + sum_wgts;
        weight_mat(p,:) =
        std_wgts_asset_130_30_shortclass(weight_mat(p,:),
                        H{h}, abs_sum_wgts, deposit_wgts,
                                    short_low_up_bounds);
        end
end

std_weight_mat = weight_mat;
end
```

Figure 6.7. *Main repair strategy Phase 2 implementation in MATLAB®: Main function (for a color version of this figure, see www.iste.co.uk/pai/metaheuristics.zip)*

```
function C = group_assets_130_30(individual_size,
                                        individual)

  M = cell(1, 2);
  p = 1;
  N = [1: individual_size];
     for c = 1: individual_size
           if (individual(c) >= 0)
             M{1}(p)=c;
             p = p+1;
           end
     end

     if (length(M{1})==0)
     disp('Empty long positions')
     C{1}= [];
     C{2}= N;
     else
     C{1} = M{1};
      C{2} = setdiff(N,M{1});
     end
  end
```

Figure 6.8. *Weight repair strategy Phase 2 implementation in MATLAB®:*
group_assets_130_30 *function (for a color version of*
this figure, see www.iste.co.uk/pai/metaheuristics.zip)

```
function  weight_vector =
std_wgts_asset_130_30_longclass(weight_vector, M,
                              wgt_sum, TW, low up bounds)

  % adjust lower bounds of assets
   L = wgt_sum;
   F =   TW - sum(low_up_bounds(1,M));
   term = F /L;
   weight_vector(M) = low_up_bounds(1,M)+
                            (weight_vector(M)* term);

  % adjust upper bounds of assets
   kr = 1;
   r = [];
   ex_flag = true;
   q = setdiff(M, r);
   while (ex_flag == true)
      ex_flag = false;
      for j = 1: length(q)
           if (weight_vector(q(j)) > low_up_bounds(2,q(j)))
           ex_flag = true;
           r(kr) = q(j);
           kr = kr+1;
           end
      end
```

```
    q = setdiff(M, r);

    if (ex_flag == true)
        L = sum(weight_vector(q));
        F = TW - ( sum(low_up_bounds(1,q))+ sum(
                                low_up_bounds(2,r)) );
        term = F/L;
        weight_vector(q) = low_up_bounds(1,q) +
                            (weight_vector(q)* term);
        weight_vector(r) = low_up_bounds(2,r);
    end

  end
end
```

Figure 6.9. *Weight repair strategy Phase 2 implementation in MATLAB®:*
std_wgts_asset_130_30_longclass *function (for a color*
version of this figure, see www.iste.co.uk/pai/metaheuristics.zip)

```
function weight_vector =
std_wgts_asset_130_30_shortclass(weight_vector, M,
                                abswgt_sum, TW, low_up_bounds)
% adjust lower bounds of assets
L = abswgt_sum;
F =   TW - sum(low_up_bounds(1,M));
if (L==0)
    term - F/length(M);
    weight_vector(M) = low_up_bounds(1,M)+  term;
else
    term = F /L;
    weight_vector(M) = low_up_bounds(1,M)+
        (abs(weight_vector(M)) * term);
end
% adjust upper bounds of assets
kr = 1;
r = [];
ex_flag = true;
q = setdiff(M, r);
while (ex_flag == true)
    ex_flag = false;
    for j = 1: length(q)
    if (weight_vector(q(j)) > low_up_bounds(2,q(j)))
    ex_flag = true;
    r(kr) = q(j);
    kr = kr+1;
    end
    end
```

```
          q = setdiff(M, r);
          if (ex_flag == true)
          L = sum(abs(weight_vector(q)));
          F = TW - (sum(low_up_bounds(1,q))+ sum(
                                    low_up_bounds(2,r)) );
             if  (length (q)~=0)
                if (L==0)
                term = F;
                weight_vector(q(1))= term;
                else
                term = F/L;
                weight_vector(q) = low_up_bounds(1,q) +
                                (abs(weight_vector(q))* term);
                end
             end
          weight_vector(r) = low_up_bounds(2,r);
          end
end
end
```

Figure 6.10. *Weight repair strategy Phase 2 implementation in MATLAB® :*
std_wgts_asset_130_30_shortclass function (for a color
version of this figure, see www.iste.co.uk/pai/metaheuristics.zip)

```
function  [psi, G]  = ConstrViolnFun 130 30( weight mat,
      betas_assets, C_param, alpha_param, beta_param,
                                    gencount)
          [row_mat, ~]= size(weight_mat);
          epsilon = 0.001;
          for i=1:row_mat

          x_chromo = weight_mat(i,:);

          % compute penalty function G
          portfolio_beta_term = sum(betas_assets.* x_chromo);
          g1_term = abs((portfolio_beta_term) - 1)-epsilon;

          if (g1_term <=0 )
           G(i)=0;
          else
           G(i)=1;
          end

          % compute constraint violation function
          penalty_term= power(C_param*gencount, alpha_param);
          psi(i) = penalty_term *( G(i)*power(g1_term,
                                    beta_param));
          end
end
```

Figure 6.11. *MATLAB® function for computation of constraint violation*
function for 130-30 portfolio optimization ([6.13]–[6.14]) (for a color
version of this figure, see www.iste.co.uk/pai/metaheuristics.zip)

```
function popln_fitness = CompFitness_130_30(popln_mat,
          return_dat,  covariance_dat, riskfree,  psi_fun)

[popln_size, ~]=size(popln_mat);

for i = 1: popln_size

   weight = popln_mat(i,:);
   popln_fitness(i) =  (((return_dat * weight')-riskfree)/
      sqrt(weight*covariance_dat * weight')) - psi_fun(i);
end
end
```

Figure 6.12. *MATLAB® function for computation of fitness function for 130-30 portfolio optimization [6.12]*

```
. . .

% while loop for generation cycles  begins

while (gen indx <= total_generations)

    % dynamic beta for each generation
    dynamic_beta = 0.5+(1-0.5)*rand(1,1);

    % obtain trial vector population
    trial vector_popln =
    DE_Rand4BestDir5_Operator(feas_parent_popln,
       feas_parent_popln_fitness,dynamic_beta,
       popln_size, chromosm_length);

    % obtain offspring population
     offsprng_popln = DE_bin_Crossover(feas_parent_popln,
            trial_vector_popln, pr_recombi,
                                chromosm_length);
     % undertake weight repair strategy Phase 1
     mutat_popln_bound =
            weight_std_130_30_boundsconstr(offsprng_popln,
                                bounds);
    % undertake weight repair strategy Phase 2
    feas_mutat_popln =
      weight_std_130_30_budgetconstr(mutat_popln_bound,
                  long_pos_bounds, short_pos_bounds);

    % compute constraint violation function
    [feas_mutat_popln_psi, feas_mutat_popln_G1] =
          ConstrViolnFun_130_30 (feas_mutat_popln,
             Beta_assets, C_dp, alpha_dp, beta_dp,
                             gen_indx);
    % compute fitness function values
    feas_mutat_popln_fitness =
          CompFitness_130_30(feas_mutat_popln, mean_data,
             cov data, riskfree,  feas mutat popln psi);
```

```
% set the population for the next generation
[next_gen_pool, next_gen_pool_fitness, Psi_fun ] =
    DE_selection_penalty_13030 (feas_parent_popln,
        feas_parent_popln_fitness, feas parent popln psi,
        feas_mutat_popln, feas_mutat_popln_fitness,
        feas_mutat_popln_psi,  popln_size);

% induct best individual into Hall of Fame
    for i=1:popln_size
        if (Psi_fun(i)== 0)
        if (next_gen_pool_fitness(i) > HOF_fitness)
        HOF_fitness = next_gen_pool_fitness(i)
        HOF_individual = next_gen_pool(i,:);
        end
        else continue;
        end
    end

% increment generation counter
    gen_indx = gen_indx + 1;

% form the parent population for the next generation

    feas_parent_popln = next_gen_pool;
    feas_parent_popln_fitness = next_gen_pool_fitness;

end  % while loop for  generations ends

. . .
```

Figure 6.13. *Code fragment demonstrating the generation cycles of DE HOF (Rand4/Best/Dir5) strategy during 130-30 portfolio optimization (for a color version of this figure, see www.iste.co.uk/pai/metaheuristics.zip)*

Project

Gordon Fowler [FOW 07] in his paper *"Understanding 130/30 Equity Strategies"* asserted that

"...Although 130/30 has become the common terminology for this class of strategies (perhaps because no one has come up with a better name), nothing is set in stone that says these could not be 140/40 strategies, 150/50 strategies, 160/60 strategies, and so on. Much depends on the nature of the portfolio manager's research. If the research is generating just a few ideas, using a lower ratio would be preferable.If the research is generating an abundance of opportunities, then a higher ratio can be sustained. ..."

To explore Gordon Fowler's assertion, download a historical data set for an equity index of your choice from a reliable finance website.

(i) Following the discussion in section 6.3, implement 130-30, 140-40, 150-50, 160-60 portfolio optimization strategies over the stock universe selected, using MATLAB® Portfolio object available in its Financial Toolbox™.

(ii) What are the information ratios of these portfolios?

(iii) Compare the performances of these portfolios with their long-only counterparts. Do these report better performances than their long-only counterparts?

(iv) Modify DE HOF (*Rand4/Best/Dir5*) algorithm to work on the constrained optimization of 130-30, 140-40, 150-50 and 160-60 strategies. What are the results obtained?

(v) Following the discussion in Chapter 4 Risk-budgeted Portfolio Optimization, what if you chose to impose a risk budget on the 130-30 portfolios? Explore.

Suggested Further Reading

Andrew Lo and Pankaj Patel's paper on *130/30: the New Long-Only* [LO 07] is a good read on the subject of 130-30 portfolio optimization.

Pai and Michel's [PAI 12b] work on *Integrated Metaheuristic Optimization of 130-30 Investment Strategy based Long-Short Portfolios* chose to explore 130-30 portfolios with the twin objectives of maximizing return and minimizing risk while ignoring the portfolio beta constraint (included in the 130-30 portfolio model discussed in this chapter). Transforming the twin objectives into a single criterion objective function by using a weighted formulation, the work explored two metaheuristics strategies chosen from two different genres, viz. Evolution Strategy with Hall of Fame and Differential Evolution (*Rand/1/Bin*) with Hall of Fame to obtain optimal portfolios. The efficiencies of the optimal portfolios obtained were analyzed using Efficiency Improvement Possibility function (BRI 04, BRA 10) a variant of Luenberger's [LUE 92] Shortage Functions.

Steve Johnson's [JOH 13] article *"The decline, fall and afterlife of 130/30"* that appeared in *Financial Times* (May 12, 2013), presented a crisp and critical outlook of 130-30 funds as viewed during the prevailing times of its publication.

Metaheuristic Portfolio Rebalancing with Transaction Costs

This chapter discusses metaheuristic rebalancing of portfolios with the additional constraint of curtailing transaction costs. The portfolio rebalancing strategy strives to maximize the Diversification Ratio of the rebalanced portfolio while trying to ensure that the risk of the rebalanced portfolio does not exceed the same of the original portfolio. Evolution Strategy with Hall of Fame is employed to optimize the portfolio rebalancing model. The experimental analysis has been undertaken over a high-risk portfolio of equities invested in the S&P BSE 200 index (Bombay Stock Exchange, India, March 1999–March 2009). The MATLAB® demonstrations of the functions that illustrate the working of the metaheuristic portfolio rebalancing model are discussed last.

7.1. Portfolio rebalancing

It is anybody's surmise that fund managers in particular and investment firms in general have to necessarily grapple with strategies, policies and market behavior before they decide on the right mix of assets for their portfolio, that conforms to their investment objectives and constraints, while balancing risk with performance. *Asset allocation* is a key factor in long-term investment performance. However, it is not a one-shot deal but a dynamic process, since over a period of time market forces can tend to fluctuate dramatically pushing the portfolios away from their original targets. An untended portfolio can result in a *weight drift* that can result in its exposure to more risk than what the investors had wanted or expected or in general can acquire risk and return characteristics that are inconsistent with the investor's goals and preferences, besides diluting the diversification index. The drift in weights therefore, can lead to portfolios tending to become more volatile resulting in portfolios that are less diversified and hence more exposed to undesirable risks. Hence, the need to *rebalance* a portfolio.

Portfolio rebalancing involves buying and selling portions of the portfolio to either set the weights back to its original state or if risk, returns and diversification are of greater concern, to devise a new asset allocation by readjusting the weights of each asset so that these objectives are met with. The rebalancing process serves to readjust the weights of each asset in the portfolio to fulfill a newly devised asset allocation that serves to realign the risk return characteristics of the drifted portfolio. Of the several approaches to rebalancing [JAC 10], *Active Rebalancing* is one where portfolios are rebalanced as and when the need is felt, based on the analysis of expected market conditions. It is a tactical asset allocation that is based on analysis of expected market conditions. The portfolio rebalancing model discussed in this chapter adopts active rebalancing.

Despite its benefits, portfolio rebalancing has its costs too, viz. capital gains taxes, transaction costs to execute and process trades besides, administrative costs and/or management fees, which can eat into the returns of the rebalanced portfolio. Termed generally as *Transaction costs*, portfolio rebalancing quite often includes the additional objective of minimizing its transaction costs so that the investor obtains a reasonable return after deduction of transaction costs besides the already included ones involved with adjusting the risk, return, and diversification characteristics of the drifted portfolio. Therefore, it is quite expected that investors desire a rebalanced portfolio that is *self-financing* and leaves respectable returns after deduction of all transaction costs. The portfolio rebalancing model adopted in this work incorporates this aspect in its rebalancing model and strives to obtain the optimal proportion of assets to buy/sell, not only to adjust the risk – return – diversification index expected of the rebalanced portfolio but also to render it self-financed.

EXAMPLE.– Gita and Gautier are two investors who chose to invest 60% of their capital of ₹10, 00, 000 on equity funds and 40% of the same on bond funds. Figure 7.1(a) shows the portfolio asset mix and value on January 02, 2014, the date of investment.

After one year (January 02, 2015), with the equities outperforming bonds, both of them find that the allocation of assets have changed in their respective portfolios. The equities rose to 71% and bonds decreased to 29%. Figure 7.1(b) illustrates the asset mix and value of the untended portfolio on January 02, 2015.

Now, Gita being a risk-averse investor desires investment security and decides to adhere to her risk-return tolerance level. She therefore decides to rebalance her portfolio. Figure 7.1(c) illustrates the asset mix and value of Gita's rebalanced portfolio on January 02, 2015. On the other hand, Gautier decides to stay put with his, pleased with the 16.67% appreciated returns fetched by the untended portfolio.

One year later (January 02, 2016), the markets turn turbulent with the equity funds performing poorly losing 10% while the bond funds performed well appreciating 15%. Gita and Gautier both review the closing balances of their respective portfolios on January 02, 2016. The portfolio values are as illustrated in Figure 7.1(d). It can be seen that while Gita's rebalanced portfolio was able to cushion her from the market turbulence yielding 0% losses, Gautier's portfolio suffered a loss of 2.7%! Thus for the given circumstances rebalancing the portfolio was the optimal decision that one could have taken.

Needless to say, if the markets had rallied resulting in equity funds performing better, then Gautier's portfolio would have yielded appreciated returns. It is therefore a matter of choice between the upside potential of one's portfolio or investment security, largely dictated by the investor's risk tolerance levels.

7.2. Portfolio rebalancing mathematical model

Let P_{Orignl} represent the original portfolio allocation. We assume that the portfolio kept untended for a long period of time (perhaps) needs to be optimally rebalanced to yield P_{Rebal}, the optimal rebalanced portfolio. The aim of the portfolio rebalancing model therefore is to obtain the optimal buy/sell weights, that is the proportion of weights of individual assets in the original portfolio that need to be sold or bought, to rebalance the portfolio to adhere to the investor's expected risk tolerance levels.

Let $\bar{W} = (w_1, w_2, ... w_N)'$ represent the weight allocations for the optimal original portfolio P_{Orignl} and $\bar{X} = (x_1, x_2, ... x_N)'$ be the desired optimal allocations of the rebalanced portfolio P_{Rebal}. Let $x_i^+, i = 1, 2, ... N$ and $x_i^-, i = 1, 2, ... N$ be the proportions of weights that need to be bought or sold from $\bar{W}$ to rebalance the portfolio. We assume that each asset i is characterized by the mutually exclusive pair $[x_i^+, x_i^-]$, with x_i^+ set to zero, if a sell decision was made for the asset and x_i^- set to zero if a buy decision was made for the asset. Let p be the transaction cost rate and u_i the upper limit of the proportion of assets that can be bought. Since transaction costs can burn away the returns of a rebalanced portfolio, u_i acts as a ceiling to curtail transactions costs that are incurred during buying of assets.

The single objective of the portfolio rebalancing model to be discussed here is to maximize the diversification ratio of P_{Rebal} which is tantamount to minimizing its risk. Diversification Ratio (DR) as a popular diversification index method was introduced in Chapter 3, section 3.1.

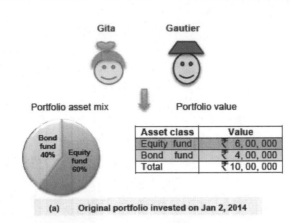

Portfolio asset mix

Portfolio value

Asset class	Value
Equity fund	₹ 6, 00, 000
Bond fund	₹ 4, 00, 000
Total	₹ 10, 00, 000

(a)   Original portfolio invested on Jan 2, 2014

Portfolio asset mix

Portfolio value

Asset class	Value
Equity fund	₹ 8, 50, 000
Bond fund	₹ 3, 50, 000
Total	₹ 12, 00, 000

(b)   Untended portfolio as on Jan 2, 2015

Asset class	Value
Equity fund	₹ 7, 20, 000
Bond fund	₹ 4, 80, 000
Total	₹12, 00, 000

(c)   Gita's rebalanced portfolio as on Jan 2, 2015

Closing balance of
Gita's Rebalanced portfolio
on   Jan 02, 2016

Closing balance of
Gautier's untended portfolio
on Jan 02, 2016

Asset class	Value
Equity fund	₹ 6, 48, 000
Bond fund	₹ 5, 52, 000
Total	₹ 12, 00, 000

Asset class	Value
Equity fund	₹ 7, 65, 000
Bond fund	₹ 4, 02, 500
Total	₹ 11, 67, 500

(d) Gita's rebalanced portfolio and Gautier's untended portfolio value as on Jan 2, 2016

Figure 7.1. *Rebalancing versus Non-Rebalancing of portfolios – an example*

The constraints imposed on the rebalancing model are: (1) the rebalanced portfolio should be self financed, that is the optimal rebalanced portfolio should yield respectable returns after deduction of transaction costs, and (2) risk of P_{Rebal} should not exceed that of P_{Orignl}, (i.e.) the rebalanced portfolio should adhere to the investor's risk tolerance that was reflected in the original portfolio, besides other bound constraints imposed on the buy/sell weights.

The portfolio rebalancing model is defined as below:

$$\text{Max}\left(\frac{\bar{\sigma}.\bar{X}}{\sqrt{\bar{X}'.V.\bar{X}}}\right) \qquad [7.1]$$

where $\bar{\sigma} = (\sigma_1, \sigma_2, ... \sigma_N)$ are the standard deviations of the returns on the assets i, i =1, 2, ...N and V is the *variance-covariance matrix of returns* on the assets of the portfolio.

Subject to,

i) $0 \le x_i^+ \le u_i$ (bounds on weights of buy assets)   [7.2]

ii) $0 \le x_i^- \le w_i$ (bounds on weights of sell assets)   [7.3]

iii) $x_i = w_i + x_i^+ - x_i^-$ (weights of the rebalanced portfolio)   [7.4]

iv) $0 \le x_i \le 1$ (bounds on weights of rebalanced portfolio)   [7.5]

v) $\displaystyle\sum_{i=1}^{N} x_i + p.\sum_{i=1}^{N}\left(x_i^+ + x_i^-\right) = 1$ (self financing portfolio)   [7.6]

vi) $\sqrt{\left(\bar{X}'.V.\bar{X}\right)} \le Risk^{Orignl}$ (ceiling on the rebalanced portfolio risk)   [7.7]

where $Risk^{Orignl}$ is the risk of the original portfolio P_{Orignl}.

The objective of the portfolio rebalancing model is therefore to find the optimal $\bar{X}$, which obviously is dependent on the optimal buy/sell weights x_i^+ / x_i^-.

As discussed already in the earlier chapters, application of metaheuristics to optimization problems demands prudent mechanisms to tackle constraints. Two popular methods of constraint handling viz. weight repair strategy and penalty function strategy have already been discussed in this book (Chapters 4, 5 and 6). We now employ the same strategies to tackle the string of constraints represented by [7.2]–[7.7], for solving the portfolio rebalancing model using metaheuristics. Thus while the non-linear constraint of ceiling on the rebalanced portfolio risk represented by [7.7] is tackled using Joines and Houck's penalty function strategy [JOI 94] that employs dynamic penalties (discussed and demonstrated in Chapter 4, sections 4.3.1 and 4.3.2), the linear constraints of bounds, self-financing portfolio and the others are tackled using a unified weight repair strategy.

The transformed portfolio rebalancing model that employs Joines and Houck's penalty function strategy to absorb the non-linear constraint represented by [7.7] into its penalized objective function is as follows:

$$\text{Max}\left(\frac{\bar{\sigma}.\bar{X}}{\sqrt{\bar{X}'.V.\bar{X}}} - \psi(\bar{X},V,Risk^{Originl},t)\right) \qquad [7.8]$$

where $\quad \psi(\bar{X},V,Risk^{Orignl},t) = (C.t)^{\alpha}\left(G.\phi\left(\bar{X},V,Risk^{Orignl}\right)^{\beta}\right),$

$$\phi\left(\bar{X},V,Risk^{Orignl}\right) = \left|\sqrt{\bar{X}'.V.\bar{X}} - Risk^{Orignl}\right| - \varepsilon,$$

$$G = \begin{cases} 0, & \phi\left(\bar{X},V,Risk^{Orignl}\right) \le 0 \\ 1, & otherwise \end{cases}, \qquad [7.9]$$

C, α, β are coefficients on which the quality of the solution depends and t is the generation counter, subject to [7.2]–[7.6] as the linear constraints. ε is the tolerance level.

The transformed model represented by [7.8]–[7.9] as the objective function and [7.2]–[7.6] as the constraints, is solved using a metaheuristic strategy, viz. Evolution Strategy with Hall of Fame (ES HOF).

7.3. Evolution Strategy with Hall of Fame for Portfolio Rebalancing

7.3.1. *Evolution Strategy – a brief note*

Evolution Strategy is a metaheuristic strategy that evokes elitism using Hall of Fame and was detailed in Chapter 2, section 2.4. To briefly recall, ES HOF works over an initial random population of chromosomes representative of a candidate solution set, with each gene of the chromosome representing the design variables of the problem. In the event of a constrained optimization problem, the metaheuristic method may choose to adopt strategies that can transform the population of chromosomes representing a candidate solution set into a population of chromosomes that represents a feasible solution set to the problem. Weight repair strategy and Penalty function strategy are two such popular strategies that have been focused upon in this book.

In the next stage, genetic inheritance operators such as crossover and mutation (arithmetic variable point crossover and real number uniform mutation, specifically, and discussed in Chapter 2, section 2.4.1) are executed over the initial population termed as the parent population, to yield the offspring population. The offspring population of chromosomes, like its parents, undergoes transformation with the help of weight repair or penalty function strategies to satisfy all the constraints and thereby represent another feasible solution set to the problem.

The selection operator determines the choice of best fit individuals from the parent and offspring populations (a practice predominantly followed in this book) for the next generation. The best among the individuals so selected is inducted and/or competes with the chromosome in the Hall of Fame. The entire cycle of operations continues generation after generation, with the Hall of Fame recording the best individual obtained thus far, until the termination criterion is met, at which point the generation cycle ends. The individual in the Hall of Fame now represents the optimal solution and the values of the design variables of the problem represented by its genes represent the optimal values of the variables describing the problem.

7.3.2. *Optimal rebalanced portfolio using ES HOF*

The optimal rebalanced portfolio is obtained by getting ES HOF to work on the constrained optimization problem described by [7-8]–[7.9] as the objective function and [7.2]–[7.6] as the constraints. The optimal X arrived at is the optimal buy/sell weights (x_i^+ / x_i^-) of the N assets comprising the original portfolio. $W \pm (x_i^+ / x_i^-)$, where W is the original portfolio allocation weights, yields the final optimal rebalanced portfolio weights.

The chromosome of ES HOF comprises N genes representing buy/sell weights (x_i^+ / x_i^-) of the respective assets. Since buy/sell decisions and the respective values are randomly generated for the initial population, it is convenient to view each gene as a pair $[x_i^+, x_i^-]$, with x_i^+ set to zero if a sell decision is randomly generated for the asset with a random value x_i^- and vice-versa when a buy decision is randomly generated for the asset. The initial population of chromosomes is randomly generated in such a way that each of the N genes that hold x_i^+ or x_i^- with its buy or sell decision randomly decided, satisfy their respective bounds described by [7.2]–[7.3]. ES HOF invokes the weight repair strategy `PortfolioRebalancing_WeightRepair` to standardize the weights in such a way that all the constraints represented by [7.2]–[7.6] are satisfied and the population of chromosomes, termed as the parent population, represent a feasible solution set of buy/sell weights. The fitness function values of the population are computed by obtaining the rebalanced weights X as $x_i = w_i + x_i^+ - x_i^-$ and using [7.8]–[7.9].

The genetic inheritance operators of arithmetic variable point crossover and real number uniform mutation are executed over random selection of parent pairs to yield the offspring population. The offspring population essentially needs to be normalized so that the chromosomes satisfy their respective bounds represented by [7.2]–[7.3]. The weight repair strategy PortfolioRebalancing_WeightRepair is invoked over the normalized offspring population to standardize the buy/sell weights and thereby transform them into a feasible solution set. The fitness values of the offspring population are computed as was done for the parent population.

The best fit amongst the parent and offspring populations are selected in the ratio of $\mu{:}\lambda$ for the next generation NEXTGEN. The best fit chromosome amongst those in NEXTGEN and whose penalty function value is zero ($\psi = 0$ in [7.9]) is inducted into the Hall of Fame. NEXTGEN is set as the parent population for the next generation.

The generation cycles continue with the best fit chromosome of NEXTGEN in each generation competing with the chromosome in the Hall of Fame. Once the termination criterion which is set to be a definite number of generations, is met with, the generation cycle ends and the chromosome in the Hall of Fame is output as the optimal solution. The buy/sell weights represented by the chromosome in the Hall of Fame which denotes the optimal (x_i^+ / x_i^-), yield the optimal rebalanced weight X as $x_i = w_i + x_i^+ - x_i^-$. Equation [7.8] yields the maximal diversification ratio of the optimal rebalanced portfolio.

Figure 7.2 illustrates the process flow chart of ES HOF working to obtain the optimal rebalanced portfolio.

7.3.3. *Weight repair strategy for portfolio rebalancing*

Algorithm `PortfolioRebalancing_WeightRepair` method is adapted from a similar procedure discussed by Pai [PAI 17] over fuzzy rebalancing of portfolios. Let Z be a random vector of *BUY/SELL* weights x_i^+ / x_j^-, $i, j = 1, 2, ... N$. To recall, for each asset i in the chromosome comprising the population, the decision to *BUY* or *SELL* is randomly generated and remembered. The random vector is normalized so that each asset weight in the chromosome, and hence the population, satisfies the respective bounds imposed on the *BUY* and *SELL* weights specified by [7.2]–[7.3].

The objective of `PortfolioRebalancing_WeightRepair` is to transform the candidate solution vector Z into a feasible solution vector by undertaking weight repair to enable it to satisfy the constraints represented by [7.4]–[7.6]. This is equivalent to adjusting the *BUY/ SELL* weights x_i^+ and x_j^- such that,

$$\sum\left(x_i^+\right) = a.\sum\left(x_j^-\right) \quad \text{where} \quad a = \frac{(1-p)}{(1+p)} \tag{7.10}$$

If $DIFF = \sum\left(x_i^!\right) - a.\sum\left(x_j^-\right)$ equals 0, the procedure is done.

If $(DIFF > 0)$ then compute $term = DIFF/NZ$, where NZ are the non-zero weights in Z and redistribute $DIFF$ to *BUY* and *SELL* as,

$$\begin{cases} x_i^+ = x_i^+ - term \\ x_j^- = x_j^- + \dfrac{term}{a} \end{cases} \tag{7.11}$$

otherwise, as

$$\begin{cases} x_i^+ = x_i^+ + term \\ x_j^- = x_j^- - \dfrac{term}{a} \end{cases} \tag{7.12}$$

If the redistributed weights in Z violate their lower bounds ([7.2]–[7.3]) then call *ADJUST_LOWBOUNDS_PFREBAL ()*, otherwise call *ADJUST_UPBOUNDS_ PFREBAL ()* at the end of which the entire weight vector satisfies the constraints represented by [7.2]–[7.6] yielding a feasible solution set.

ADJUST_LOWBOUNDS_PFREBAL () proceeds to determine which of the *BUY/SELL* class of weights in a chromosome violates its lower bound constraints. Since the rebalanced weight vector is already normalized to satisfy its respective bound constraints ([7.2]–[7.3]), the initial redistribution of *DIFF* to the vector can upset only one of them. The function upgrades the deficit weights (R) to their lower bounds by adding weights. If *DEFICIT* is the sum total of the weights that were added, the procedure proceeds to adjust *DEFICIT* by subtracting an equal share from such of those weights (*Q*) which can accommodate a deduction without falling below their respective lower bounds, so that *DEFICIT* becomes close to zero.

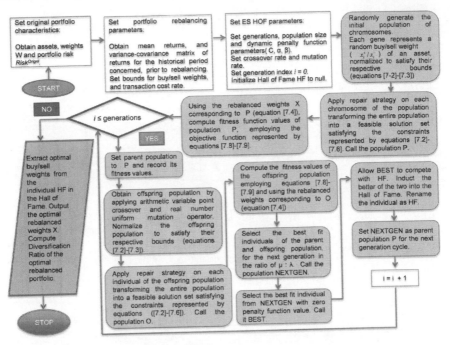

Figure 7.2. *Process flow chart of Evolution Strategy with Hall of Fame for Portfolio Rebalancing with Transaction costs (for a color version of this figure, see www.iste.co.uk/pai/metaheuristics.zip)*

To elaborate, let *FIRST* indicate the category that violates its lower bounds and *SECOND* the alternate one. Let *R* denote those weights in *FIRST* which violate their lower bounds and *Q* those that satisfy their lower bounds. The function upgrades the weights in *R* to their lower bounds and if *DEFICIT* is the sum total of the weights that were added, proceeds to adjust *DEFICIT* by subtracting an equal share from such of those weights in *Q* which can accommodate a cut without falling below their respective lower bounds, so that *DEFICIT* becomes close to *EPSILON*, a very small quantity. In the event of *DEFICIT* > *EPSILON*, the balance amount in *DEFICIT* is adjusted against the weights in *SECOND*, by adding an appropriate share even if the same results in some weights exceeding their upper bounds. It is left to ADJUST_UPBOUNDS_PFREBAL() function to handle the excesses concerned. At the end of its execution, ADJUST_LOWBOUNDS_PFREBAL() renders all the weights in the candidate solution vector to have satisfied their respective lower bounds besides, constraints represented by [7.4]–[7.6].

```
Algorithm PortfolioRebalancing_WeightRepair()
```

/* Let Z be the candidate solution vector normalized
to satisfy bounds (equations [7.2]-[7.3]). Let BUY
and SELL be the set of weights representing the
buy/sell decision. The objective is to repair the
weights such that constraints represented by
equations [7.2]-[7.6]) are satisfied by Z*/

begin

Compute DIFF = $\sum(x_i^+) - a.\sum(x_j^-)$;

if (DIFF ==0)   /* Z satisfies constraints,
                                              then exit */
then   exit();
end

Compute term = DIFF/NZ, where NZ are the non-zero
weights in Z;

if (DIFF > 0)
then   Redistribute DIFF by subtracting *term* from
            weights of assets in BUY and adding *term/a* to
            weights of assets in SELL, (i.e.)

$$x_i^+ = x_i^+ - term$$
$$x_j^- = x_j^- + \frac{term}{a} \; ^i$$

else   /* DIFF <0 */
            Redistribute DIFF by adding *term* to weights
            of assets in BUY and subtracting *term/a* from
            weights of assets in SELL, (i.e.)

$$x_i^+ = x_i^+ + term$$
$$x_j^- = x_j^- - \frac{term}{a} \; ^i$$

end   /* the excess weights of BUY/SELL are first
                   absorbed by the sets appropriately*/

```
Algorithm PortfolioRebalancing_WeightRepair Contd.


if     (the redistributed buy/sell weights in  Z
       satisfy their lower bounds (equations
       [7.2]- [7.3]))
then   continue;
else   call ADJUST_LOWBOUNDS_PFREBAL();
                          /* adjust lower bounds*/
end

if     (the lower bounds adjusted Z satisfies its
       upper bounds (equations [7.2]-[7.3]))
then   continue;
else   call  ADJUST_UPBOUNDS_PFREBAL();
                          /* adjust upper bounds */
end

/*lower  and  upper  bounds  satisfied  Z  now
represents a feasible solution vector satisfying
equations [7.2]-[7.6]*/

end

end PortfolioRebalancing_WeightRepair
```

In the last phase, the lower bound adjusted candidate solution vector goes through its upper bound adjustment process through function *ADJUST_UPBOUNDS_PFREBAL()*. *ADJUST_UPBOUNDS_PFREBAL()* now works to adjust the violations in upper bounds if any, by leveling off weights (R) that overshoot their upper bounds. Let *EXCESS* be the sum total of the weights sheared off. *EXCESS* is now equally distributed between the rest of the weights (Q) provided the weights accepting the new share of weights do not overshoot their respective upper bounds. If the balance amount in *EXCESS* after redistribution is close to zero, then the procedure is done and the feasible solution vector is returned. Otherwise, a prudent realignment of weights is undertaken not just to clear off *EXCESS* but also to keep the adjusted weights well within their bounds, thereby yielding a feasible solution set.

To elaborate, if all weights, in particular those belonging to *SECOND* are within the upper bound limits then the function terminates releasing the vector which is now a feasible solution vector. Otherwise it proceeds to bifurcate *SECOND* as *R* – the set of weights which overshoot their upper bounds and *Q*- the set that satisfies their upper bounds. The weights in *R* are leveled off to their respective upper bounds and the *EXCESS* which is the sum total of the weights sheared off, are equally distributed between those of *Q* provided the weights accepting the new share of weights do not overshoot their upper bounds. If the balance amount in *EXCESS* after redistribution is less than *EPSILON*, the function terminates to return the feasible solution vector. On the other hand if *EXCESS* > *EPSILON*, then there is little option but to adjust it again by adding it to weights in *FIRST*. At this stage, to prevent the weight adjustment from boomeranging back to *SECOND* in the event of violation of upper bounds, a prudent realignment of *FIRST* is undertaken not just to adjust *EXCESS* but also to keep the adjusted weights in *FIRST* well within their bounds. This case occurs when *FIRST* represents the sell category of assets and *SECOND* the buy category of assets.

The final weight adjustment involves the following computations:

Let *TOTAL* be the sum of weights of *FIRST* before adjusting *EXCESS* and *NZ* the set of non-zero weights in *FIRST*. The function now resets the non-zero weights of *FIRST* and gives each weight $y_i \in NZ$ their minimum due equivalent to their respective lower bounds with an increment proportional to their original weights, computed over *ACTUAL*, which is the actual sum of weights that needs to be redistributed. The computations yield,

$$ACTUAL = TOTAL - \frac{EXCESS}{a} - \sum_{y_i \in NZ, y_i \neq 0} lowerbounds(y_i) \qquad [7.13]$$

$$y_i^{adj} = lowerbounds(y_i) + \frac{y_i}{TOTAL} \cdot ACTUAL \qquad [7.14]$$

It can be easily seen that the new adjusted weights y_i^{adj} in *FIRST* cannot exceed their respective upper bounds after adjustment due to their proportional increments over *ACTUAL* which is less than *TOTAL*.

Thus, at the end of these processes, **Algorithm** PortfolioRebalancing_ WeightRepair() delivers a population of chromosomes that satisfy all the constraints represented by [7.2]–[7.6] and hence represent a feasible solution set.

EXAMPLE.– Let W = (0.25, 0.15, 0.1, 0.1, 0.05, 0.05, 0.2, 0.05, 0.03, 0.02) be the weights of the original portfolio of ten assets. Let us suppose that the following random vector with a random BUY/SELL decision, ascribed to each of the assets shown in brackets as B/S respectively, was generated to determine the rebalancing proportions of buy/sell weights (x_i^+ / x_i^-). The objective is to repair the rebalancing buy/sell weights (x_i^+ / x_i^-) so that it represents a feasible solution vector satisfying the constraints [7.2]–[7.6].

(0.0064 (B),   0.02 (B),   0.0191 (S), 0.0038 (B),   0.0076 (B),   0.0242 (S), 0.0242 (B), 0.0134 (B),   0.0158 (S),   0.001(S))

Let the lower and upper bound pairs for each of the buy/sell proportions of weights of the assets be as follows:

([0, 0.025], [0, 0.025],   [0, 0.1],   [0, 0.025],   [0, 0.025],   [0, 0.05], [0, 0.025], [0, 0.025],   [0, 0.03],   [0, 0.02]).

It can be observed that while all BUY decisions are bounded by [0, 0.025] satisfying [7.2] with u_i = 0.025, all SELL decisions are bound by their respective original portfolio weights satisfying [7.3].

Let the transaction cost rate p = 0.0044. Therefore $a = \dfrac{(1-p)}{(1+p)} = 0.9912$.

The weight repairing is now done as follows:

The sum of all BUY weights, $\sum\left(x_i^+\right)$ = 0.0755, the sum of all SELL weights $\sum\left(x_i^-\right)$ = 0.0601 and $DIFF = \sum\left(x_i^+\right) - a.\sum\left(x_i^-\right) = 0.0159$. Since $DIFF > 0$, *term* = $DIFF/10$ = 0.0016. Following [7.11] weights are repaired by distributing $DIFF$ over the buy/sell weights to yield,

$\left.\begin{cases} x_i^+ = x_i^+ - 0.0016 \\ x_j^- = x_j^- + 0.0016 \end{cases}\right\}$ that results in the repaired vector as,

(0.0048 (B),   0.0184 (B),   0.0207 (S),   0.0023 (B),   0.006 (B) ,   0.0258 (S),   0.0226 (B),   0.0118 (B),   0.0174 (S),   0.0026 (S)).

With each of the repaired weights satisfying their respective bounds, the repaired vector is delivered as the final buy/sell weight vector.

It can be easily checked that from [7.4], which yields the rebalanced weight vector X = (0.2548, 0.1684, 0.0793, 0.1023, 0.0560, 0.0242, 0.2226, 0.0618, 0.0126, 0.0174), [7.5] and [7.6] are satisfied. Thus X is the final rebalanced portfolio weight vector that is a feasible solution vector satisfying all the constraints represented by [7.2]–[7.6]. In the event of buy/sell weights violating their bounds during the redistribution of weights, procedures $ADJUST\_LOWBOUNDS\_$ $PFREBAL()$ and $ADJUST\_UPBOUNDS\_PFREBAL()$ are appropriately called for, to tackle the deficits or excesses.

Thus, the procedure PortfolioRebalancing_WeightRepair works on each chromosome of the parent and offspring populations to transform them into a feasible solution set. The MATLAB$^®$ implementation of procedure PortfolioRebalancing_WeightRepair is discussed in section 7.6 A and illustrated in Figure 7.10, with functions $ADJUST\_LOWBOUNDS\_PFREBAL()$ and $ADJUST\_UPBOUNDS\_PFREBAL()$ illustrated as MATLAB$^®$ functions in Figure 7.11 and Figure 7.12 respectively. Interested readers are encouraged to work on these functions, testing it over appropriate weight vectors to comprehend the nuances of the unified weight repair strategy.

7.4. Experimental results

7.4.1. *ES HOF-based rebalancing of a high risk S&P BSE200 portfolio*

The metaheuristic portfolio rebalancing discussed in this chapter and illustrated in Figure 7.2 was experimented over a high-risk portfolio comprising the top 15 percentile of high volatility stocks of S&P BSE200 (March 1999–March 2009) ordered according to their historic volatilities. Table 7.1 shows the list of 32 assets selected for the experiments.

Making use of the historical data set from March 03, 1999–December 29, 2006 the optimal portfolio allocations were computed and the portfolio invested on January 02, 2007. Termed *original portfolio* (to distinguish it from the rebalanced portfolio) the characteristics of the original portfolio have been shown in Table 7.2. The original portfolio reported a diversification ratio of 2.7822 with an expected portfolio annualized return and annualized risk of 88.74% and 33.60%, respectively.

The original portfolio was kept untended for a year, January 03, 2007–January 02, 2008 and the rebalancing of the portfolio, using Evolution Strategy with Hall of Fame, was undertaken on January 03, 2008. The historical data set considered for rebalancing was from March 03, 1999–January 02, 2008. The transaction cost rate p was set to 0.0044. The upper bound u_i for all buy decisions to curtail transaction costs was set to 0.025. Table 7.3 shows the control parameters of ES HOF set for the portfolio rebalancing problem concerned. Table 7.4 shows the buy/sell weights (x_i^+ / x_i^-) and the characteristics of the optimal rebalanced portfolio. For ease of representation the buy weights (x_i^+) are shown positive and the sell weights (x_i^-) are shown negative. The optimal rebalanced portfolio reported a diversification ratio of 2.7580 and an expected portfolio annualized return and annualized risk of 92.04% and 32.75%, respectively. It can be observed that the risk of the rebalanced portfolio did not exceed that of the original portfolio risk, which in fact was one of the constraints set by the investor ([7.7]) and all other constraints given by [7.2]–[7.6] were also seen satisfied.

7.4.2. *Convergence characteristics of ES HOF*

Observing the convergence characteristics of metaheuristics algorithms is an essential part of their study. A discussion on how an empirical metric such as convergence of the objective function (fitness function) or a distribution-based criterion such as P measure [FEO 06] could be employed to study the convergence characteristics of metaheuristics algorithms, was included in Chapter 2. Following the same, ES HOF was observed for its convergence behavior, by way of both the objective functions as well as P Measures.

ES HOF was run several times over rebalancing of the high risk S&P BSE200 portfolio. The objective function values (fitness function values) of the chromosomes inducted into the Hall of Fame during the generation cycles were recorded. Figure 7.3 illustrates the objective function values of the HOF chromosomes in five different runs. As can be seen, for the portfolio rebalancing problem which is a maximization problem, ES HOF yields HOF chromosomes whose fitness function values rise with each new chromosome inducted into HOF and stabilizes thereafter, close to 200 generations, indicating convergence.

The P measures of the new generation of chromosomes created by selecting the best fit among the parent and offspring populations, during each generation cycle were also observed. Chapter 2, section 2.5.5 discusses P Measures. Figure 7.4 shows the trace of the P measures during the generation cycles of ES HOF for the portfolio rebalancing problem, for five different runs. It can be clearly seen that in a matter of a few generations, P measures have begun crowding around a specific region and converging towards 0, indicative of low diversity and hence better convergence.

ESSAR SHIPPING PORTS & LOGS	NAGARJUNA CONSTRUCTION CO	PRAJ INDUSTRIES LIMITED
HINDUSTAN ZINC LIMITED	ROLTA INDIA LIMITED	SHRIRAM TRANSPORT FINANCE
UNITED BREWERIES HOLDINGS LTD	UNITECH LIMITED	VIDEOCON INDUSTRIES LTD
MANGALORE REFINERY & PETRO	PANTALOON RETAIL INDIA LTD	FINANCIAL TECHN (INDIA) LTD
JAIN IRRIGATION SYSTEMS LTD	GTL LTD	ISPAT INDUSTRIES LTD
BHUSHAN STEEL LIMITED	JSW STEEL LIMITED	ESSAR OIL LTD
AREVA T&D INDIA LTD	NEYVELI LIGNITE CORPORATION	WELSPUN-GUJARAT STAHL LTD
RAJAJ HINDUSTHAN LIMITED	MOSER BAER INDIA LTD	GUJARAT NRE COKE LTD
KOTAK MAHINDRA BANK LTD	MERCATOR LINES LIMITED	IVRCL INFRASTRUCTURES & PROJ
STEEL AUTHORITY OF INDIA	IFCI LIMITED	UNITED PHOSPHORUS LTD
JAI CORP LTD	BOMBAY DYEING & MFG CO LTD	

Table 7.1. *High risk portfolio of 32 assets selected from S&P BSE200 (March 1999–March 2009) to demonstrate metaheuristic portfolio rebalancing*

Asset	Weight	Asset	Weight
ESSAR SHIPPING PORTS & LOGS	0.0248	JSW STEEL LIMITED	0.0010
HINDUSTAN ZINC LIMITED	0.0137	NEYVELI LIGNITE CORPORATION	0.0149
UNITED BREWERIES HOLDINGS LT	0.0010	MOSER BAER INDIA LTD	0.0151
MANGALORE REFINERY & PETRO	0.0010	MERCATOR LINES LIMITED	0.0316
JAIN IRRIGATION SYSTEMS LTD	0.0512	IFCI LIMITED	0.0010
BHUSHAN STEEL LIMITED	0.0209	BOMBAY DYEING & MFG CO LTD	0.0695
AREVA T&D INDIA LTD	0.0316	PRAJ INDUSTRIES LIMITED	0.0635
BAJAJ HINDUSTHAN LIMITED	0.0576	SHRIRAM TRANSPORT FINANCE	0.0687
KOTAK MAHINDRA BANK LTD	0.0323	VIDEOCON INDUSTRIES LTD	0.0595
STEEL AUTHORITY OF INDIA	0.0010	FINANCIAL TECHN (INDIA) LTD	0.0059
JAI CORP LTD	0.0409	ISPAT INDUSTRIES LTD	0.0308
NAGARJUNA CONSTRUCTION CO	0.0010	ESSAR OIL LTD	0.0617
ROLTA INDIA LIMITED	0.0020	WELSPUN-GUJARAT STAHL LTD	0.0575
UNITECH LIMITED	0.1115	GUJARAT NRE COKE LTD	0.0425
PANTALOON RETAIL INDIA LTD	0.0250	IVRCL INFRASTRUCTURES & PROJ	0.0435
GTL LTD	0.0010	UNITED PHOSPHORUS LTD	0.0171
Diversification Ratio		2.7822	
Expected Portfolio Annualized Return		88.74%	
Annualized Risk		33.60%	

Table 7.2. *Optimal original portfolio characteristics*

Control parameter	Value
Chromosome length (portfolio size)	32
Population size	320
Generations	1000
(C, α, β)	(0.5, 2, 2)
Crossover rate	0.61
Mutation rate	0.01

Table 7.3. *Control parameters of Evolution Strategy with Hall of Fame for metaheuristic portfolio rebalancing*

Asset	Optimal Buy/Sell Weights (x_i^+ / x_i^-)	Optimal rebalanced portfolio weights (X)
ESSAR SHIPPING PORTS & LOGS	-0.0012	0.0236
HINDUSTAN ZINC LIMITED	-0.0010	0.0127
UNITED BREWERIES HOLDINGS LTD	0.0231	0.0241
MANGALORE REFINERY & PETRO	0	0.0010
JAIN IRRIGATION SYSTEMS LTD	-0.0017	0.0495
BHUSHAN STEEL LIMITED	0.0011	0.0220
AREVA T&D INDIA LTD	-0.0013	0.0303
BAJAJ HINDUSTHAN LIMITED	-0.0030	0.0546
KOTAK MAHINDRA BANK LTD	-0.0009	0.0314
STEEL AUTHORITY OF INDIA	-0.0009	0.0001
JAI CORP LTD	0.0154	0.0563
NAGARJUNA CONSTRUCTION CO	0	0.0010
ROLTA INDIA LIMITED	0	0.0020
UNITECH LIMITED	-0.0208	0.0907
PANTALOON RETAIL INDIA LTD	0.0128	0.0378
GTL LTD	0	0.0010
JSW STEEL LIMITED	-0.0009	0.0001
NEYVELI LIGNITE CORPORATION	0.0012	0.0161
MOSER BAER INDIA LTD	0	0.0151
MERCATOR LINES LIMITED	0	0.0316
IFCI LIMITED	0	0.0010

BOMBAY DYEING & MFG CO LTD	-0.0187	0.0508
PRAJ INDUSTRIES LIMITED	-0.0090	0.0545
SHRIRAM TRANSPORT FINANCE	0.0003	0.0690
VIDEOCON INDUSTRIES LTD	0.0074	0.0669
FINANCIAL TECHN (INDIA) LTD	0.0040	0.0099
ISPAT INDUSTRIES LTD	-0.0009	0.0299
ESSAR OIL LTD	-0.0027	0.0590
WELSPUN-GUJARAT STAHL LTD	-0.0048	0.0527
GUJARAT NRE COKE LTD	0.0028	0.0453
IVRCL INFRASTRUCTURES & PROJ	-0.0009	0.0426
UNITED PHOSPHORUS LTD	0	0.0171
Diversification Ratio	2.7580	
Expected Portfolio Annualized Return	92.04%	
Annualized Risk	32.75%	

Table 7.4. *Optimal rebalanced portfolio characteristics*

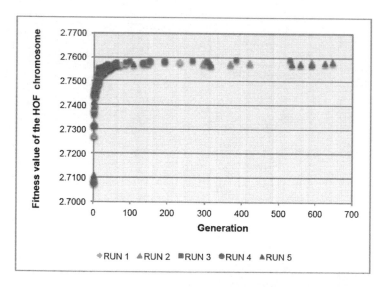

Figure 7.3. *Convergence characteristics of ES HOF during portfolio rebalancing: Trace of the fitness function value of HOF chromosome during generation cycles of some sample runs (for a color version of this figure, see www.iste.co.uk/pai/metaheuristics.zip)*

7.4.3. *Consistency of performance of ES HOF*

As discussed in Chapter 2, considering the stochastic nature of the population-based metaheuristics algorithms, to test for performance consistency, it is essential and useful to undertake an empirical testing by repeatedly running the metaheuristic algorithm for a definite number of runs. ES HOF was repeatedly run over the specific high-risk portfolio discussed in section 7.4.1. The summary of the optimal rebalanced portfolio characteristics during five such sample runs have been shown in Table 7.5.

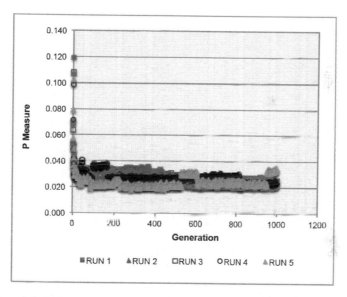

Figure 7.4. *Convergence characteristics of ES HOF during portfolio rebalancing: Trace of the P measures of the populations during generation cycles, for some sample runs (for a color version of this figure, see www.iste.co.uk/pai/metaheuristics.zip)*

7.5. Comparison of Non-Rebalanced and Rebalanced portfolios

In this section, we explore and analyze the following questions on portfolio rebalancing vis-à-vis non-rebalancing, which is significant from an investment management perspective:

– in the absence of portfolio rebalancing, how much would the weight drift be for the non-rebalanced portfolio?

– non-rebalanced versus rebalanced portfolio – which of these is better and when?

7.5.1. *Weight drift analysis for the Non-Rebalanced portfolio*

An untended portfolio tends to drift and in course of time can turn more volatile and/or acquire characteristics that are inconsistent with the investor's goals and preferences. On the other hand, however, rebalancing involves costs and hence questions, such as how often, how far and how much, need to be addressed before indulging in rebalancing.

A weight drift analysis, which involves computing the day to day drift, helps analyze the drift in weights before a decision can be taken by the investor. Let $w_i^{(old)}$ be the original weight allocated to asset i, $w_i^{(new)}$ the drifted weight, $\mu_i^{(d)}$ the return of the asset i on day d and $P_i^{(d)}$ the total return of the portfolio on the day d. The drifted weights are given by

$$w_i^{(new)} = w_i^{(old)} * (1 + \mu_i^{(d)}) / (1 + P_i^{(d)})$$ [7.15]

For a sample portfolio of 32 high-risk assets invested in the S&P BSE200 index, a weight drift analysis was experimented upon. The original portfolio allocation was done on January 02, 2007. After leaving the portfolio untended for almost a year, the weight drifts were tracked during the trading days for the period from January 02, 2008 to January 15, 2008. Figure 7.5 illustrates the weight drifts of the assets in the portfolio shown as a stacked line chart. The Relative Standard Deviation (%) of the drift in weights of the individual assets in the specific portfolio varied from 1.305% to 7.087%. It could now be left to the discretion of the investor to decide on whether the portfolio should be rebalanced or continue to remain non-rebalanced.

7.5.2. *Non-Rebalanced versus Rebalanced portfolios – which of these is better?*

Qian [QIA 14] investigated the intriguing question of "To rebalance or not to rebalance?" and the following are significant assertions made by him with regard to a *long-only portfolio*, which is of relevance to the portfolio discussed in this work:

1) the returns of a Rebalanced portfolio can never exceed that of a Non-Rebalanced portfolio termed Buy-and-Hold portfolio (Jensen's inequality);

2) the risk of a Rebalanced portfolio will always be better adjusted than a Buy-and-Hold portfolio;

3) the Diversification index of a Buy-and-Hold portfolio over a period of time will show a downward trend when compared to that of Rebalanced portfolios due to concentration.

ES HOF Runs	Diversification Ratio	Annualized Risk(%)	Expected portfolio annual return (%)
Run 1	2.7580	32.75	92.04
Run 2	2.7582	32.51	91.89
Run 3	2.7591	32.68	92.83
Run 4	2.7582	32.69	92.49
Run 5	2.7583	32.74	92.25

Table 7.5. *Summarized characteristics of the optimal rebalanced portfolios for S&P BSE200 (March 1999–March 2009) dataset, obtained by ES HOF during five sample runs*

Investigation of Qian's assertions to the high risk portfolio of S&P BSE200 discussed in section 7.3.1 showed that all three assertions were meticulously obeyed. The Diversification Ratio, Risk, Return characteristics of the Rebalanced and Non-Rebalanced portfolio were observed during the trading days of the tracking period (January 02, 2008–January16, 2008), using the historical data set from January 03, 2007 to the trading day concerned, to compute the Diversification Ratios and Risks.

Figure 7.6 shows the Diversification Ratios of the Rebalanced and Non-Rebalanced portfolios and verifies assertion (3) that the Diversification Ratios of the Non-Rebalanced portfolio is smaller than those of the Rebalanced portfolio. Figure 7.7 illustrates the agreement with assertion (2) where the risks of the Rebalanced portfolios are better adjusted than those of Non-Rebalanced portfolio. Figure 7.8 verifies that assertion (1) is true in that the returns of the Rebalanced portfolio cannot exceed those of the Non-Rebalanced portfolio – for a long only portfolio especially. The returns of the Rebalanced portfolio are the ones after deduction of transaction costs.

Qian's observations are significant in the sense that it helps the investor of a long only portfolio to take a decision on which of the major objectives – Risk or Return – is of concern to him/her and accordingly decide on whether to rebalance or not to rebalance.

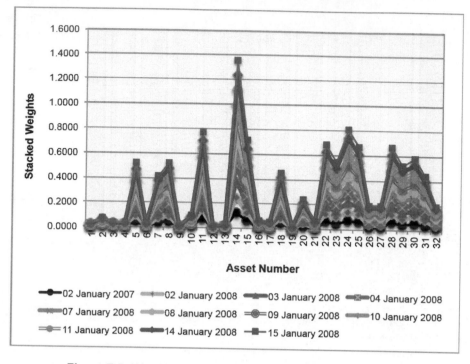

Figure 7.5. *Weight drifts of the non-rebalanced portfolio during the trading days of the tracking period from January 02, 2008 to January 15, 2008, shown as a stacked line chart (for a color version of this figure, see www.iste.co.uk/pai/metaheuristics.zip)*

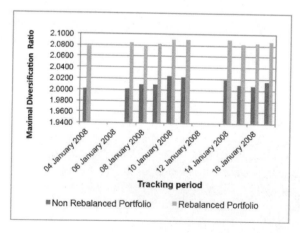

Figure 7.6. *Non Rebalanced versus Rebalanced portfolios: Diversification Ratio*

7.5.3. *Risk-Return performance of the Rebalanced and Non-Rebalanced portfolios*

The Risk-Return performance of a Rebalanced and Non-Rebalanced portfolio were studied during a long-term tracking period of January 2008–September 2008, by tracing their respective efficient frontiers, using their historical return series.

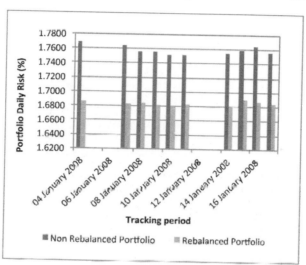

Figure 7.7. *Non-Rebalanced versus Rebalanced portfolios: Daily risk (%)*

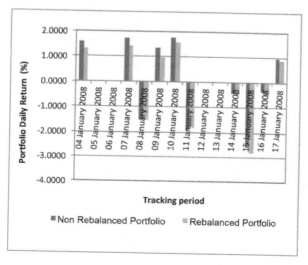

Figure 7.8. *Non-Rebalanced versus Rebalanced portfolios: Daily return (%)*

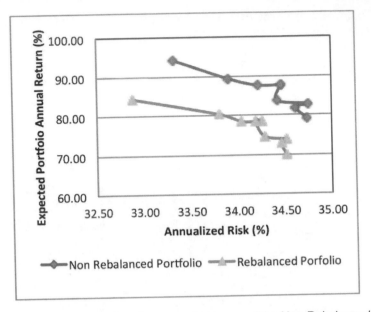

Figure 7.9. *Risk versus Return performance of the Non-Rebalanced and Rebalanced portfolio during the tracking period: January–Sept, 2008, with portfolio rebalancing done on January 02, 2008*

Figure 7.9 illustrates the efficient frontiers for the Non-Rebalanced and Rebalanced portfolio. Qian's assertions can also be observed on the efficient frontiers in that the efficient frontiers of the rebalanced portfolios have moved leftwards indicating a risk adjusted performance while the efficient frontier of the Non-Rebalanced portfolio points northwards indicating a better return when compared with its respective competitor.

7.6. MATLAB® demonstrations

In this section we demonstrate MATLAB® functions associated with the ES HOF based portfolio rebalancing, as listed below. The MATLAB® coding style has been kept direct and simple to favor novices in MATLAB®.

A. Weight repair strategy.

B. Computing constraint violation function.

C. Computing fitness function.

A. *Weight repair strategy*

The weight repair strategy adopted by ES HOF and described by Algorithm `PortfolioRebalancing_WeightRepair()` in this chapter is presented as a MATLAB® function in Figure 7.10. For ease of implementation the buy weights are represented as positive weights and sell weights are represented as negative weights during weight repair.

`weight_mat` refers to a population of buy/sell weights with dimension `[row_mat, col_mat]`. `TrCost` refers to the proportional transaction cost p. `Wgtlimits{i}` is a cell array that stores all the lower and upper bounds of each of the buy/sell weights of chromosome `i`, belonging to the population `weight_mat`. Implementation of [7.10]–[7.12] can be easily seen in the MATLAB® function. `Pos_Weights` refers to buy weights with the sell weight components set as 0 and `Neg_Weights` refers to sell weights with the buy weights components set as 0. `LOWLIMIT_FLAG` and `UPLIMIT_FLAG` serve to aid invocation of sub functions `adjustPosNegWgts_lowbounds()` and `adjustPosNegWgts_upbounds()` respectively, if the weights violate their respective limits during weight repair.

The function `adjustPosNegWgts_lowbounds()` representing function `ADJUST_LOWBOUNDS_PFREBAL()` in **Algorithm** Portfolio Rebalancing_WeightRepair is illustrated in Figure 7.11. The function `adjust PosNegWgts_upbounds()` representing function `ADJUST_UPBOUNDS_PFREBAL()` in **Algorithm** `PortfolioRebalancing_WeightRepair` is illustrated in Figure 7.12.

B. *Computing constraint violation function*

For the portfolio rebalancing problem, the non-linear constraint that the rebalanced portfolio risk should not exceed that preferred by the investor for the original portfolio and represented by [7.7], was tackled using Joines and Houck's penalty function strategy. Thus a constraint violation function represented by $\psi(\bar{X}, V, Risk^{Orignl}, t)$ ([7.9]) served to tackle the non-linear constraint by absorbing it into the objective function ([7.8]). The MATLAB® function to compute the constraint violation function value for the population of chromosomes is illustrated in Figure 7.13.

Of the input parameters to the function, `weight_mat`, `covar_mat` and `orignl_risk` represent the population of chromosomes, the variance-covariance matrix of the assets and the risk of the original portfolio. `C_param`, `beta_param` and `alpha_param` represent the parameters of the dynamic penalty function strategy, (C, α, β). `gencount` represents the generation count t.

The output parameters [G, psi] represent the penalties and the constraint violation function values. It needs to be recalled here that only those chromosomes whose psi equals 0, are eligible to compete with the HOF chromosome. This prerequisite ensures that only feasible solution sets can compete to enter HOF.

```
function std_weight_mat =
PortfolioRebalancing_WeightRepair (weight_mat,
                                   Wgtlimits, TrCost)

[row_mat, col_mat] = size(weight_mat);

a = (1-TrCost)/(1+TrCost);

for i =1:row_mat
 low_up_bounds = Wgtlimits{i};
 Pos_Weights = weight_mat(i,:) .*
               (weight_mat(i,:)>=0); % buy weights
 Neg_Weights = -(weight_mat(i,:) .*
               (weight_mat(i,:)<0; % sell weights

 X_Plus  = sum(Pos_Weights);
 X_Minus = sum(Neg_Weights);
 NZ      = sum(Pos_Weights ~=0) +
                        sum(Neg_Weights ~= 0);

 X_Minus_Whole = a*X_Minus;
 if (X_Plus > X_Minus_Whole)
       DIFF = X_Plus - X_Minus_Whole;
       SIGNAL = 1; % sum of buy weights  greater
                   % than sum of sell weights
 else
 if (X_Plus < X_Minus_Whole)
       DIFF = X_Minus_Whole- X_Plus;
       SIGNAL =0; % sum of sell weights greater
                  % than sum of buy weights
 else continue;
 end
 end
```

Figure 7.10. *MATLAB® function for weight repairing buy/sell weights (Algorithm* PortfolioRebalancing_WeightRepair() *) (for a color version of this figure, see www.iste.co.uk/pai/metaheuristics.zip)*

```
LOWLIMIT_FLAG=1;
UPLIMIT_FLAG =1;
if (DIFF ~=0)
    term = DIFF/NZ; % redistribute excess weights
    if (SIGNAL == 1)
        for j=1:col_mat
            if (Pos_Weights(1,j) >0)
            Pos_Weights(1,j) = Pos_Weights(1,j) -
                                            term;
            end
            if Neg_Weights(1,j) >0
            Neg_Weights(1,j) = Neg_Weights(1,j) +
                                            term/a;
            end
        end
    else
    if (SIGNAL == 0)% redistribute excess weights
        for j=1:col_mat
            if (Neg_Weights(1,j) >0)
            Neg_Weights(1,j) = Neg_Weights(1,j) -
                                            term/a;
            end
            if Pos_Weights(1,j) >0
                Pos_Weights(1,j) = Pos_Weights(1,j) +
                                            term;
            end
        end
    end
  end
end
```

Figure 7.10. *Contd.*

```
for j=1:col mat
                P = Pos_Weights(1,j);
                N = Neg_Weights(1,j);
                l = low_up_bounds(1,j);
                u = low_up_bounds(2,j);
                if (P ~= 0)
                    if ((P >= l) && (P <= u))
                        continue;
                    else
                        LOWLIMIT_FLAG =0;
                    end
                end

                if (N ~= 0)
                    if ((N >= l) && (N <=u))
                        continue;
                    else
                        LOWLIMIT_FLAG =0;
                    end
                end
end
if (LOWLIMIT_FLAG ==0)
[Pos_Weights(1,:),Neg_Weights(1,:),UPLIMIT_FLAG]
    = adjustPosNegWgts_lowbounds(Pos_Weights(1,:),
        Neg_Weights(1,:), low_up_bounds, SIGNAL, a);
end;

if (UPLIMIT_FLAG ==0)
[Pos_Weights(1,:), Neg_Weights(1,:)] =
   adjustPosNegWgts_upbounds( Pos_Weights(1,:),
   Neg_Weights(1,:), low_up_bounds, SIGNAL, a);
end;

std_weight_mat(i,:) = Pos_Weights(1,:)-
                              Neg_Weights(1,:);
end
end
```

Figure 7.10. *Contd.*

```
% standardize lower bounds

function [ PosWgt_Adj,NegWgt_Adj, UPBOUNDS_FLAG ] =
adjustPosNegWgts_lowbounds( PosWgtsVec, NegWgtsVec,
                            lowupbounds, Signal, a )
[~, col_vec]= size(PosWgtsVec);

% whichever category (buy or sell) exceeds its sum
% of weights is First_Weights, the other is
% Second_Weights

if (Signal ==1)
    First_Weights = PosWgtsVec;    % Test and adjust
                                   % positive weights first
    Second_Weights = NegWgtsVec;
else
    First_Weights = NegWgtsVec;    % Test and adjust
                                   % negative weights first
    Second_Weights = PosWgtsVec;
end

% R: those weights that fell below their lower
% bound and are now adjusted
R=[];
c_R=0;
DEPOSIT = 0;
EPSILON = 0.0001;
for i=1:col_vec
    if ((First_Weights(1,1)~=0) &&(First_Weights(1,i) <
                                   lowupbounds(1,i)))
        DEFICIT = (lowupbounds(1,i)-First_Weights(1,i));
        DEPOSIT - DEPOSIT - DEFICIT;
        First_Weights(1,i) = lowupbounds(1,i);
        c_R = c_R+1;
        R(c_R) = i;
    end
end

% Q: those weights which satisfy their lower bounds
Q = setdiff(1:col_vec, R);
sharing_wgts = sum(First_Weights(1,Q)~=0);
if (sharing_wgts ~=0)
    redistr_share = DEPOSIT/(sharing_wgts);
    [~,t] = size(Q);
```

Figure 7.11. *MATLAB® function for weight repairing buy/sell weights (function* `ADJUST_LOWBOUNDS_PFREBAL` *in Algorithm* `PortfolioRebalancing_` `WeightRepair()` *) (for a color version of this figure, see www.iste.co.uk/pai/metaheuristics.zip)*

```
      for i=1:t
      if
      (First_Weights(1,Q(i))>0)&&((First_Weights(1,Q(i))-
              abs(redistr_share))>= lowupbounds(1,Q(i)))
      First_Weights(1,Q(i)) = First_Weights(1, Q(i)) -
                                      abs(redistr_share);
      DEPOSIT = DEPOSIT-redistr_share;

      if (abs(DEPOSIT) <= EPSILON)
      break;
      else continue;
      end
      end
      end
end

if (abs(DEPOSIT) > EPSILON)

    non_zero_wgts = sum(Second_Weights(1,:)~=0);
    if (Signal ==1)
    redistr_share = DEPOSIT/(a*non_zero_wgts);
    else
    redistr_share = (DEPOSIT/non_zero_wgts);
    end
    for i=1:col_vec
      if (Second_Weights(1,i) ~= 0)
      Second_Weights(1,i) = Second_Weights (1,i) +
                                    abs(redistr_share);
      end
    end
end

UPBOUNDS_FLAG =1;
for j=1:col_vec
    if ((Second_Weights(1,j)~=0)&&(Second_Weights(1,j) >
                                    lowupbounds(2,j)))
    UPBOUNDS_FLAG = 0;
    end
end;
if (Signal ==1)
    PosWgt_Adj = First_Weights;
    NegWgt_Adj = Second_Weights;
else
    PosWgt_Adj = Second_Weights;
    NegWgt_Adj = First_Weights;
end
end
```

Figure 7.11. *Contd.*

```
% standardize upper bounds

function [ PosWgt_Adj, NegWgt_Adj ] =
    adjustPosNegWgts_upbounds( PosWgtsVec, NegWgtsVec,
                                lowupbounds, Signal, a )
[~, col_vec]= size(PosWgtsVec);

% whichever category (buy or sell) exceeds its sum of
% weights is First_Weights, the other is Second_Weights

if (Signal ==1)
    First_Weights = PosWgtsVec; % Test and adjust
                               % positive weights first
    Second_Weights = NegWgtsVec;
else
    First_Weights = NegWgtsVec; % Test and adjust
                               % negative weights first
    Second_Weights = PosWgtsVec;
end

% R: those weights that exceeded  their upper bounds and
% are now adjusted
R=[];
c_R=0;
DEPOSIT = 0;
EPSILON = 0.0001;
for i=1:col_vec
    if ((Second_Weights(1,i)~=0) &&
        (Second_Weights(1,i) > lowupbounds(2,i)))
        EXCESS = (-lowupbounds(2,i)+Second_Weights(1,i));
        DEPOSIT = DEPOSIT + EXCESS;
        Second_Weights(1,i) = lowupbounds(2,i);
        c_R = c_R+1;
        R(c_R) = i;
    end
end

%Q: those weights which satisfy their upper bounds
Q = setdiff([1:col_vec], R);
sharing_wgts = sum(Second_Weights(1,Q)~=0);
```

Figure 7.12. *MATLAB® function for weight repairing buy/sell weights (function* ADJUST_UPBOUNDS_PFREBAL *in Algorithm* PortfolioRebalancing_ WeightRepair() *) (for a color version of this figure, see www.iste.co.uk/pai/metaheuristics.zip)*

```
if (sharing_wgts ~=0)
    if (Signal==1)
        redistr_share = DEPOSIT/(a * sharing_wgts);
    else
        redistr_share = DEPOSIT/ sharing_wgts;
    end
    [~,t] = size(Q);


    for i=1:t
      if (Second_Weights(1,Q(i))>0)&&
      ((Second_Weights(1,Q(i))+redistr_share)<=
                                  lowupbounds(2,Q(i)))
        Second_Weights(1,Q(i)) = Second_Weights(1, Q(i)) +
                                  redistr_share;
        DEPOSIT = DEPOSIT-redistr_share;
        if ((DEPOSIT) <= EPSILON)
        break;
        else continue;
        end
      end
    end
end

if (DEPOSIT > EPSILON)

actual_total = sum(First_Weights(1,:));
NZ_FirstWeights_Indx = find(First_Weights(1,:));
total = actual_total -(DEPOSIT/a)-
sum(lowupbounds(1,NZ_FirstWeights_Indx));
for i=1:col_vec
if (First_Weights(1,i) ~= 0)
    proportion = (First_Weights(1,i)/actual_total)*total;
    First_Weights(1,i) = lowupbounds(1,i) + proportion;
end
end
end
if (Signal ==1)
    PosWgt_Adj = First_Weights;
    NegWgt_Adj = Second_Weights;
else
    PosWgt_Adj = Second_Weights;
    NegWgt_Adj = First_Weights;
end

end
```

Figure 7.12. *Contd.*

```
function  [G, psi]  = compute constrvioln fn Rebal(
      weight_mat, covar_mat, orignl_risk,  C_param,
      beta_param, alpha_param, gencount)

[row_mat,  ~]= size(weight_mat);
psi(1:row_mat) = zeros(1, row_mat);
G(1:row_mat) = zeros(1,row_mat);
epsilon=0.001;

for i=1:row_mat

    % select each chromosome from the population
    x_chrom = weight_mat(i,:);

    % compute portfolio risk for the chromosome
    portfolio_risk = sqrt(x_chrom * covar_mat *
                                    x_chrom');
    % phi: rebalanced portfolio risk constraint
    phi = abs(portfolio_risk - orignl_risk)-
                                    epsilon;
    % compute penalties G
    g = 1-(phi <=0);
    G(i) = g;

    % compute  constraint  violation function psi
    penalty_term=
            power(C_param*gencount,alpha_param);
    psi(i) = penalty_term * sum( g.*power(phi,
                                    beta_param));

end

end
```

Figure 7.13. MATLAB® function for computing constraint
violation function for portfolio rebalancing (for a color version
of this figure, see www.iste.co.uk/pai/metaheuristics.zip)

C. Computing fitness function

Figure 7.14 illustrates the MATLAB® function that computes the fitness function
values from the penalized objective function shown in [7.8], for the population of
individuals popln_mat. covariance_dat and psi denote the variance-
covariance matrix and the constraint violation function values respectively.
obj_val indicates the penalized objective function values that represent the
fitness values of the population of chromosomes.

```
function [obj val ] = Rebal comp fitness(popln mat,
                              covariance_dat,    psi)

 [popln_size, ~]= size(popln_mat);
 obj_val = zeros(popln_size,1);

 stdev_assets = sqrt(diag(covariance_dat));

 for i = 1:popln_size

   weight = popln_mat(i,:);

   % compute portfolio risk P
   P = sqrt(weight * covariance_dat * weight');
   obj_val (i) = ((sum(stdev_assets .* weight')) /
                              P) - psi(i);

 end

end
```

Figure 7.14. *MATLAB® function for computing fitness function values for the portfolio rebalancing problem (for a color version of this figure, see www.iste.co.uk/pai/metaheuristics.zip)*

Project

Three risk aggressive investors, Gita, Gautier and Ganesh independently decide to invest in 30 high beta stocks and five bonds. The following objectives and constraints were decided upon in common:

(i)   maximize Sharpe Ratio of the portfolio, and

(ii)   preference for an 80/20 fully invested portfolio.

Gita with her laid back approach works out the optimal portfolio allocation and decides to keep it untended for the next two years!

Gautier too decides to keep his portfolio untended for the next two years just as Gita decided, but is wary enough to cushion his risk by including risk budgets on his portfolio. He therefore brings in the following risk-budgeting constraint:

(iii)   impose a Risk Budget of 15.5% with regard to the absolute contribution to risk, for selective high risk assets

Metaheuristic Portfolio Rebalancing with Transaction Costs   275

Ganesh decides to subscribe to (i) and (ii) alone for his portfolio, but is determined that he would rebalance his portfolio at the end of one year.

(a) Frame the mathematical model for Gita/Ganesh and Gautier's portfolio optimization.

(b) Obtain Gita/Ganesh's optimal portfolio allocation using MATLAB Financial Toolbox^{TM}.

(c) Execute Evolution Strategy with Hall of Fame to decide on Gautier's optimal portfolio.

(d) At the end of two years how much did Gita's portfolio drift? Undertake a weight drift analysis of her portfolio.

(e) At the end of two years how much did Gautier's portfolio drift? Compare Gita's and Gautier's portfolio performance. Is Gautier's untended portfolio less risky than that of Gita's?

(f) How did Ganesh's portfolio perform at the end of one year? If he decided to rebalance his portfolio using Evolution Strategy with Hall of Fame, what would be the optimal buy/sell weights delivered by the method?

(g) Test Qian's [QIA 14] assertions on Non-Rebalanced versus Rebalanced portfolios with regard to Ganesh's portfolio.

(h) If Ganesh opted for Differential Evolution strategy to obtain his optimal rebalanced portfolio, what would be the optimal buy/sell weights delivered by it? Compare the characteristics of the optimal rebalanced portfolios obtained by Evolution Strategy with Hall of Fame and Differential Evolution.

Suggested Further Reading

White papers and articles on portfolio rebalancing published by investment firms, such as *"Best practices for portfolio rebalancing"* by Vanguard Research – 2010, 2015, (JAC 10, ZIL 15), *"Portfolio rebalancing in theory and practice"* by Vanguard Investment Counseling and Research-2007 [TOK 07] and *"The art of rebalancing"* by Smith Barney Citigroup-2005 [SMI 05], are good reads on the critical issue of portfolio rebalancing.

Portfolio Rebalancing problem models can also be formulated with multiple objectives and constraints. In such cases multi-objective metaheuristic optimization strategies need to be employed to solve the models. Deb's book on *Multi-Objective Optimization using Evolutionary Algorithms* [DEB 03] and Coello *et al.'s* book on

Evolutionary Algorithms for solving Multi-Objective Problems [COE 07] are good textbooks to know more about multi-objective metaheuristic optimization.

Fuzzy decision theory based portfolio rebalancing with multiple objectives and constraints, using metaheuristics, was explored by Pai [PAI 17].

Conclusion

The problem of Portfolio Optimization in finance can become complex when myriad objectives and constraints induced by market norms, investor preferences and investment strategies, to list a few, are inducted into the problem model. With the complex mathematical models finding little help from traditional or analytical methods to arrive at the optimal portfolios, a voluntary and natural choice has been to turn to non-traditional algorithms and non-orthodox approaches from the ever-expanding discipline of Metaheuristics in order to arrive at the optimal portfolios.

This interdisciplinary book, therefore, elucidates a collection of practical and strategic Portfolio Optimization models in Finance, that employ Metaheuristics for their effective solutions and demonstrates the results using MATLAB® implementations, on live portfolios invested across global stock universes.

The first part of the book, which laid the foundation for the discussions in the rest of the book, introduced the cornerstones of the subject matter, viz. Portfolio Optimization and Metaheuristics. While Chapter 1 targeting non-finance readers discussed the fundamentals of portfolio optimization, Chapter 2 targeting non-computer science/metaheuristics readers presented a brief primer on Metaheuristics, restricting its discussion to two strategies from the genres of Evolution Strategy and Differential Evolution, on which the rest of the discussion in the book is dependent upon.

The second part of the book spanning Chapters 3 through 7, discussed strategic portfolio optimization problem models built over popular investment strategies and theories followed by the investment and finance industry, namely heuristic selection, risk budgeting, market neutral investing, 130-30 portfolio construction and portfolio rebalancing, but relying on Metaheuristics to arrive at the optimal portfolio allocations.

So what are the lessons learned?

Let us try to garner answers from the book, by rephrasing the question as,

"Therefore, how does one get started to strategically solve a distinct portfolio optimization problem model of one's choice?" and posing the following sub-queries to find complete answers.

What are the objectives of the problem model?

Ensure what the objective (objectives) of the problem model is (are) to be. In the case of the classical Markowitz model, the objectives were always bi-criterion, viz. maximizing return and minimizing risk (Chapter 1). A host of single criterion objectives such as maximizing Sharpe Ratio (Chapters 1, 4, 6), maximizing return (Chapter 5), maximizing Diversification Ratio (Chapter 7), besides minimizing risk, to quote a few, may be framed.

This book focused on single objective portfolio optimization models. However, in the case of multiple objectives (two or more), a weighted formulation that transforms the bi-criterion or multi-criterion objective function into a single criterion objective function, for example, linear scalarization, can be adopted. The other option is to tackle the multi-criterion objectives as they are and employ strategies to obtain what are called Pareto-optimal solutions to the problem model.

What are the constraints to be imposed on the problem model?

List out the constraints that the problem model is subjected to. The constraints may be linear or non-linear. Thus, basic, bound, class or group, budget, turnover, leveraged bounds, net market exposure, portfolio beta and self-financing portfolio constraints (Chapters 1, 4, 5, 6, 7) are examples of linear constraints. On the other hand constraints such as risk budgeting (Chapters 4, 5) and ceiling on the rebalanced portfolio risk (Chapter 7) are examples of non-linear constraints. Sometimes certain constraints can render the problem difficult for direct solving using traditional methods. For example, inclusion of cardinality constraint (Chapter 1) can turn the problem model into a mixed integer quadratic programming model making it difficult for direct solving using traditional methods. Needless to say, in such cases alternate methods of solving the problem have to be explored (Chapter 3: section 3.5.3).

How to handle constraints?

If traditional methods or commercial solvers (MATLAB® solvers, for instance) can tackle all the constraints as they are for the problem model, then all is done. However, many a time it may be difficult to tackle non-linear constraints for they are not amenable to the traditional method used. In such a case, a common method used is to employ what is called penalty function, which imposes a penalty that is proportional to the square of its violation. The penalty function in general serves to absorb the constraints in the objective function yielding what is called a penalized objective function, which transforms the constrained optimization problem model into an unconstrained optimization model. An unconstrained optimization model obviously can be easily solved using a variety of traditional methods. Chapter 4, section 4.3.1 discussed constraint handling using penalty function strategy.

On the other hand, when the choice is Metaheuristics, it has been acknowledged that constraint handling is a major hurdle. Nevertheless there are several methods that can be employed to overcome the issue. Two strategies described in this book and predominantly used to tackle a variety of constraints both linear and non-linear imposed on the portfolio optimization models discussed in the book, viz. Repair strategy and Penalty function strategy (Chapter 4: sections 4.3.1, 4.5, Chapter 5: sections 5.3, 5.4.3, Chapter 6: sections 6.4.1, 6.4.2, Chapter 7: sections 7.2, 7.3.3) can be adopted. However, it needs to be reiterated here that repair strategies are not global and quite often have to be designed for the problem model in question. Again there may arise situations where it is difficult to design a repair procedure for the problem model in hand. Despite this disadvantage and their complex process of handling constraints, repair strategies have been commended for their speed and performance in delivering feasible solution sets.

Thus at this stage, when the choice of solution strategy for the portfolio optimization problem model is metaheuristics, a transformed mathematical model with penalized objective functions and/or repair strategies to effectively tackle a definite set of constraints could be formulated.

Which metaheuristic strategy to adopt?

It is difficult to give a straightforward answer to this question, for the reality is, a metaheuristic strategy that is good for one problem model may not be suitable enough to deliver results for another problem model. David H Wolpert and William G Macready [WOL 97] in their paper "*No free lunch theorems for optimization*" published in *IEEE Transactions on Evolutionary Computation* asserted that "...if some algorithm a_1's performance is superior to that of another algorithm a_2 over some set of optimization problems, then the reverse must be true over the set of all other optimization problems…" Adding to the woes is the repertoire of strategies that are available in this fast growing field and therefore making the right choice calls for discretion and a strong understanding of the problem model and the objective functions.

How to implement a metaheuristic strategy?

Metaheuristic strategies are amenable for implementation in any language or software of one's choice. However, as demonstrated in the book (sections titled "MATLAB® demonstrations" in all the chapters) considering the availability of a repertoire of functions and toolboxes available in MATLAB®, implementation of the strategies in MATLAB® can be a programmer's delight. A useful strategy to follow during coding of metaheuristics is to adopt a functional style, where the complete metaheuristic strategy is broken down into components representing processes and their respective genetic inheritance operators that work over them, with individual functions written for each of the components. This way it is easier to manage the components first before the entire program is managed. Besides, the components available as functions promote reusability and reengineering, in an alternative metaheuristic method belonging to the same genre.

How to assess the performance of the metaheuristic algorithm?

Metaheuristic strategies being stochastic in nature need to go through an elaborate experimental analysis while assessing their performance over the problem concerned. Besides, most metaheuristic strategies are sensitive to the control parameters that define the strategy. Hence in many cases, tuning of control parameters to enable the algorithm to suit the problem in hand may have to be undertaken. Quite often one may be lucky to find some benchmarks defined in the literature for some specific algorithms or problem models.

To assess the performance of metaheuristic strategies, several measures exist. In this book, two measures, namely Population Convergence (P-Measure) and convergence of objective function, were adopted (Chapter 2: sections 2.4.4, 2.5.5). Besides the above, an elaborate empirical testing to assess the consistency of performance of the algorithms will have to be undertaken.

Should one compare performances of metaheuristic algorithms from different genres?

As the last but optional step, it pays to compare the results obtained by two or more metaheuristic algorithms on the same problem model, notwithstanding Wolpert and Macready's *No free lunch theorem*. Since metaheuristic algorithms only yield near-optimal or acceptable solutions, an appropriate comparison with its counterpart can possibly serve to exude more confidence in the results obtained.

This book, in the author's opinion, only serves to catch a glimpse of the exciting possibilities of applications of Computational Intelligence to the mystical world of Finance, in general, or an interesting application of Metaheuristics to the discipline of Portfolio Optimization in particular. Interested readers and workers are encouraged to explore this interdisciplinary area, which offers huge potential for research, application and intelligent problem solving.

Bibliography

[BAC 00] BACK T., FOGEL D.B., MICHALEWICZ Z., *Evolutionary Computation I: Basic Algorithms and Operators*, CRC Press, 2000.

[BES 10] BEST M., *Portfolio Optimization*, Chapman and Hall/CRC, 2010.

[BLI 07] BLITZ D.C., VLIET P., The Volatility Effect: Lower risk without Lower return, ERIM Report Series Research in Management, ERS-2007-044-F&A, July 2007.

[BRA 10] BRANDOUY O., BRIEC W., KERSTENS K. *et al.*, "Portfolio Performance Gauging in Discrete Time using a Luenberger Productivity Indicator", *Journal of Banking and Finance*, vol. 34 no. 8, pp. 1899–1910, 2010.

[BRI 04] BRIEC W., KERSTENS K., LESOURD J.B., "Single period Markowitz portfolio selection performance gauging and duality: A variation on the Luenberger shortage function", *Journal of Optimization theory and Applications*, vol. 120, no.1, pp. 1–27, 2004.

[CHA 00] CHANG T.J., MEADE N., BEASLEY J.B. *et al.*, "Heuristics for cardinality constrained portfolio optimization", *Computers and Operations Research*, vol. 27, pp. 1271–1302, 2000.

[CHO 08] CHOUEIFATY Y., COIGNARD Y., "Toward Maximum Diversification", *The Journal of Portfolio Management*, pp. 40–51, 2008.

[CHO 13] CHOUEIFATY Y., FROIDURE T., REYNIER J., "Properties of the Most Diversified Portfolio", *Journal of Investment Strategies*, vol. 2, no. 2, pp. 1–22, 2013.

[COE 07] COELLO C.A.C., LAMONT G.B., DAVID V.V.A., *Evolutionary Algorithms for Solving Multi-Objective Problems*, Springer, 2007.

[COL 04] COLLETTE Y., SIARRY P., *Multiobjective Optimization, Principles and Case Studies*, Springer-Verlag Berlin Heidelberg, 2004.

[DEB 03] DEB K., *Multi-objective Optimization using Evolutionary Algorithms*, John Wiley, 2003.

[DRE 06] DREO J., PETROWSKI J., TAILLARD E. *et al.*, *Metaheuristics for Hard Optimization: Methods and Case Studies*, Springer, 2006.

[EIB 08] EIBEN A.E., SMITH J. E., *Introduction to Evolutionary Computing*, Springer, 2008.

[ELT 14] ELTON E.J., GRUBER M.J., BROWN S.J. *et al.*, *Modern Portfolio Theory and Investment Analysis,* 9th ed., Wiley, 2014.

[ENG 07] ENGELBRECHT A., *Computational Intelligence: an Introduction*, Wiley, 2007.

[EVE 11] EVERITT B.S., LANDAU S., LEESE M. *et al.*, *Cluster Analysis*, 5th ed., Wiley, 2011.

[FEO 06] FEOKTISTOV V., *Differential Evolution in Search of Solutions*, Springer, 2006.

[FOW 07] FOWLER Jr. G.B., "Understanding 130/30 Equity Strategies", http://www.cfapubs. org/doi/pdf/10.2469/cp.v24.n3.4848, Sept. 2007.

[GIL 11] GILLI M., MARINGER D., SCHUMANN E., *Numerical Methods and Optimization in Finance*, Academic Press, 2011.

[GRI 00] GRINOLD R.C., Kahn R.N., *Active Portfolio Management*, 2nd ed., McGraw-Hill, New York, 2000.

[JAC 99] JACOBS B.I., LEVY K.N., STARER D., "Long-Short Portfolio Management: An Integrated Approach", *The Journal of Portfolio Management*, vol. 25, no.2, pp. 23–32, 1999.

[JAC 05] JACOBS B.I., LEVY K.N., *Market Neutral Strategies*, John Wiley, 2005.

[JAC 10] JACONETTI C.M., KINNIRY JrF.M., ZILBERING Y., Best Practices for Portfolio Rebalancing, Vanguard Research, http://www.vanguard.com/pdf/icrpr.pdf, July 2010.

[JOH 07] JOHNSON G., ERICSON S., SRIMURTHY V., "An Empirical Analysis of 130/30 Strategies: Domestic and International 130/30 Strategies Add Value Over Long-Only Strategies", *The Journal of Alternative Investments*, pp. 31–42, 2007.

[JOH 13] JOHNSON S., "The decline, fall and afterlife of 130/30", *Financial Times*, https://www.ft.com/content/fdbf6284-b724-11e2-841e-00144feabdc0, May 12, 2013.

[JOI 94] JOINES J.A., HOUCK C.R., "On the use of non-stationary penalty functions to solve nonlinear constrained optimization problems with Gas", *Proceedings of the First IEEE Conference on Evolutionary Computation*, pp. 579–584, 1994.

[JUR 13] JURCKZENKO E., MICHEL T., TEILETCHE J., Generalized Risk-Based Investing, Available at SSRN: https://ssrn.com/abstract=2205979 or http://dx.doi.org/10.2139/ssrn.2205979, 2013.

[JUR 15] JURCKZENKO E., MICHEL T., TEILETCHE J., "A Unified framework for Risk-based Investing", *Journal of Investment Strategies*, vol. 4, no. 4, pp. 1–29, September 2015.

[KAU 05] KAUFMAN L., ROUSSEEUW P.J., *Finding Groups in Data: An Introduction to Cluster Analysis*, Wiley, 2005.

[LAL 07] LALOUX L., CIZEAU P., POTTERS M. *et al.*, "Random Matrix Theory and financial correlations", *Mathematical Models and Methods in Applied Sciences*, World Scientific Publishing Company, 2007.

[LO 07] LO A., PATEL P., "130/30: The New Long Only", *Journal of Portfolio Management*, vol. 34, no. 2, pp. 12–38, 2007.

[LOE 07] LOEB G.M., *The Battle for Investment Survival*, Wiley, 2007.

[LUE 92] LUENBERGER D.G., "Benefit functions and duality", *Journal of Mathematical Economics*, vol. 21, pp. 461–481, 1992.

[MAL 06] MALGORZATA S., KRZYCH J., "Automatic trading agent. RMT based Portfolio theory and portfolio selection", *Acta Physica Polonica B*, vol. 37, no. 11, 2006.

[MAR 52] MARKOWITZ H., "Portfolio Selection", *The Journal of Finance*, vol. 7, no. 1, pp. 77–91, Mar., 1952.

[MAR 05] MARINGER D., *Portfolio Management with Heuristic Optimization*, Springer, 2005.

[MET 90] METHA M.L., *Random Matrices*, Academic Press, 1990.

[MIC 93] MICHAUD R., "Are Long-Short Equity Strategies Superior?", *Financial Analysts Journal*, vol. 49, pp. 44–50, 1993.

[MIC 96] MICHALEWICZ Z., DASGUPTA D., LE RICHE R.G. *et al.*, "Evolutionary algorithms for Industrial Engineering Problems", *International Journal of Computers and Industrial Engineering*, vol. 30, no. 4, pp. 851–870, 1996.

[MIC 04] MICHALEWICZ Z., FOGEL D.B., *How to Solve it: Modern Heuristics*, Springer, 2004.

[OSY 02] OSYCZKA A., *Evolutionary Algorithms for Single and Multicriteria Design Optimization*, Physica-Verlag, Heidelberg, 2002.

[PAI 09] PAI G.A.V., MICHEL T., "Evolutionary optimization of constrained k-means clustered assets for diversification in small portfolios", *IEEE Transactions on Evolutionary Computation*, vol. 13, no. 5, pp. 1030–1054, October 2009.

[PAI 11] PAI G.A.V., MICHEL T., "Metaheuristic Optimization of Risk Budgeted Global Asset Allocation Portfolios", *Proc. of 2011 World Congress on Information and Communication Technologies*, pp. 154–159, Mumbai, India, 2011.

[PAI 12a] PAI G.A.V., MICHEL T., "Differential Evolution based optimization of Risk Budgeted Equity Market Neutral Portfolios", *Proc. IEEE World Congress on Computational Intelligence*, pp. 1888–1895, Brisbane, Australia, June 10–15, 2012.

[PAI 12b] PAI G.A.V., MICHEL T., "Integrated Metaheuristic Optimization of 130-30 Investment Strategy based Long-Short Portfolios", *Intelligent Systems in Accounting, Finance and Management*, vol. 19, pp. 43–74, 2012.

[PAI 14] PAI G.A.V., "Multi-Objective Differential Evolution Based Optimization of Risk Budgeted Global Asset Allocation Portfolios", *Proc. 2014 2nd International Symposium on Computational and Business Intelligence*, pp. 17–20, 2014.

[PAI 17] PAI G.A.V., "Fuzzy decision theory based metaheuristics portfolio optimization and active rebalancing using interval type-2 fuzzy sets", *IEEE Transactions On Fuzzy Systems*, vol. 25, no. 2, April 2017.

[PAP 05] PAPP G., PAFKA S.Z., NOWAK M.A. *et al.*, "Random matrix filtering in portfolio optimization", *Acta Physica Polonica B*, vol. 36, no. 9, 2005.

[PFA 16] PFAFF B., *Financial Risk Modelling and Portfolio Optimization with R*, 2nd ed., Wiley, 2016.

[PRI 97] PRICE K., STORN R., "Differential Evolution: A simple evolution strategy for fast optimization", *Dr Dobb's Journal of Software Tools*, vol. 22, no. 4, pp. 18–24, April 1997.

[QIA 14] QIAN E.E., "To rebalance or not to rebalance: A statistical comparison of terminal wealth of fixed weight and buy-and-hold portfolios", http://papers.ssrn.com/sol3/papers.cfm?abstract_id=2402679, Jan. 26, 2014.

[SCH 05] SCHERER B., MARTIN D., *Introduction to Modern Portfolio Optimization with NUOPT and S-PLUS*, Springer, 2005.

[SIA 16] SIARRY P., *Metaheuristics*, Springer, 2016.

[SIM 13] SIMON D., *Evolutionary Optimization Algorithms*, Wiley, 2013.

[SMI 05] SMITHBARNEY CITIGROUP, "The Art of Rebalancing", http://www.retailinvestor.org/pdf/SmithBarney.pdf, 2005.

[SOR 13] SORENSEN K., GLOVER F., "Metaheuristics", in GASS S. and FU M. (eds) *Encyclopedia of Operations Research and Management Science*, 3rd ed., Springer, London, 2013.

[SOR 15] SORENSEN K., "Metaheuristics – the metaphor exposed", *International Transactions in Operational Research*, vol. 22, no. 1, pp. 3–18, January 2015.

[STO 95] STORN R., PRICE K., Differential Evolution – A simple and efficient adaptive scheme for global optimization over continuous spaces, Technical Report: TR-95-012, Intl. Computer Science Institute, Berkeley, CA, 1995.

[STO 97] STORN R., PRICE K., "Differential Evolution – A simple and efficient heuristic for global optimization over continuous spaces", *Journal of Global Optimization*, vol. 11, pp. 341–359, Dec 1997.

[TOK 07] TOKAT Y., "Portfolio rebalancing in theory and practice", Vanguard Investment Counseling and Research, https://personal.vanguard.com/pdf/flgprtp.pdf, 2007.

[VIN 05] VINCENZO T., LILLO F., GALLEGATI M. *et al.*, "Cluster analysis for portfolio optimization", *arXiv:physics/0507006*, VI, July 2005.

[WOE 93] WOERHEIDE W., PERSSON D., "An index of Portfolio Diversification", *Financial Series Review*, vol. 2, no. 2, pp. 73–85, 1993.

[WOL 97] WOLPERT D.H., MACREADY W.G., "No free lunch theorems for optimization", *IEEE Transactions on Evolutionary Computation*, vol. 1, no. 1, pp. 67–82, 1997.

[YAO 02] YAO F., XU B., DOUCET K., *Streetsmart Guide to Managing your Portfolio*, McGraw-Hill, 2002.

[ZIL 15] ZILBERING Y., JACONETTI C.M., KINNIRY JR. F.M., "Best practices for portfolio rebalancing", Vanguard Research, https://www.vanguard.com/pdf/ISGPORE.pdf, Nov. 2015.

Index

Other titles from

in

Computer Engineering

2017

HÉLIODORE Frédéric, NAKIB Amir, ISMAIL Boussaad, OUCHRAA Salma,
SCHMITT Laurent
Metaheuristics for Intelligent Electrical Networks
(Metaheuristics Set – Volume 10)

MA Haiping, SIMON Dan
Evolutionary Computation with Biogeography-based Optimization
(Metaheuristics Set – Volume 8)

PÉTROWSKI Alain, BEN-HAMIDA Sana
Evolutionary Algorithms
(Metaheuristics Set – Volume 9)

2016

BLUM Christian, FESTA Paola
Metaheuristics for String Problems in Bio-informatics
(Metaheuristics Set – Volume 6)

DEROUSSI Laurent
Metaheuristics for Logistics
(Metaheuristics Set – Volume 4)

DHAENENS Clarisse and JOURDAN Laetitia
Metaheuristics for Big Data
(Metaheuristics Set – Volume 5)

LABADIE Nacima, PRINS Christian, PRODHON Caroline
Metaheuristics for Vehicle Routing Problems
(Metaheuristics Set – Volume 3)

LEROY Laure
Eyestrain Reduction in Stereoscopy

LUTTON Evelyne, PERROT Nathalie, TONDA Albert
Evolutionary Algorithms for Food Science and Technology
(Metaheuristics Set – Volume 7)

MAGOULÈS Frédéric, ZHAO Hai-Xiang
Data Mining and Machine Learning in Building Energy Analysis

RIGO Michel
Advanced Graph Theory and Combinatorics

2015

BARBIER Franck, RECOUSSINE Jean-Luc
COBOL Software Modernization: From Principles to Implementation with the BLU AGE® Method

CHEN Ken
Performance Evaluation by Simulation and Analysis with Applications to Computer Networks

CLERC Maurice
Guided Randomness in Optimization
(Metaheuristics Set – Volume 1)

DURAND Nicolas, GIANAZZA David, GOTTELAND Jean-Baptiste,
ALLIOT Jean-Marc
Metaheuristics for Air Traffic Management
(Metaheuristics Set – Volume 2)

MAGOULÈS Frédéric, ROUX François-Xavier, HOUZEAUX Guillaume
Parallel Scientific Computing

MUNEESAWANG Paisarn, YAMMEN Suchart
Visual Inspection Technology in the Hard Disk Drive Industry

2014

BOULANGER Jean-Louis
Formal Methods Applied to Industrial Complex Systems

BOULANGER Jean-Louis
Formal Methods Applied to Complex Systems:
Implementation of the B Method

GARDI Frédéric, BENOIST Thierry, DARLAY Julien, ESTELLON Bertrand,
MEGEL Romain
Mathematical Programming Solver based on Local Search

KRICHEN Saoussen, CHAOUACHI Jouhaina
Graph-related Optimization and Decision Support Systems

LARRIEU Nicolas, VARET Antoine
Rapid Prototyping of Software for Avionics Systems: Model-oriented
Approaches for Complex Systems Certification

OUSSALAH Mourad Chabane
Software Architecture 1
Software Architecture 2

PASCHOS Vangelis Th
Combinatorial Optimization – 3-volume series, 2ⁿᵈ Edition
Concepts of Combinatorial Optimization – Volume 1, 2ⁿᵈ Edition
Problems and New Approaches – Volume 2, 2ⁿᵈ Edition
Applications of Combinatorial Optimization – Volume 3, 2ⁿᵈ Edition

QUESNEL Flavien
Scheduling of Large-scale Virtualized Infrastructures: Toward Cooperative
Management

RIGO Michel
Formal Languages, Automata and Numeration Systems 1:
Introduction to Combinatorics on Words
Formal Languages, Automata and Numeration Systems 2:
Applications to Recognizability and Decidability

SAINT-DIZIER Patrick
Musical Rhetoric: Foundations and Annotation Schemes

TOUATI Sid, DE DINECHIN Benoit
Advanced Backend Optimization

2013

ANDRÉ Etienne, SOULAT Romain
The Inverse Method: Parametric Verification of Real-time Embedded
Systems

BOULANGER Jean-Louis
Safety Management for Software-based Equipment

DELAHAYE Daniel, PUECHMOREL Stéphane
Modeling and Optimization of Air Traffic

FRANCOPOULO Gil
LMF — Lexical Markup Framework

GHÉDIRA Khaled
Constraint Satisfaction Problems

ROCHANGE Christine, UHRIG Sascha, SAINRAT Pascal
Time-Predictable Architectures

WAHBI Mohamed
Algorithms and Ordering Heuristics for Distributed Constraint Satisfaction
Problems

ZELM Martin *et al.*
Enterprise Interoperability

KORDON Fabrice, HADDAD Serge, PAUTET Laurent, PETRUCCI Laure
Distributed Systems: Design and Algorithms

KORDON Fabrice, HADDAD Serge, PAUTET Laurent, PETRUCCI Laure
Models and Analysis in Distributed Systems

LORCA Xavier
Tree-based Graph Partitioning Constraint

TRUCHET Charlotte, ASSAYAG Gerard
Constraint Programming in Music

VICAT-BLANC PRIMET Pascale *et al.*
Computing Networks: From Cluster to Cloud Computing

2010

AUDIBERT Pierre
Mathematics for Informatics and Computer Science

BABAU Jean-Philippe *et al.*
Model Driven Engineering for Distributed Real-Time Embedded Systems 2009

BOULANGER Jean-Louis
Safety of Computer Architectures

MONMARCHE Nicolas *et al.*
Artificial Ants

PANETTO Hervé, BOUDJLIDA Nacer
Interoperability for Enterprise Software and Applications 2010

SIGAUD Olivier *et al.*
Markov Decision Processes in Artificial Intelligence

SOLNON Christine
Ant Colony Optimization and Constraint Programming

AUBRUN Christophe, SIMON Daniel, SONG Ye-Qiong *et al.*
Co-design Approaches for Dependable Networked Control Systems

2009

FOURNIER Jean-Claude
Graph Theory and Applications

GUEDON Jeanpierre
The Mojette Transform / Theory and Applications

JARD Claude, ROUX Olivier
Communicating Embedded Systems / Software and Design

LECOUTRE Christophe
Constraint Networks / Targeting Simplicity for Techniques and Algorithms

2008

BANÂTRE Michel, MARRÓN Pedro José, OLLERO Hannibal, WOLITZ Adam
Cooperating Embedded Systems and Wireless Sensor Networks

MERZ Stephan, NAVET Nicolas
Modeling and Verification of Real-time Systems

PASCHOS Vangelis Th
Combinatorial Optimization and Theoretical Computer Science: Interfaces and Perspectives

WALDNER Jean-Baptiste
Nanocomputers and Swarm Intelligence

2007

BENHAMOU Frédéric, JUSSIEN Narendra, O'SULLIVAN Barry
Trends in Constraint Programming

JUSSIEN Narendra
A to Z of Sudoku

2006

BABAU Jean-Philippe *et al.*
From MDD Concepts to Experiments and Illustrations – DRES 2006

HABRIAS Henri, FRAPPIER Marc
Software Specification Methods

MURAT Cecile, PASCHOS Vangelis Th
Probabilistic Combinatorial Optimization on Graphs

PANETTO Hervé, BOUDJLIDA Nacer
*Interoperability for Enterprise Software and Applications 2006 / IFAC-IFIP
I-ESA '2006*

2005

GÉRARD Sébastien *et al.*
Model Driven Engineering for Distributed Real Time Embedded Systems

PANETTO Hervé
Interoperability of Enterprise Software and Applications 2005

Printed and bound by CPI Group (UK) Ltd, Croydon, CR0 4YY